Tax Incentives and
Capital Spending

Studies of Government Finance
TITLES PUBLISHED

Brookings Conference ...

Tax Incentives and

Capital Spending

GARY FROMM *Editor*

Papers presented at a conference of experts
held on November 3, 1967

Studies of Government Finance

THE BROOKINGS INSTITUTION

WASHINGTON, D.C.

© 1971 by

THE BROOKINGS INSTITUTION
1775 Massachusetts Avenue, N.W., Washington, D.C. 20036

ISBN 0 8157 2942 1 (cloth)
ISBN 0 8157 2941 3 (paper)

Library of Congress Catalog Card Number 79-115225
North-Holland ISBN 0 7204 3048-8

Distributed outside the United States and Canada by
NORTH-HOLLAND PUBLISHING COMPANY – AMSTERDAM

THE BROOKINGS INSTITUTION is an independent organization devoted to nonpartisan research, education, and publication in economics, government, foreign policy, and the social sciences generally. Its principal purposes are to aid in the development of sound public policies and to promote public understanding of issues of national importance.

The Institution was founded December 8, 1927, to merge the activities of the Institute for Government Research, founded in 1916, the Institute of Economics, founded in 1922, and the Robert Brookings Graduate School of Economics and Government, founded in 1924.

The general administration of the Institution is the responsibility of a Board of Trustees charged with maintaining the independence of the staff and fostering the most favorable conditions for creative research and education. The immediate direction of the policies, program, and staff of the Institution is vested in the President, assisted by an advisory committee of the officers and staff.

In publishing a study, the Institution presents it as a competent treatment of a subject worthy of public consideration. The interpretations and conclusions in such publications are those of the author or authors and do not necessarily reflect the views of the other staff members, officers, or trustees of the Brookings Institution.

Foreword

THE INVESTMENT TAX CREDIT was enacted in 1962, when the economy of the United States was lagging far behind its potential. Together with revisions in depreciation guidelines, the credit was meant to spur lagging replacement and net additions to capital in order to increase the national growth rate.

Whether the investment tax credit was the best means for achieving this purpose remains debatable. Moreover, estimates of the effect of the credit on investment vary widely. These questions are still unsettled though the credit was suspended for five months beginning in October 1966 and was repealed at the end of 1969.

This volume brings together several papers prepared by economic analysts in an effort to answer these questions by estimating the effects of the investment tax credit and accelerated depreciation on the level of investment expenditure. They were presented at a conference held at the Brookings Institution in November 1967.

The paper by Robert E. Hall and Dale W. Jorgenson was an outgrowth of Jorgenson's investment studies for the Brookings econometric model project. Those of Robert E. Coen and Charles W. Bischoff are adapted from their doctoral dissertations at Stanford University and Yale University, respectively. Coen's work was done during his tenure as a Brookings Research Fellow. Bischoff's investment functions, later slightly revised, were incorporated into the Federal Reserve Board–Massachusetts Institute of Technology model. The paper by Lawrence Klein and Paul Taubman results from a study of the impact of the investment credit made with the Wharton School model sponsored by the U.S. Treasury Department.

The conference was part of the Brookings Institution's program of Studies of Government Finance, a special program of research and education in taxation and government expenditures supervised by the National Committee on Government Finance. The committee was established in 1960 by the trustees of the Brookings Institution; its program is supported with funds provided by the Ford Foundation.

Robert Hall and Dale Jorgenson also wish to acknowledge the assistance of the National Science Foundation, whose grant financed part of their research. Charles Bischoff wishes to thank Albert Ando, Robert Hall, Edwin Kuh, and Franco Modigliani for their comments on his paper, and the National Science Foundation and the Cowles Foundation for Research in Economics for grants that supported his research. Robert Coen acknowledges the help of Robert Eisner, who directed his research, and that of Samuel B. Chase, Jr., and Bert G. Hickman, who made helpful suggestions on earlier drafts of his paper.

Mendelle Berenson edited the manuscript, Evelyn Fisher verified the data and bibliographical references, and Penelope Stafford prepared the index. The views expressed in this volume are those of the authors and are not presented as the views of the Ford Foundation, the National Committee on Government Finance, or the staff members, officers, or trustees of the Brookings Institution.

KERMIT GORDON
President

April 1970
Washington, D.C.

Studies of Government Finance

Studies of Government Finance is a special program of research and education in taxation and government expenditures at the federal, state, and local levels. This program, which was supported by a special grant from the Ford Foundation, was undertaken and supervised by the National Committee on Government Finance appointed by the trustees of the Brookings Institution.

MEMBERS OF THE ADVISORY COMMITTEE

Contents

Tables and Figures

Bischoff

Coen

Harberger

CHAPTER I

Introduction

GARY FROMM *Washington, D.C.*

THE PURPOSE OF THE PAPERS presented at the Brookings Conference on the Effects of Tax Policy on Investment was to develop models of fixed investment behavior of United States business firms and to evaluate the impact on capital spending of federal tax incentives enacted since the end of the Second World War. The conference did not resolve the issue of the effectiveness of the tax incentives that were used. Four papers were prepared by competent scholars. Each had the objective of measuring the same phenomenon. Each obtained a significantly different answer.

Yet this is no cause for despair. The analyses undertaken in this volume are substantially more sophisticated and comprehensive than the simplistic approaches applied heretofore. Merely relating changes in tax rates or depreciation allowances to changes in the ratio of investment to gross national product, as has been done in the past, is inadequate for evaluating incentives in a world in which many influences impinge directly and indirectly on capital outlays.

Although the papers in the succeeding chapters do not give *the* answer to the impact question, they go a long way toward formulating the theoretical framework and developing the methodology for analyzing the effect of various economic factors on investment. It is hoped that further improvements in theory and refinements in the data will lead to more definitive conclusions.

The common impression that the tax structure and administrative provisions that affect after-tax rates of return and individuals' after-tax income from business investment have been relatively stable for many years is far from the truth. From 1929 through 1965 there were twenty changes in federal depreciation regulations, four changes in tax credits for equipment expenditures, fourteen changes in corporation income tax rates, and seventeen changes in individual income tax rates. The total is fifty-five tax changes in thirty-six years—more than one per year—and this does not include alterations in excise, gift, or estate tax rates or in personal exemptions and deductions.

Many of the changes were not designed or enacted to affect investment, yet, potentially, they all can do so. For example, some modifications in depreciation regulations were made on equity grounds, while others were intended to limit tax avoidance. Measures to stimulate or deter capital spending have included accelerated amortization of certified facilities during the Second World War and the Korean war, modified depreciable assets lives, accelerated depreciation methods, and, in the 1960s, tax credits for new investment.

Tax credits granted on the basis of investment outlays were first introduced into the United States tax system in 1962. After extended congressional discussion of various alternatives, the bill finally enacted provided for a 7 percent credit (3 percent for utilities) on equipment with useful lives of eight years or more. (Reduced credits were given for investments with useful lives of four to eight years; no credit was given for investments with useful lives of less than four years.) Credits amounting to more than $25,000 were limited to a maximum reduction of tax liability of 50 percent (25 percent before March 1967); amounts in excess of this limitation could be carried forward for five years to reduce future tax liabilities. Originally, the reduction in liability had to be subtracted from the depreciable basis of the property; this provision, known as the Long amendment, was repealed in 1964. In October 1966 the tax credit was suspended until December 1967, but the suspension was repealed after only five months when the pace of economic activity slackened markedly. Later, as prices rose sharply and investment expenditures remained very high, Congress terminated the credit in the Tax Reform Act of 1969, effective as of April 18, 1969.

The Models and the Estimates

The investment model formulated by Robert Hall and Dale Jorgenson is based on neoclassical economic theory. In this model producers are said to maximize profits and to take account of an implicit rental price of capital. It is assumed that the underlying production function is of the Cobb-Douglas type and that the elasticity of substitution between labor and capital is equal to unity. The parameters of the model are estimated from annual data in 1965 dollars for investment in manufacturing and nonfarm non-manufacturing industries in the United States for the period 1929–65. Separate investment functions were fitted for equipment and for structures in each sector.

Given the above assumptions and estimated parameters, the model is employed to quantify the investment effects of the adoption of accelerated depreciation in 1954, the adoption of new, shorter lifetimes for depreciating investment and the investment tax credit in 1962, and the cut in the corporate profits tax rate in 1964. The effects of the 1966–67 suspension of the tax credit and accelerated depreciation for structures are projected to 1970. The impacts are estimated for the suspension that actually took place and for the longer suspension that was originally proposed.

On the basis of their analysis of this experience, Hall and Jorgenson conclude that tax policy has been highly effective in changing the level and timing of fixed investment outlays. They also find that tax policy has affected the composition of expenditures. Accelerated depreciation has resulted in a shift away from equipment toward greater spending for structures. The investment tax credit, which was limited to equipment, shifted investment away from structures toward equipment. Both changes in tax policy are said to have stimulated the level of investment very substantially.

Charles Bischoff's model of the investment process is similar in spirit, and in many details, to the Hall and Jorgenson model. He criticizes their model, however, because of the restrictive nature of some of the assumptions built into it, and he develops and applies a less restrictive and more general set of assumptions.

The most important of Bischoff's generalizations is that factor proportions may not be freely variable at all times, but only before fixed capital goods are put into place. This "putty-clay" hypothesis is shown to imply that measures that alter the relative price of capital services (including, among others, tax credits, depreciation rules, and profits taxes) should affect capital goods spending more gradually than do changes in output. Unlike Bischoff's, the Hall and Jorgenson model does not provide separate lag distributions for output and relative prices. Bischoff's empirical results using quarterly data on investment in producers' durable equipment in 1958 dollars for the period 1951–65 indicate that allowing for separate lag distributions substantially improves the predictive power of the model, and that changes in relative prices affect equipment spending more gradually than do changes in output, as predicted by the putty-clay hypothesis.

Bischoff relaxes other restrictions in the following ways: (1) The assumption that the production function underlying the demand for capital is of the Cobb-Douglas type is replaced by the assumption that the underlying function has a constant but unspecified elasticity of substitution. (2) The implicit assumption that expectations are static is replaced by the assumption that expected output and expected relative prices are generated via distributed lag mechanisms. (3) The assumption that the before-tax cost of capital relevant to investment decisions by firms is a constant is replaced by the assumption that the after-tax cost of capital may be approximated by a linear function of the corporate bond yield, the corporate dividend-price ratio, the degree of corporate leverage, and the corporate tax rate.

Bischoff finds that changes in the relative prices of capital goods —including changes resulting from the investment tax credit—appear to have a statistically significant effect on equipment spending. His estimate of the long-run price elasticity of demand for equipment is close to unity. Other things being equal, the stimulus to equipment spending provided by the investment tax credit is estimated to exceed the revenue losses from the credit. For accelerated depreciation, however, the estimated effects are considerably smaller than revenue losses.

Robert Coen estimates the effect of various tax incentives for investment —accelerated depreciation, the investment tax credit, and reductions in tax rates on business income—on total plant and equipment expenditures of manufacturing firms. Tax incentives are presumed to influence capital expenditures in two ways. First, by reducing the implicit rental price of capital, they increase firms' desired stocks of capital. Second, by increasing the flow of internal funds available for financing purchases of capital goods, they facilitate adjustments of capital stocks to desired levels.

The initial step in the analysis is measurement of changes in the rental price of capital and in cash flow that were brought about by changes in tax policy. Coen finds that during the 1954–61 period, a switch from straight-line to double-declining-balance depreciation reduced the rental price of capital of manufacturing firms by 4 percent on the average. An equivalent reduction in the rental price would have occurred if accelerated depreciation had not been granted, but instead the tax rate on business income had been reduced by approximately 4 percentage points. By 1966, a combination of tax incentives had reduced the rental price by 19 percent, or the equivalent of a 20-percentage-point reduction in the tax rate. Coen also found that, by reducing tax liabilities, accelerated depreciation increased cash flow by $5.1 billion (1954 dollars) during the 1954–61 period. The effect was equivalent to a reduction of approximately 3 percentage points in the tax rate. In 1966 alone, firms enjoyed an increased cash flow of $3.1 billion as a result of all tax incentives—the equivalent of a 9-percentage-point reduction in the tax rate.

The next step in Coen's analysis involves determination of the responsiveness of investment to changes in the rental price of capital and in cash flow by statistically fitting an investment relation to quarterly data for 1950–66. The relation depicts investment as the process by which firms adjust their actual capital stocks to desired levels, with the adjustment speed dependent on the adequacy of cash flow to finance desired capital expenditures. Firms are assumed to minimize costs of production, so that their desired stocks of capital depend on expected future output and relative prices of factors of production, the price of capital being an implicit rental price. Expected output is specified as a weighted average of current and past values of new orders, with the weights following an inverted-V pattern. Similarly, expected relative factor prices are specified as a weighted average of current and past prices. Several variants of this basic model are tested. The preferred investment relation suggests that if cash flow is small relative to the size of the gap, firms close about 10 percent of the difference between desired and actual stocks each quarter. If cash flow is about equal to the gap, the adjustment speed increases to about 28 percent per quarter. The relation also implies that a 1 percent increase in expected output increases the desired capital stock by 0.9 percent, while a 1 percent decrease in the rental price of capital increases the desired stock by 0.3 percent.

The effects of tax policy can be calculated by combining the results of the two-step analysis. Coen estimates that accelerated depreciation increased expenditures by $2 billion (1954 dollars) from the beginning of 1954 to mid-1962; this compares with tax savings to firms (revenues lost to the federal treasury) of $5.1 billion over the same period. From mid-1962 through the third quarter of 1966, all tax incentives increased expenditures by $2.8 billion, compared with tax savings of $8.6 billion. Thus, based on Coen's estimates, the impact of tax incentives has been disappointing in light of their costs.

Lawrence Klein and Paul Taubman give estimates of the effects of the investment tax credit and accelerated depreciation on nonfarm fixed investment; and they make a comparison of their methods with those in the other studies presented at the conference. Unlike the other authors, they did not estimate new investment functions with explicit tax credit variables. Instead, these equations (based on quarterly data for the period 1948–64) were taken from the then current version of the Wharton School model. Tax changes were translated into effects on the rate of return and entered as shifts in interest rate terms in the equations for manufacturing, regulated industry, and all other nonfarm investment. For the investment tax credit, the increase in the rate of return was computed for each of the three industry groups.

The effects differ among groups because, for example, utilities were granted a lower maximum credit rate and their capital has longer economic lives. Differences also arise from the mix between eligible and noneligible investment, and the distinction between the statutory and effective rate. The impacts on cash flow resulting from both the investment tax credit and accelerated depreciation also were estimated. All effects were evaluated within the Wharton model; hence, feedbacks from the national economy are included, an aspect missing from the other papers.

In contrast to Hall and Jorgenson, Klein and Taubman allowed for the fact that a temporary tax credit suspension (as in 1966–67) should have greater impact on investment than a permanent suspension. Assuming that it had not been revoked in March 1967, the suspension of the credit and accelerated depreciation would have reduced investment by an estimated $2.3 billion in 1967. About half this effect occurs because of feedbacks within the model. Without adjustments for the temporary nature of the suspension, the impact was estimated to be $1.6 billion (both amounts in 1958 dollars).

This study also goes into substantial detail on problems involved in computing the rental price of capital. It deals with some important omissions still evident in the estimates of others at the time of the conference. These include the failure to account for state and local taxes on property and profits; the accelerated amortization provisions under the program of certificates of necessity; and, for structures, the conversion of accelerated depreciation into capital gains.

The Conference Discussion

In opening the conference discussion, Franklin Fisher stressed the underlying lack of agreement in the economics profession about the determinants of investment. In his comment, he notes that each of the studies translates the effects of tax policy into its impact on proxy variables (such as rental prices or interest rates) and speculates on the possibility of testing the impact of tax policy directly. This is of special concern because business-men were slow to adopt accelerated depreciation methods after 1954. Fisher also takes exception, as did several other participants in the con-ference, to intermingling the effects of changes in output and other variables in attempting to determine the impact of changes in taxes.

The assumptions about the determinants of desired capital stock are also an issue. Fisher expresses doubt that those underlying many models are realistic and pleads for tests to ascertain whether excluded factors, such as liquidity (which does not enter either the Hall and Jorgenson or Bischoff models), really do affect investment.

The problem of aggregation across firms also is raised and it is noted that investment functions for the economy as a whole may not be valid if they depend on assumptions that the production functions of firms can be aggregated. An additional difficulty is that capital markets may be imperfect and may not permit firms to make optimum adjustments to desired invest-ment positions.

Fisher also finds disparities among the assumptions the studies make about the length and form of lag distributions. In part the statistical question of the autocorrelation of equation residuals affects the nature of the lag distribution and the interpretation of the results of the timing of responses to tax policy. Fisher finds this problem more severe for some of the papers (especially Coen's) than for others.

Simultaneity poses a related issue. Fisher observes that, at the level of the firm, output and desired capital stock are part of the same decision and that investment (by all firms) affects output and vice versa. Thus autocorrela-tion in the disturbances means that output and output-related variables should not be treated as determined outside the model, as they are in all four papers.

Fisher hesitantly chooses the Bischoff and Klein and Taubman results in preference to those of Coen and Hall and Jorgenson. He is suspicious of Coen's results, on the grounds of estimation procedures and the specifica-tion of distributed lags, and of those of Hall and Jorgenson, because their model imposes too many restrictive assumptions.

Arnold Harberger expressed many of the same concerns as Fisher. Observing that models may be soundly based in theory and yet have widely different implications, he notes that "an infinite number of hypotheses [are] capable of explaining a given finite body of data."

Harberger stresses both the effect of tax measures on the rate of interest and feedbacks on investment. For example, if cuts in taxes raise interest rates, the stimulative impact on investment would be reduced from what it otherwise would have been. This effect is reinforced if the tax incentives are restricted to certain sectors of the economy or types of investment and thus cause a shift of capital spending from noncovered to covered sectors.

Errors of measurement in the basic data also are given attention by Harberger. Whether intermingling variations in rental price and output or separating them is more desirable depends in part on whether these variables can be accurately determined. If so, then Coen's results are preferred; if not—which is more likely, especially for rental prices—then the treatments by Hall and Jorgenson and by Bischoff should be chosen.

Harberger concludes with the rough judgment that the tax incentives of the past decade played an important role in maintaining full employment in the face of a strong balance-of-payments constraint that required higher than normal interest rates. Without the incentives, investment in the noncovered sectors would have been substantially higher; with them, total investment and income were raised significantly.

One new issue raised in the discussion by the conference participants is that estimates derived from investment functions are inappropriate as measures of the elasticity of substitution. Another is the need to take account of expectations of the prices of investment goods. Furthermore, there was widespread sentiment for checking the sensitivity of results to different underlying assumptions about investment behavior and alternative values of input variables.

If any general conclusion can be drawn from the discussion, it is that the subject is far from closed. While universally applauding the high quality of the studies that were presented, those attending called for additional study before any firm conclusions are made. Suggestions were made to analyze data from individual firms (perhaps from federal tax returns) and from surveys of investment expectations.

CHAPTER II

Application of the Theory of Optimum Capital Accumulation

ROBERT E. HALL *Massachusetts Institute of Technology*

DALE W. JORGENSON *Harvard University*

TAX MEASURES FOR CONTROLLING investment expenditures by providing incentives or disincentives through tax credits and accelerated depreciation are now a permanent part of the fiscal policies of the United States and many other countries. The quantitative study of tax incentives, however, has lagged far behind the study of policies that operate directly upon income. For example, the multiplier effect of the tax cut of 1964 has been estimated with some care; much less is known about the quantitative effect of the investment tax credit of 1962. In view of the many current proposals to apply the tax incentive system in other sectors, notably low-cost housing, policies of this kind clearly call for extensive empirical study.

The effectiveness of tax policy in altering investment expenditures has been established in a qualitative sense by a number of authors; their argument can be stated in its essence as follows: If capital services cost less as a result of tax incentives, businessmen will employ more of them.[1] This

---

[1] The effects of tax policy on investment behavior are analyzed from this point of view by, among others, E. Cary Brown, "The New Depreciation Policy under the Income Tax: An Economic Analysis," *National Tax Journal*, Vol. 8 (March 1955), pp. 81–98; E. Cary Brown, "Tax Incentives for Investment," in American Economic Association, *Papers and Proceedings of the Seventy-fourth Annual Meeting, 1961* (*American Economic Review*, Vol. 52, May 1962), pp. 335–45; Norman B. Ture, "Tax Reform: Depreciation Problems," in American Economic Association, *Papers and Proceedings of the Seventy-fifth Annual Meeting, 1962* (*American Economic Review*, Vol. 53, May 1963), pp. 334–53,

view is not free of ambiguities even at the qualitative level. For example, a reduction in the tax rate would appear to reduce the burden of the corporate income tax and to act as a stimulus to investment. But as Samuelson has demonstrated, a reduction in the tax rate may make assets more attractive, less attractive, or equally attractive to the investor, depending on depreciation allowances for tax purposes.[2] At a further remove, a change in the tax rate may increase, decrease, or leave unchanged the prevailing cost of money.[3] The effect of a reduction in taxes depends on the responsiveness of saving, as well as that of investment, to the proposed change.[4]

Even where the qualitative implications of a tax change are clear and unambiguous, no answers are given to the important questions for economic policy: How much investment? When will it occur? A stimulus to investment may have large or small effects. The resulting investment expenditures may take place immediately or over a considerable period of time. To determine the effects precisely, a quantitative analysis of investment behavior is required. In two previous papers we have presented an econometric model designed specifically to study the effects of tax policy on investment behavior.[5] We have estimated the unknown parameters of this model from annual data on investment expenditures for the nonfarm sector of the United States beginning with 1929. Given the empirical results, we have

esp. pp. 341–45; Sam B. Chase, Jr., "Tax Credits for Investment Spending," *National Tax Journal*, Vol. 15 (March 1962), pp. 32–52; and Richard A. Musgrave, "Effects of Tax Policy on Private Capital Formation," in Commission on Money and Credit, *Fiscal and Debt Management Policies* (Prentice-Hall, 1963), pp. 53–54 and 117–29.

[2] Paul A. Samuelson, "Tax Deductibility of Economic Depreciation To Insure Invariant Valuations," *Journal of Political Economy*, Vol. 72 (December 1964), pp. 604–06.

[3] The effects of changes in the corporate tax rate on the cost of capital is the subject of much controversy. Recent contributions to the discussion include those of Robert J. Gordon, "The Incidence of the Corporation Income Tax in U.S. Manufacturing, 1925–62," *American Economic Review*, Vol. 57 (September 1967), pp. 731–58; Marian Krzyzaniak and Richard A. Musgrave, *The Shifting of the Corporation Income Tax: An Empirical Study of Its Short-run Effect upon the Rate of Return* (Johns Hopkins Press, 1963); and John G. Cragg, Arnold C. Harberger, and Peter Mieszkowski, "Empirical Evidence on the Incidence of the Corporation Income Tax," *Journal of Political Economy*, Vol. 75 (December 1967), pp. 811–21.

[4] Little is known about the effects of the rate of return on saving. Harberger assumes that changes in the rate of return leave saving unchanged. See Chap. 7.

[5] Robert E. Hall and Dale W. Jorgenson, "Tax Policy and Investment Behavior," *American Economic Review*, Vol. 57 (June 1967), pp. 391–414, and Robert E. Hall and Dale W. Jorgenson, "The Role of Taxation in Stabilizing Private Investment," in Vincent P. Rock (ed.), *Policymakers and Model Builders: Cases and Concepts* (Washington: Gordon and Breach, 1969).

calculated the effects of tax policy on investment behavior in the postwar period. Specifically, we have studied the effects of the adoption of accelerated depreciation in 1954, new lifetimes for depreciation in 1962, the investment tax credit in 1962 and its modification in 1964, and suspension of the investment tax credit in 1966–67.

The purpose of this study is similar to that of our previous work. We first reestimate our econometric model of investment behavior, taking into account data that have become available since our earlier work. We have revised our econometric technique to take advantage of recently developed methods of estimation. With these changes we obtain a new set of investment functions for the nonfarm sector of the United States, which we employ to characterize the effects of the various measures adopted between 1954 and 1967. We calculate both the impact of the suspension of the tax credit actually in effect from October 1966 to March 1967 and the hypothetical results of the originally proposed suspension through December 1967.

The evolution of tax policies during the postwar period provides a broad range of experience for a quantitative study of their effects on investment behavior. On the basis of our analysis, we conclude that tax policy has been highly effective in changing the level and timing of investment expenditures. It has also affected the composition of investment expenditures in the nonfarm sector. The adoption of accelerated methods for depreciation and the reduction in depreciation lifetimes for tax purposes increased investment expenditures substantially. They also resulted in a shift in the composition of investment away from equipment toward structures. Limited to equipment, the investment tax credit has been a potent stimulus to the level of investment; it has also shifted the composition of investment toward equipment.

An econometric model of investment behavior has a decisive advantage over a purely qualitative analysis of the effects of tax policy as a basis for policy making. At the same time our study has significant limitations that must be made explicit at the outset. Our calculations are based on a partial equilibrium analysis of investment behavior. A general equilibrium analysis would be required to determine the full effects of a change in tax policy. We calculate the effects of tax policy on investment behavior given the prices of investment goods, the cost of financial capital, and the level and price of output. Obviously, the results derived from a complete econometric model—incorporating our econometric model of investment and an explanation of the prices of investment goods, the cost of financial capital, and the level and price of output—could differ substantially. Since no econometric model of this scope is currently available, such a general equilibrium analysis of tax policy, however desirable, is not now feasible. For quantitative analysis we are forced to choose between an econometric model of investment behavior that adequately reflects the direct effects of tax policy on investment and general equilibrium analysis based on the more traditional ad hoc explanations of investment behavior. This important gap in the study of macroeconometric models could be remedied by combining our model of investment behavior with an explanation of the supply of investment goods, the supply of and demand for consumer goods, and the supply of saving.

Theory of Investment Behavior

Our econometric model of investment behavior is based on the theory of optimal capital accumulation. This theory can be approached from two alternative and equivalent points of view.[6] In the first, the objective of the firm may be taken as the maximization of its market value. Given a recursive description of technology—output depending on the flow of current input and of capital services, and capital depending on the level of investment and the past value of capital—maximization of the market value of the firm implies that the marginal product of each current input is equal to its real price and the marginal product of each capital service is equal to its real rental. In the second approach, the objective of the firm is maximization of profit, defined as the difference between current revenue and current outlay less the rental value of capital services. The rental price of capital services is determined from the condition of market equilibrium that equates the value of an asset and the sum of discounted values of all capital services from that asset. These two approaches lead to the same theory of the firm. In this study, the maximization of profit is taken as the objective of the firm and an appropriate price of capital services determined from the price of capital assets. Tax policy affects investment behavior through the price of capital services.

There are, however, two objections to the theory of optimal capital accumulation as a basis for an econometric model of investment behavior. First, a substantial body of survey data suggests that "marginalist" considerations such as the cost of capital and tax policy are irrelevant to

---

[6] These alternative points of view on the theory of optimal capital accumulation are described in more detail in Dale W. Jorgenson, "The Theory of Investment Behavior," in Robert Ferber (ed.), *Determinants of Investment Behavior*, a Conference of the Universities-National Bureau Committee for Economic Research (Columbia University Press for the National Bureau of Economic Research, 1967).

business decisions to invest. This evidence has, however, been carefully analyzed by William H. White, who concludes that the survey data are defective even by the standards of noneconometric empirical work and that no reliance can be placed on conclusions drawn from them.[7] A second objection is that previous attempts to analyze investment behavior on the basis of neoclassical theory have not been successful. This objection is valid so far as the first such attempts are concerned. Negative results have been reported by Jan Tinbergen, Charles Roos, and Lawrence Klein for models incorporating marginalist considerations.[8] However, an econometric model based on current formulations of the neoclassical theory provides a better explanation of investment expenditures than its competitors, the flexible accelerator model studied intensively by Robert Eisner, and the models containing combinations of capacity utilization, liquidity, and the rate of interest studied by Locke Anderson and by John Meyer and Robert Glauber.[9] Further, the predictive performance of the neoclassical model is as satisfactory as that of models based on alternative theories of investment behavior.[10]

[7] William H. White, "Interest Inelasticity of Investment Demand—The Case from Business Attitude Surveys Re-examined," *American Economic Review*, Vol. 46 (September 1956), pp. 565–87.

[8] Negative results were reported in Jan Tinbergen, *Statistical Testing of Business-Cycle Theories*, Vol. 1, "A Method and Its Application to Investment Activity" (Geneva: League of Nations, 1939). Subsequently, similar results were reported in Charles F. Roos, "The Demand for Investment Goods," in American Economic Association, *Papers and Proceedings of the Sixtieth Annual Meeting, 1947* (*American Economic Review*, Vol. 38, May 1948), pp. 311–20; Charles F. Roos and Victor S. Von Szeliski, "The Demand for Durable Goods," *Econometrica*, Vol. 11 (April 1943), pp. 97–122; Lawrence R. Klein, *Economic Fluctuations in the United States, 1921–1941* (Wiley, 1950), esp. pp. 14–40; Lawrence R. Klein, "Studies in Investment Behavior," in Universities-National Bureau Committee for Economic Research, *Conference on Business Cycles* (National Bureau of Economic Research, 1951).

[9] Robert Eisner, "Realization of Investment Anticipations," in James S. Duesenberry, Gary Fromm, Lawrence R. Klein, and Edwin Kuh (eds.), *The Brookings Quarterly Econometric Model of the United States* (Chicago: Rand McNally, 1965; Amsterdam: North-Holland, 1965); W. H. Locke Anderson, *Corporate Finance and Fixed Investment* (Harvard University, Graduate School of Business Administration, Division of Research, 1964); and John R. Meyer and Robert R. Glauber, *Investment Decisions, Economic Forecasting, and Public Policy* (Harvard University, Graduate School of Business Administration, Division of Research, 1964). See also Dale W. Jorgenson, Jerald Hunter, and M. Ishag Nadiri, "A Comparison of Alternative Econometric Models of Quarterly Investment Behavior," *Econometrica*, Vol. 38 (March 1970), pp. 187–212.

[10] The predictive performance of these alternative econometric models is compared in

In addition to the direct support for the neoclassical theory from econometric studies of investment behavior, indirect support overwhelmingly favorable to it is provided by econometric studies of cost and production functions.[11] Current empirical research emphasizes such technical questions as the appropriate form for the production function and the statistical specification of econometric models of production. As an example, Nerlove has recently surveyed the literature, running to more than forty references, devoted solely to estimation of the elasticity of substitution.[12] In it, the neoclassical theory of the firm is taken as a point of departure. The purpose of the empirical research reviewed by Nerlove is to give more precise results within the framework provided by neoclassical theory.

Rental Price of Capital

To be noted first in this detailed analysis of the relationship between tax policy and investment behavior is that the objective of the firm is to maximize profit. Profit Z_B' is defined in a special sense as the difference between current revenue and current outlay less the rental value of capital services:

$$Z_B' = pQ - wL - cK, \tag{2.1}$$

where

p = the price of output
Q = the quantity of output
w = the price of labor input
L = the quantity of labor input
c = the rental price of capital
K = the quantity of capital.

Dale W. Jorgenson, Jerald Hunter, and M. Ishag Nadiri, "The Predictive Performance of Econometric Models of Quarterly Investment Behavior," *Econometrica*, Vol. 38 (March 1970), pp. 213–24.

[11] Three hundred forty-five references, almost all presenting the results of econometric tests of the neoclassical theory of the firm, are listed in a recent survey of the econometric literature on cost and production functions. See A. A. Walters, "Production and Cost Functions: An Econometric Survey," *Econometrica*, Vol. 31 (January–April 1963), pp. 1–66.

[12] Marc Nerlove, "Recent Empirical Studies of the CES and Related Production Functions," in Murray Brown (ed.), *The Theory and Empirical Analysis of Production* (Columbia University Press for the National Bureau of Economic Research, 1967).

Profit is maximized at each point of time subject to a production function,

$$Q = \Phi(L, K).$$ (2.2)

Investment I is the sum of changes in capital stock $\dot{K}$ and of replacement. We assume that replacement is proportional to capital so that investment may be determined from the relationship,

$$I = \dot{K} + \delta K,$$ (2.3)

where δ is the rate of replacement.

Necessary conditions for profit maximization are that the marginal product of current input is equal to its real price,

$$\partial \Phi / \partial L = w/p;$$ (2.4)

similarly, the marginal product of capital input is equal to its real rental,

$$\partial \Phi / \partial K = c/p.$$ (2.5)

Second, the price of new capital goods q must equal the present value of future rentals.[13] In the absence of direct taxation this relationship takes the form

$$q(t) = \int_{t}^{\infty} e^{-r(s-t)} c(s) e^{-\delta(s-t)} \, ds,$$ (2.6)

where

r = the rate of return
c = the rental price of capital input
$e^{-\delta(s-t)}$ = the quantity of capital input at time s resulting from the purchase of one unit of the capital asset at time t.

If prices of new investment goods are expected to remain stationary,[14]

$$c = q(r + \delta).$$ (2.7)

---

[13] Here we assume that investment is fully reversible. A discussion of the relationship between the price of capital goods and the present value of future rentals where investment is irreversible may be found in Kenneth J. Arrow, "Optimal Capital Policy with Irreversible Investment," in James N. Wolfe (ed.), *Value, Capital and Growth: Papers in Honour of Sir John Hicks* (Edinburgh: Edinburgh University Press, 1968).

[14] A detailed derivation is given in Jorgenson, "The Theory of Investment Behavior."

For the nonfarm sector of the U.S. economy, taxes are imposed on current revenue less outlay on current input and less certain deductions on capital account. As an approximation, taxation is represented in the nonfarm sector by the corporate income tax. It is assumed that business income is taxed at a constant marginal rate with deductions allowed for interest payments and for depreciation on capital assets. In addition a tax credit is allowed on the acquisition of new investment goods. Where the before-tax rate of return ρ reflects deductions of interest allowed for tax purposes, the relationship between the price of new capital goods and the present value of all future rentals and tax deductions becomes

$$q(t) = \int_t^\infty e^{-(1-u)\rho(s-t)}[e^{-\delta(s-t)}(1-u)c(s)+uq(t)D(s-t)]ds+kq(t). \qquad (2.8)$$

The rental value of capital services after taxes is $(1-u)c$, where u is the tax rate. The depreciation formula $D(s-t)$ gives the depreciation allowance per dollar of initial investment for tax purposes at time t on an asset of age $(s-t)$. Note that depreciation allowances depend on the price at which the asset is acquired $q(t)$, not the price of assets at the time depreciation is allowed as a charge against income $q(s)$. Finally, the tax credit is $kq(t)$, where k is the proportion of the value of the asset allowable as a credit against taxes; the tax credit is not deducted from the amount of depreciation to be claimed. This formulation is inappropriate to the tax credit for the years 1962 and 1963, during the period the Long amendment was in effect. Under this amendment the tax credit was deducted from allowable depreciation so that

$$q(t) = \int_t^\infty e^{-(1-u)\rho(s-t)}[e^{-\delta(s-t)}(1-u)c(s)+uq(t)(1-k)D(s-t)]ds+kq(t).$$
$$(2.9)$$

As before, it is assumed that the prices of new investment goods (and the rate of the investment tax credit) are expected to remain stationary. The relationship between the price of capital services c and the price of capital assets q after repeal of the Long amendment was

$$c = q[(1-u)\rho+\delta](1-k-uz)/(1-u), \qquad (2.10)$$

where

$$z = \int_t^\infty e^{-(1-u)\rho(s-t)}D(s-t)ds \qquad (2.11)$$

may be interpreted as the present value of depreciation deductions totaling one dollar over the lifetime of the investment. Before repeal of the Long amendment, when the tax credit was deducted from the allowable depreciation base, the relationship was

$$c = q[(1-u)\rho+\delta](1-k)(1-uz)/(1-u). \tag{2.12}$$

Considering the impact of changes in the tax structure on the price of capital services, an increase in the investment tax credit k will always reduce the price of capital services. Where the investment tax credit is deducted from allowable depreciation, this credit has precisely the effect of a direct subsidy to the purchase of investment goods.[15] Second, an increase in the present value of depreciation deductions z, resulting from a reduction in lifetimes of investment goods allowable for tax purposes or from the use of accelerated depreciation formulas, reduces the price of capital services.

The effect of a change in the tax rate u on the price of capital services depends on the effect of such a change on the rate of return. If the before-tax rate of return ρ is held constant, a change in the tax rate is neutral in its effects on the price of capital services if the combined value of depreciation allowances and the investment tax credit is equal to the value of "economic" depreciation, where economic depreciation corresponds to

$$D(s-t) = \delta e^{-\delta(s-t)}. \tag{2.13}$$

The present value of economic depreciation z^* is

$$z^* = \int_t^\infty e^{-(1-u)\rho(s-t)} \delta e^{-\delta(s-t)} \, ds,$$
$$= \delta/(1-u)\rho+\delta. \tag{2.14}$$

Provided that

$$k+uz = uz^*,$$

then

$$c = q(\rho+\delta),$$

so that the price of capital services is unaffected by changes in the tax rate.[16]

---

[15] A direct subsidy at the rate k results in a cost of acquisition of investment goods $q(1-k)$. With tax rate u and present value of depreciation z, the same formula is obtained for the rental price of capital as for the investment tax credit, $c = q(1-k)[(1-u)\rho+\delta] \times (1-uz)/(1-u)$.

[16] Similar results are given in E. Cary Brown, "Business-Income Taxation and Investment Incentives," in Lloyd A. Metzler and others, *Income, Employment and Public Policy: Essays in Honor of Alvin H. Hansen* (W. W. Norton, 1948); and in Samuelson, "Tax Deductibility of Economic Depreciation To Insure Invariant Valuations."

On the other hand, if the after-tax rate of return $r = (1-u)\rho$ is held constant, a change in the tax rate is neutral if the combined value of depreciation allowances and the investment tax credit is equal to the value of immediate expensing of assets. Provided that

$$k + uz = u,$$

then

$$c = q(r + \delta);$$

thus the price of capital services is unaffected by changes in the tax rate.[17]

Therefore, if the before-tax cost of capital is fixed, changes in the tax rate have no effect on the price of capital services when the combined effect of the investment tax credit and depreciation allowances for tax purposes is equivalent to economic depreciation. Second, if the after-tax cost of capital is fixed, changes in the tax rate are neutral when the combined effect is equivalent to immediate expensing of assets. Thus the neutrality of changes in the tax rate depends on whether the burden of the tax is borne by the firm (before-tax cost of capital constant) or shifted (after-tax cost of capital constant). To resolve the controversy surrounding the incidence of the corporate income tax requires a general equilibrium analysis based on an econometric model including saving as well as investment.[18] Here it is assumed that the burden of the tax is borne by the firm, that is, that the before-tax rate of return is unaffected by changes in the tax rate.

Depreciation Formulas

STRAIGHT LINE. Prior to the Revenue Act of 1954, essentially the only depreciation formula permitted for tax purposes was the straight-line formula, with a constant stream of depreciation over the lifetime of the

[17] Similar results are given in Brown, "Business-Income Taxation and Investment Incentives"; in Richard A. Musgrave, *The Theory of Public Finance* (McGraw-Hill, 1959); and in Vernon L. Smith, "Tax Depreciation Policy and Investment Theory," *International Economic Review*, Vol. 4 (January 1963), pp. 80–91.

[18] For recent contributions to this controversy, see Gordon, "Incidence of the Corporation Income Tax in U.S. Manufacturing"; Krzyzaniak and Musgrave, *Shifting of the Corporation Income Tax*; and Cragg and others, "Empirical Evidence on the Incidence of the Corporation Income Tax." Our assumption of "no shifting"—that is, the before-tax rate of return is unaffected by changes in the tax rate—is supported by the results reported by Gordon. Alternative assumptions are suggested by Cragg and others and by Krzyzaniak and Musgrave. None of these empirical results is based on a complete econometric model appropriate to a general equilibrium analysis of the incidence of the corporate income tax.

asset. This formula can be expressed

$$D(\tau) = 1/T, \qquad 0 \leqq \tau \leqq T, \qquad (2.15)$$

where T is the lifetime and $\tau = s - t$ is the age of the asset. The present value of depreciation deductions under the straight-line formula is

$$z = [1/(1-\mu)\rho T][1 - e^{-(1-\mu)\rho T}]. \qquad (2.16)$$

Under the Revenue Act of 1954, three depreciation formulas were allowed for tax purposes. As alternatives to the straight-line formula, taxpayers were permitted to employ the sum-of-the-years-digits and declining-balance formulas. These two formulas are known as accelerated methods of depreciation because for a given lifetime and cost of capital they result in higher present values of depreciation deductions than the straight-line method.

SUM-OF-THE-YEARS-DIGITS. In the sum-of-the-years-digits method the deduction for depreciation declines linearly over the lifetime of the asset, starting at twice the corresponding straight-line rate; the depreciation formula is [19]

$$D(\tau) = 2(T-\tau)/T^2 \qquad 0 \leqq \tau \leqq T. \qquad (2.17)$$

The present value of depreciation deductions under this formula is [20]

$$z = [2/(1-u)\rho T]\{1 - [1 - e^{-(1-u)\rho T}]/[(1-u)\rho T]\}. \qquad (2.18)$$

DECLINING BALANCE. In the declining-balance method of depreciation, the deduction drops exponentially over the lifetime of the asset starting at a fixed proportion of the straight-line rate. If this proportion θ is 2, the method is referred to as double declining balance; if the proportion is 1.5 the method is called 150 percent declining balance. Tax provisions permit taxpayers to switch from the declining-balance to straight-line depreciation at any point during the lifetime of the asset. Obviously, the switchover point that maximizes the present value of the depreciation deduction T^* occurs where the flow of declining-balance depreciation equals the flow of straight-line depreciation after the switch. The declining-balance depreciation formula is

$$D(\tau) = \begin{cases} (\theta/T)e^{-(\theta/T)\tau}, & 0 \leqq \tau \leqq T^*, \\ \dfrac{e^{-(\theta/T)T^*}}{T-T^*}, & T^* \leqq \tau \leqq T. \end{cases} \qquad (2.19)$$

---

[19] This is formula (7) in our earlier paper, Hall and Jorgenson, "Tax Policy and Investment Behavior," p. 394.

[20] See formula (8), *ibid.*

When (2.19) is solved for the optimal switchover point,

$$T^* = T[1 - (1/\theta)].\qquad(2.20)$$

The present value of depreciation under the declining-balance method is [21]

$$
\begin{aligned}
z = {}& \frac{\theta/T}{(1-u)\rho + (\theta/T)}\,[1 - e^{-[(1-u)\rho + (\theta/T)]T^*}] \\
&+ \frac{e^{-(\theta/T)T^*}}{(1-u)\rho(T-T^*)}\,[e^{-(1-u)\rho T^*} - e^{-(1-u)\rho T}].
\end{aligned}\qquad(2.21)
$$

Production Functions

Econometric implementation of a theory of investment behavior based on the neoclassical theory of optimal capital accumulation requires an appropriate form for the production function. The choice of the form has been the subject of much empirical research, which is currently focused on the choice of an appropriate value for the elasticity of substitution. Summarizing his recent survey of this research, Zvi Griliches finds that "the studies based on cross-sectional data yield estimates which are on the whole not significantly different from unity. The time series studies report, on the average, substantially lower estimates." [22]

In an attempt to reconcile this basic conflict between the estimates based on time series and on cross-sectional data, Griliches modifies in three ways the regression of output per employee on the real wage (both in logarithms) employed by Arrow, Chenery, Minhas, and Solow: [23] (1) measures of labor quality are introduced into the regression; (2) regional dummy variables are introduced to take account of possible differentials in price of output and labor quality by region; and (3) allowance is made for the possibility of serial correlation in the error term due to persistence of omitted variables. [24] The resulting cross-sectional estimates of the elasticity of substitution are similar to previous estimates. Only one (out of seventeen) of

---

[21] This result corrects an error in formula (9), *ibid*. Fortunately, this error did not affect any of the empirical results presented in that or the subsequent paper, Hall and Jorgenson, "Role of Taxation in Stabilizing Private Investment."

[22] Zvi Griliches, "Production Functions in Manufacturing: Some Preliminary Results," in Brown, *Theory and Empirical Analysis of Production*, p. 285.

[23] Kenneth J. Arrow, Hollis B. Chenery, B. S. Minhas, and Robert M. Solow, "Capital-Labor Substitution and Economic Efficiency," *Review of Economics and Statistics*, Vol. 43 (August 1961), pp. 225–50.

[24] Griliches, "Production Functions in Manufacturing," p. 290.

these estimates of the elasticity of substitution is significantly different from unity, and that one is above unity.[25] Allowing for serial correlation of the errors in successive years, Griliches obtains estimates for successive cross sections that he characterizes as ". . . not . . . very different from unity, the significant deviations if anything occurring above unity rather than below it." [26] "I do not intend to argue," Griliches concludes from these and additional estimates of the elasticity of substitution, "that these results prove that the Cobb-Douglas [elasticity of substitution equal to unity] is the right form for the manufacturing production function, only that there is no strong evidence against it. Until better evidence appears, there is no reason to give it up as the maintained hypothesis." [27] On the basis of the results presented by Griliches and the work that both he and Nerlove surveyed,[28] we adopt the Cobb-Douglas production function for our theory of investment behavior. This form was used in our earlier studies.[29]

Capital Accumulation

If there is no lag in the completion of investment projects, the level of investment appropriate for optimal capital accumulation may be determined from the conditions necessary for maximization of profit. In the theory of investment behavior described below, the assumption is that the actual level of capital stock may differ from the optimal level. More specifically, given capital stock, the levels of output and current input are assumed to be determined from the production function and the marginal productivity condition for current input. The desired level of capital is determined from the actual level of output, given the marginal productivity condition for capital input, while the actual level of capital is determined by past investment. Finally, time is required for the completion of new investment projects. Projects are initiated at every point in time so that the actual level of capital plus the backlog of uncompleted projects is equal to the desired level of capital.

If the production function has the Cobb-Douglas form, the marginal

---

[25] *Ibid.*, p. 292.

[26] *Ibid.*

[27] *Ibid.*, p. 297.

[28] Nerlove, "Recent Empirical Studies of the CES and Related Production Functions."

[29] Hall and Jorgenson, "Role of Taxation in Stabilizing Private Investment"; and Hall and Jorgenson, "Tax Policy and Investment Behavior."

productivity condition for capital input may be written

$$\alpha(Q/K^*) = (c/p), \tag{2.22}$$

where α is the elasticity of output with respect to capital input and K^* is the desired level of capital. To solve for desired capital,

$$K^* = \alpha(pQ/c). \tag{2.23}$$

To represent the theory of investment, the proportion of investment projects initiated in time t and completed in period $t+\tau$ was designated μ_τ. It is assumed that the sequence of proportions μ_τ depends only on the time elapsed between initiation of a project and its completion. New projects are held to be initiated in each period until the backlog of uncompleted projects is equal to the difference between desired and actual capital. Under this assumption new investment orders in each period are equal to the change in desired capital stock. In every period the level of actual net investment is a weighted average of projects initiated in previous periods,

$$I_t - \delta K_{t-1} = \mu_0[K_t^* - K_{t-1}^*] + \mu_1[K_{t-1}^* - K_{t-2}^*] + \dots, \tag{2.24}$$

where I_t is gross investment and δK_{t-1} is replacement investment.

To make the notation more concise, it is useful to use the lag operator S, defined as:

$$Sx_t = x_{t-1},$$

for any sequence x_t. With this notation, the expression for the level of net investment given above may be written more compactly as

$$I_t - \delta K_{t-1} = \mu(S)[K_t^* - K_{t-1}^*], \tag{2.25}$$

where

$$\mu(S) = \mu_0 + \mu_1 S + \dots, \tag{2.26}$$

is a power series in the lag operator.

Summary

To summarize, investment in period t depends on the capital stock at the beginning of the period and changes in the desired level of capital in previous periods. The form of the relationship depends on the form of the distributed lag function and the rate of replacement. The desired level of capital depends on the level of output, the price of output, and the rental price of capital input. Tax policy affects investment behavior through the rental price of capital input. This price depends on the price of investment goods, the cost of capital, the tax rate, the formulas for calculating depreciation allowances for tax purposes, and the level of the investment tax credit. A change in tax policy changes the rental price of capital input and consequently the desired level of capital stock. An increase in desired capital stock generates net investment; if the price of capital input and the other determinants of desired capital remain constant, net investment declines to zero as capital stock approaches its desired level. The change in tax policy continues to affect gross investment through replacement requirements for a permanently larger capital stock.

Econometrics of Investment Behavior

Our theory of investment behavior implies a distributed lag relationship between net investment and changes in the desired level of capital. If this theory is to be implemented econometrically, restrictions must be imposed on the sequence of μ_τ coefficients. In previous studies we have employed the restriction that this sequence has a rational generating function. With this restriction the power series $\mu(S)$ may be represented as the ratio of two polynomials in the lag operator, that is, a rational function of the lag operator,

$$\mu(S) = \gamma(S)/\omega(S). \tag{2.27}$$

The resulting rational distributed lag function may be written as a mixed moving average and autoregressive scheme in changes in the desired level of capital and net investment.[30] Second, a random component ε_t must be added to the distributed lag function,

$$\omega(S)[I_t - \delta K_{t-1}] = \gamma(S)[K_t^* - K_{t-1}^*] + \varepsilon_t. \tag{2.28}$$

Finally, an appropriate specification must be chosen for the stochastic component ε_t. In previous studies we have assumed that the random component is distributed independently and identically over time, a feature that we retain here. In addition we employ further restrictions on the sequence of coefficients μ_τ in order to economize on the number of parameters to be estimated.

The first assumption is that the distributed lag function may be represented as a finite moving average with an autoregressive error, that is

$$I_t - \delta K_{t-1} = \beta(S)[K_t^* - K_{t-1}^*] + v_t, \tag{2.29}$$

---

[30] For further discussion of this point, see Dale W. Jorgenson, "Rational Distributed Lag Functions," *Econometrica*, Vol. 32 (January 1966), pp. 135–49.

where $\beta(S)$ is a polynomial in the lag operator and v_t is an autoregressive error. It is assumed that v_t is generated by an autoregressive scheme,

$$\omega(S)v_t = \varepsilon_t, \tag{2.30}$$

where $\omega(S)$ is a polynomial in the lag operator and ε_t is distributed independently and identically over time. Multiplication of both sides of the distributed lag function by the polynomial $\omega(S)$ results in an alternative form of the distributed lag function,

$$\omega(S)[I_t - \delta K_{t-1}] = \omega(S)\beta(S)[K_t^* - K_{t-1}^*] + \omega(S)v_t$$
$$= \omega(S)\beta(S)[K_t^* - K_{t-1}^*] + \varepsilon_t, \tag{2.31}$$

which is a rational distributed lag function with independently and identically distributed error term, the specification employed in our earlier studies.

With the representation of the power series $\mu(S)$ as the ratio of two polynomials in the lag operator, it is possible to write

$$\omega(S) = \omega(S),$$
$$\gamma(S) = \omega(S)\beta(S).$$

The rational distributed lag function employed in our earlier studies is now further restricted in that the polynomial $\gamma(S)$ is the product of two polynomials, one of them $\omega(S)$, the denominator of the original representation of the power series $\mu(S)$. If this restriction is valid, it may be used to reduce the number of parameters to be estimated. Further, the implied estimator of the power series $\mu(S)$ reduces to an estimator of the polynomial $\beta(S)$, since

$$\mu(S) = \frac{\gamma(S)}{\omega(S)}$$
$$= \frac{\omega(S)\beta(S)}{\omega(S)}$$
$$= \beta(S).$$

This restriction overcomes a possible objection to an unconstrained estimator of the parameters of the power series $\mu(S)$ for a rational distributed lag function. In some circumstances relatively small variations in the coefficients of the numerator of the power series may give rise to large variations in the coefficients of the power series itself, as Griliches has suggested.[31] Under

[31] Zvi Griliches, "Distributed Lags: A Survey," *Econometrica*, Vol. 35 (January 1967), pp. 16–49.

the restrictions proposed here, the estimator of the coefficients of the power series $\mu(S)$ is independent of the estimator of the coefficients of the numerator $\omega(S)$.

As an example, if there are five terms in the original polynomial in the lag operator $\beta(S)$, the distributed lag function becomes

$$I_t - \delta K_{t-1} = \sum_{\tau=0}^{4} \beta_\tau [K^*_{t-\tau} - K^*_{t-\tau-1}] + v_t. \tag{2.32}$$

If, further, the order of the polynomial $\omega(S)$ is unity, that is, the disturbance has only first-order autocorrelation, both sides of the distributed lag function may be multiplied by $\omega(S) = 1 + \omega_1 S$ to obtain

$$[I_t - \delta K_{t-1}] + \omega_1 [I_{t-1} - \delta K_{t-2}] = \beta_0 [K^*_t - K^*_{t-1}]$$
$$+ \sum_{\tau=0}^{3} [\omega_1 \beta_\tau + \beta_{\tau+1}][K^*_{t-\tau-1} - K^*_{t-\tau-2}]$$
$$+ \omega_1 \beta_4 [K^*_{t-5} - K^*_{t-6}] + \varepsilon_t$$
$$= \sum_{\tau=0}^{5} \gamma_\tau [K^*_{t-\tau} - K^*_{t-\tau-1}] + \varepsilon_t. \tag{2.33}$$

Satisfactory specifications of the distributed lag function between net investment and changes in the desired level of capital have been obtained using polynomials $\omega(S)$ of low order. However, as many as five terms in the polynomial $\beta(S)$ have been required to obtain a satisfactory specification. In order to economize further on the number of parameters to be estimated, we have employed an approximation proposed by Shirley Almon.[32] This method assumes that the polynomial in the lag operator $\beta(S)$ has coefficients generated by a polynomial in the lag itself:

$$\beta_\tau = \pi_0 + \pi_1 \tau + \ldots + \pi_\kappa \tau^\kappa. \tag{2.34}$$

To make this an approximation at all, of course, the order of the approximating polynomial must be less than the order of the polynomial in the lag operator.

If the order of the approximating polynomial is two and there are five terms in the original polynomial in the lag operator $\beta(S)$, the distributed lag function becomes

---

[32] Shirley Almon, "The Distributed Lag between Capital Appropriations and Expenditures," *Econometrica*, Vol. 33 (January 1965), pp. 178–96.

$$I_t - \delta K_{t-1} = \sum_{\tau=0}^{4} \beta_\tau [K^*_{t-\tau} - K^*_{t-\tau-1}] + v_t,$$

$$= \sum_{\tau=0}^{4} [\pi_0 + \pi_1 \tau + \pi_2 \tau^2][K^*_{t-\tau} - K^*_{t-\tau-1}] + v_t,$$

$$= \sum_{i=0}^{2} \pi_i \sum_{\tau=0}^{4} \tau^i [K^*_{t-\tau} - K^*_{t-\tau-1}] + v_t. \qquad (2.35)$$

On transformation this function becomes

$$[I_t - \delta K_{t-1}] + \omega_1 [I_{t-1} - \delta K_{t-2}] = \sum_{i=0}^{2} \pi_i \sum_{\tau=0}^{4} \tau^i [K^*_{t-\tau} - K^*_{t-\tau-1}]$$

$$+ \omega_1 \sum_{i=0}^{2} \pi_i \sum_{\tau=0}^{4} \tau^i [K^*_{t-\tau-1} - K^*_{t-\tau-2}] + \varepsilon_t. \qquad (2.36)$$

In this distributed lag function there are only four unknown parameters: π_0, π_1, π_2, and ω_1.

Ordinary least squares may be employed to estimate the unknown parameters of a rational distributed lag function with independently and identically distributed error term ε_t. The resulting estimator is consistent; its asymptotic distribution may be characterized in precisely the same way as in our previous studies.[33]

Estimating Procedure

Provided that the restrictions on the coefficients we have proposed are valid, it is useful to take them into account in estimating the unknown parameters of the distributed lag function. First, approximation of the coefficients of the polynomial in the lag operator $\beta(S)$ by a polynomial in the lag itself results in restrictions that are linear in the unknown parameters β_τ. These restrictions are used to eliminate the parameters β_τ and express the distributed lag function in terms of the parameters π_i. The constrained distributed lag function is still linear in the unknown parameters so that ordinary least squares may be applied directly. Secondly, generation of a rational distributed lag function by autoregressive transformation of a finite moving average results in a distributed lag function that is nonlinear in its parameters. To estimate such a function, Durbin's two stage least

---

[33] Further details on properties of the least squares estimator are discussed in Jorgenson, "Rational Distributed Lag Functions," pp. 142–43.

squares is employed.[34] It begins with application of an ordinary least squares estimator to the unconstrained rational distributed lag function, and continues with estimation of the parameters of the moving average β_τ by applying least squares to the dependent and independent variables transformed in accord with the original autoregressive scheme. Parameters of the scheme ω_τ are set equal to their first-round estimates. The procedure results in estimates of the parameters β_τ, ω_τ that are asymptotically efficient.[35] It is easily seen to converge on successive iterations to the maximum likelihood estimator of the distributed lag function.

Durbin's two stage procedure may be characterized as follows: First, the parameters of the rational distributed lag function equation (2.33) are estimated without constraints—ω_1, γ_0 ... γ_5—by ordinary least squares. Second, least squares are applied to the relationship

$$[I_t - \delta K_{t-1}] + \hat{\omega}_1 [I_{t-1} - \delta K_{t-2}] = \sum_{i=0}^{2} \pi_i \sum_{\tau=0}^{4} \tau^i \{ [K_{t-\tau}^* - K_{t-\tau-1}^*]$$

$$+ \hat{\omega}_1 [K_{t-\tau-1}^* - K_{t-\tau-2}^*] \} + \hat{\varepsilon}_t, \tag{2.37}$$

where

$\hat{\omega}_1$ = the first-round estimator of the autocorrelation parameter

$\hat{\varepsilon}_t$ = the error in the distributed lag function plus the error in the first stage estimator $\hat{\omega}_1$, times the corresponding variables and parameters.

Since the first stage estimator is consistent, the error in it does not affect the asymptotic properties of the estimator of the remaining parameters π_0, π_1, and π_2.

To test the validity of the two constraints we have proposed, we begin with the unconstrained least squares estimator of the unknown parameters of the distributed lag function. This is the first stage in Durbin's two-stage estimator. We then impose the constraints, obtaining an estimator satisfying the restrictions that $\gamma(S) = \omega(S)\beta(S)$ and that $\beta(S)$ has coefficients that may be approximated by a polynomial in the lag itself. A test statistic $\mathscr{F}$

---

[34] James Durbin, "Estimation of Parameters in Time-series Regression Models," *Journal of the Royal Statistical Society*, Series B, Vol. 22 (1960), pp. 139–53.

[35] See *ibid.*, pp. 150–53.

that is asymptotically equivalent to a likelihood ratio test is:

$$\mathscr{F} = \frac{(\hat{\varepsilon}_0' \hat{\varepsilon}_0 - \hat{\varepsilon}_1' \hat{\varepsilon}_1)/(m_1 - m_0)}{\hat{\varepsilon}_1' \hat{\varepsilon}_1/(m_2 - m_1)}, \tag{2.38}$$

where

$\hat{\varepsilon}_0' \hat{\varepsilon}_0$ = the constrained estimators
$\hat{\varepsilon}_1' \hat{\varepsilon}_1$ = the unconstrained estimators
m_1 = the number of parameters to be estimated without constraints
m_0 = the number of parameters to be estimated with constraints taken into account
m_2 = the number of observations.

This statistic is asymptotically equivalent to the statistic associated with the likelihood ratio test of this hypothesis. In the example above there are seven unknown parameters in the unconstrained distributed lag function so that $m_1 = 7$. In the constrained estimator there are only four, so that $m_0 = 4$. It should be noted that acceptance of the null hypothesis at conventional levels of significance is not in itself justification for imposing the constraints; it is merely an indication that there is no strong evidence contradicting the constraints.

Estimates of the Parameters of the Investment Functions

Data Sources

The econometric model of investment behavior outlined in previous sections has been fitted to data on investment expenditures based on the 1966 capital goods study of the Office of Business Economics (OBE).[36] Data are available for structures and equipment separately for both the manufacturing and nonfarm nonmanufacturing sectors of the U.S. economy for the years 1929–65. The data are derived by allocating commodity flow data on gross private domestic investment from the national product accounts among sectors of destination. The investment data used in this study differ from those employed in our earlier studies in two ways: (1) They reflect revisions in commodity flow estimates of gross private domestic investment resulting from revisions of the U.S. national income and product

[36] These unpublished data, collected by the U.S. Department of Commerce, Office of Business Economics, were kindly made available to us by Robert Wasson of the Office of Business Economics.

accounts,[37] and (2) they incorporate estimates of government-owned capital used in private production and some other minor adjustments made by Gordon.[38]

Published price indexes for gross private domestic investment are biased because they are based in part on the price of inputs to the capital goods industries rather than the price of output. To overcome this bias we used the Bureau of Public Roads price index for structures in our previous studies. Here we use an index constructed by Gordon, based on price indexes for the output of structures from the 1966 capital goods study. In our previous study we replaced the implicit deflator for producers' durables by a deflator for consumers' durables. To avoid a possible bias resulting from differences in the cyclical behavior of consumers' and producers' price indexes, it was decided not to attempt to correct the bias in the producers' durables price index, which, in any case, is not very substantial.[39] Accordingly, the implicit deflator for producers' durables from the national product accounts is employed in this study. All price indexes have a 1965 base.

Capital stock for equipment and structures in both industry groupings is obtained from the recursive relationship,

$$K_t = I_t + (1-\delta)K_{t-1},$$

where I_t is investment in period t, derived as outlined above, and δ is the rate of replacement, taken to be 2.5 times the inverse of the Bureau of Internal Revenue's *Bulletin F* lifetime.[40] Similar rates of replacement were used by the Office of Business Economics in its 1966 capital goods study. The values of δ are the same as those employed in our previous studies:

Manufacturing equipment	0.1471
Manufacturing structures	0.0625
Nonfarm nonmanufacturing equipment	0.1923
Nonfarm nonmanufacturing structures	0.0694

[37] U.S. Department of Commerce, Office of Business Economics, *The National Income and Product Accounts of the United States, 1929–1965: Statistical Tables* (1966).

[38] Robert J. Gordon, "Problems in the Measurement of Real Investment in the U.S. Private Economy" (Ph.D. dissertation, Massachusetts Institute of Technology, 1967).

[39] Our original estimate of the rate of growth of this bias was 0.651 percent per year, or about one-third the bias for structures. See Hall and Jorgenson, "Tax Policy and Investment Behavior," p. 399.

[40] U.S. Treasury Department, Bureau of Internal Revenue, *Income Tax Depreciation and Obsolescence: Estimated Useful Lives and Depreciation Rates*, Bulletin F (revised January 1942); referred to as *Bulletin F*.

Initial values for capital stock in 1929 were estimated by cumulating net investment over the whole period for which data are available for each asset.

The desired level of capital stock depends on the value of output. As a measure of output and prices pQ, we have used gross value added at factor cost, in current dollars, defined as gross product originating in each industry less indirect business taxes. For the years 1929 to 1946 these data are identical to those of our previous studies. For the years 1947 to 1965 data were obtained from the OBE study of gross product originating in each sector.[41]

The desired level of capital also depends on the rental price for capital services. Through 1953 the rental price is that appropriate to straight-line depreciation. Since 1954 the rental price is that appropriate to sum-of-the-years-digits depreciation.[42] From October 1966 to March 1967 the appropriate rental price for structures is that for 150-percent-declining-balance depreciation.

The investment tax credit was introduced in 1962 at a rate nominally equal to 7 percent of the value of investment in equipment. In practice certain limitations on the applicability of the investment tax credit reduce its effective rate to 6 percent for manufacturing equipment and 5.8 percent for nonfarm nonmanufacturing equipment.[43] For 1962 and 1963, under the Long amendment, the base for depreciation was reduced by the amount of the tax credit; after 1964, with the repeal of the amendment, the base for depreciation is not reduced by the amount of the credit. From October 1966 to March 1967, the investment tax credit was suspended.

The rental price of capital services also depends on the tax rate u, the after-tax rate of return r, the investment goods price q, the rate of replacement δ, and the lifetime of capital goods allowable for tax purposes. We took the tax rate to be the statutory rate prevailing during most of each year. We did not allow for excess profits taxes during the middle thirties or the Korean war. For all years we took the rate of return before taxes ρ to be constant at 20 percent. This value is higher than the value of 14 percent used in our previous studies, but it is consistent with the results of Jorgenson

[41] See Jack J. Gottsegen, "Revised Estimates of GNP by Major Industries," *Survey of Current Business*, Vol. 47 (April 1967), pp. 18–24.

[42] Depreciation under the sum-of-the-years-digits formula has a higher present value for the range of lifetimes and rates of return of interest for this study. See Hall and Jorgenson, "Tax Policy and Investment Behavior," Table 1, p. 395.

[43] These estimates of the effective rate of the tax credit are based on data from tax returns for 1963. See U.S. Treasury Department, Internal Revenue Service, *Statistics of Income—1963, Corporation Income Tax Returns* (1968).

and Griliches.[44] Under the assumption of a constant before-tax rate of return, the after-tax rate $r = (1-u)\rho$ varies with the tax rate.

The investment goods price is the same as that used to deflate investment expenditures in current prices and the rate of replacement is the same as that used to calculate capital stock. Estimates of lifetimes of assets allowable for tax purposes were based on a special Treasury study,[45] and are the same as those employed in our previous studies:

Asset lifetimes
(years)

Period	Equipment	Structures
1929–54	17.5	27.8
1955	16.3	25.3
1956–61	15.1	22.8
1962–65	13.1	22.8

Equation Estimates

The previous section described a statistical technique for fitting our econometric model to data on investment expenditures. In summary this technique is based on the application of least squares in two stages. First, an unconstrained rational distributed lag function is fitted to data on net investment and changes in the desired level of capital for each class of asset for each sector. The independent variables include lagged values of net investment and current and lagged changes in the desired level of capital. We have designated the lag operators $\beta(S)$ and $\omega(S)$ as fourth- and first-order polynomials, respectively, so that one lagged value of net investment and current and five lagged changes in desired capital are included among the independent variables. The results of the first stage regressions, of the form of equation (2.33), for the periods 1935–40 and 1954–65 are presented in Table 2-1. The coefficient $-\hat{\omega}_1$ is associated with lagged values of net investment and is an estimate of the autocorrelation of the disturbances. The coefficients $\hat{\alpha}\hat{\gamma}_0 \ldots \hat{\alpha}\hat{\gamma}_5$ are associated with changes in the ratio of the value of output to the rental price of capital services.

[44] Dale W. Jorgenson and Zvi Griliches, "The Explanation of Productivity Change," *Review of Economic Studies*, Vol. 34 (July 1967), pp. 249–81.

[45] U.S. Treasury Department, Internal Revenue Service, "Statistics of Income —1959: Supplementary Depreciation Data from Corporation Income Tax Returns, with Special Appendix—Depreciation Methods and Amortization Data, 1954 through 1961" (mimeograph, June 1965).

TABLE 2-1. Fitted Investment Functions for Equipment and Structures, by Industrial Sector, 1935–40 and 1954–65, First Stage Regressions

Sector and asset class	$\hat{\omega}_1$	$\hat{\alpha}\hat{\gamma}_0$	$\hat{\alpha}\hat{\gamma}_1$	$\hat{\alpha}\hat{\gamma}_2$	$\hat{\alpha}\hat{\gamma}_3$	$\hat{\alpha}\hat{\gamma}_4$	$\hat{\alpha}\hat{\gamma}_5$	R^2_N	R^2_I	S_e	DW
Manufacturing											
Equipment	−0.4753	0.0123	0.0190	0.0071	0.0034	0.0001	0.0015	0.801	0.969	0.658	2.277
	(0.2276)	(0.0052)	(0.0058)	(0.0079)	(0.0075)	(0.0069)	(0.0057)				
Structures	−0.6109	0.0036	0.0055	0.0030	0.0035	0.0015	0.0001	0.524	0.815	0.585	1.447
	(0.3255)	(0.0042)	(0.0040)	(0.0045)	(0.0048)	(0.0046)	(0.0043)				
Nonfarm nonmanufacturing											
Equipment	0.0916	0.0317	0.0389	0.0229	0.0143	0.0054	0.0202	0.820	0.965	1.255	1.837
	(0.3319)	(0.0117)	(0.0198)	(0.0163)	(0.0138)	(0.0132)	(0.0133)				
Structures	−1.0065	0.0057	0.0082	−0.0010	−0.0025	−0.0029	−0.0046	0.987	0.967	0.531	1.931
	(0.0953)	(0.0037)	(0.0040)	(0.0044)	(0.0039)	(0.0039)	(0.0038)				

Source: Equation (2.33).
Note: t-statistics are shown in parentheses.

Measures of goodness of fit of the first stage regressions are also given in Table 2-1. Goodness of fit is measured in two ways: (1) the ratio of the explained sum of squares to the total sum of squares for gross investment, R_I^2, and (2) the ratio of the explained sum of squares to the total sum of squares for net investment, R_N^2. Neither ratio is corrected for degrees of freedom. While net investment is the dependent variable in the regression, gross investment is the variable of primary interest for policy considerations. The standard error of estimate S_e, corrected for degrees of freedom, is also presented for each of the regressions. The standard error is the same for gross and net investment. Autocorrelation of errors has already been taken into account in the generation of the distributed lag function underlying our econometric model. A test for autocorrelation may be performed by combining first and second stage results. For completeness the Durbin-Watson ratio DW is presented for each regression. The usual test for autocorrelation based on this ratio is, of course, biased toward randomness.[46]

Actual and fitted values of net investment from the first stage regressions are plotted in Figures 2-1–2-4. The overall goodness of fit is superior to that of our previous investment functions for 1931–41 and 1950–63, except for manufacturing structures. This improvement is mainly due to the change in time period and to revisions of the basic investment data; however, it is also due partly to the change in specification of the distributed lag function. The addition of three lagged changes in desired capital improves the result to some extent.

The second stage of our statistical procedure is to transform all variables in accord with the estimated autoregressive scheme of the errors from the first stage. We approximate the polynomial in the lag operator $\beta(S)$ by a polynomial in the lag itself. We have chosen a second-order polynomial for this purpose so the lag function is a parabola. The dependent variable is now net investment plus $\hat{\omega}_1$ multiplied by lagged net investment, while the independent variables are weighted sums of changes in desired capital plus $\hat{\omega}$ multiplied by the corresponding lagged value. The weights depend on the lags. The derived estimates of the parameters $\alpha\beta_0 \ldots \alpha\beta_4$ are presented in Table 2-2. Measures of goodness of fit similar to those presented for the unconstrained distributed lag functions are also given in Table 2-2. It should be noted that R^2 for these regressions is a measure of the degree of explanation of the autoregressively transformed values of net investment. The only

[46] See Griliches, "Distributed Lags," and Edmond Malinvaud, "Estimation et Prévision dans les Modèles Economiques Autorégressifs," *Revue de l'Institut International de Statistique*, Vol. 29, No. 2 (1961), pp. 1–32.

FIGURE 2-1. Net Investment in Manufacturing Equipment, 1935–40 and 1954–65, First Stage Regressions

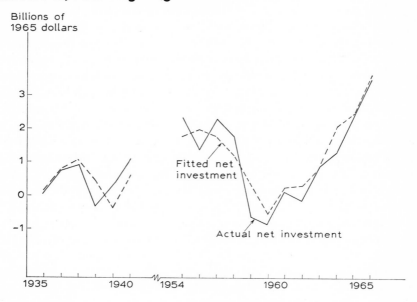

FIGURE 2-2. Net Investment in Manufacturing Structures, 1935–40 and 1954–65, First Stage Regressions

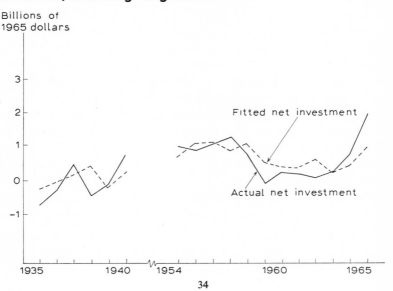

FIGURE 2-3. Net Investment in Nonfarm Nonmanufacturing Equipment, 1935–40 and 1954–65, First Stage Regressions

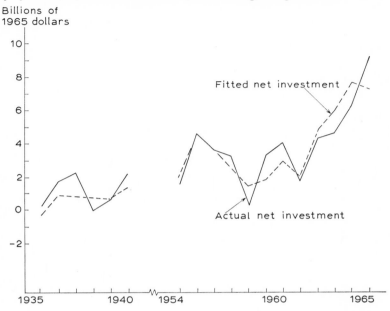

FIGURE 2-4. Net Investment in Nonfarm Nonmanufacturing Structures, 1935–40 and 1954–65, First Stage Regressions

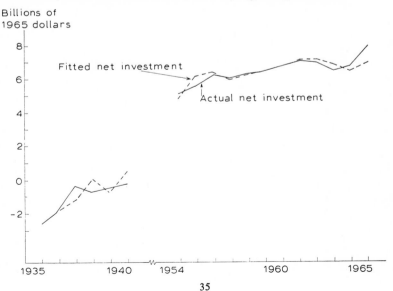

TABLE 2-2. Fitted Investment Functions for Equipment and Structures, by Industrial Sector, 1935–40 and 1954–65, Second Stage Regressions

Sector and asset class	$\hat{a}\hat{\beta}_0$	$\hat{a}\hat{\beta}_1$	$\hat{a}\hat{\beta}_2$	$\hat{a}\hat{\beta}_3$	$\hat{a}\hat{\beta}_4$	R^2	S_e	DW
Manufacturing								
Equipment	0.0130	0.0200	0.0208	0.0153	0.0036	0.602	0.620	2.099
	(0.0047)	(0.0034)	(0.0040)	(0.0040)	(0.0053)			
Structures	0.0041	0.0082	0.0093	0.0073	0.0024	0.186	0.513	1.304
	(0.0033)	(0.0030)	(0.0035)	(0.0032)	(0.0034)			
Nonfarm nonmanufacturing								
Equipment	0.0374	0.0282	0.0211	0.0160	0.0129	0.800	1.190	1.724
	(0.0083)	(0.0038)	(0.0063)	(0.0047)	(0.0090)			
Structures	0.0059	0.0105	0.0118	0.0098	0.0046	0.169	0.506	1.825
	(0.0034)	(0.0032)	(0.0035)	(0.0031)	(0.0029)			

Source: Equation (2.37).
Note: t-statistics are shown in parentheses.

measure of goodness of fit comparable to those in Table 2-1 is the standard error of estimate S_e for each of the regressions. This standard error is uniformly lower for all regressions, reflecting the fact that loss in explanatory power due to reduction in the number of parameters to be estimated is more than compensated for by the reduction in the number of degrees of freedom required for estimation. Actual and fitted values of net investment from the second stage regressions are plotted in Figures 2-5–2-8. The actual values in these plots are net investment, not the transformed net investment series that served as the left-hand variable in the second stage. The fitted values were calculated by substituting the parameter estimates from the second stage into the first stage regression equation. It would not be meaningful to plot the actual and fitted values directly from the second stage because of the autoregressive transformation.

We have generated the distributed lag function for our econometric model of investment behavior by using two restrictions: (1) The distributed lag is finite (that is, the error is autoregressive); and (2) the coefficients of the polynomial $\beta(S)$ lie along a second degree polynomial in the lag itself. The statistic derived above, based on sums of squared residuals with and without constraints, is used to test the validity of these restrictions. The resulting test statistic $\mathscr{F}$ is presented in the first column of Table 2-3. When the very low values of this statistic are compared with the critical value of the $\mathscr{F}$-ratio at the 0.05 level, 3.59, the null hypothesis is easily accepted for all regressions. We conclude that the distributed lag is finite

TABLE 2-3. Fitted Investment Functions for Equipment and Structures, by Industrial Sector, 1935–40 and 1954–65, Derived Results

Sector and asset class	$\mathscr{F}_1$ [a]	$\mathscr{F}_2$ [b]	$\hat{a}$ [c]	Mean lag (years)
Manufacturing				
Equipment	0.577	3.912	0.0727	1.67
Structures	0.138	4.764	0.0312	1.86
Nonfarm nonmanufacturing				
Equipment	0.623	0.004	0.1160	1.47
Structures	0.655	156.681	0.0426	1.92

[a] $\mathscr{F}$-statistic for the null hypothesis that the distributed lag is finite and has a parabolic shape. The critical value of $\mathscr{F}$ with 3 and 11 degrees of freedom is 3.59 at the 0.05 level.

[b] $\mathscr{F}$-statistic for the null hypothesis that there is no autocorrelation. The critical value of $\mathscr{F}$ with 1 and 14 degrees of freedom is 4.60 at the 0.05 level.

[c] Estimate of the elasticity of output with respect to the capital input.

FIGURE 2-5. Net Investment in Manufacturing Equipment, 1935–40 and 1954–65, Second Stage Regressions

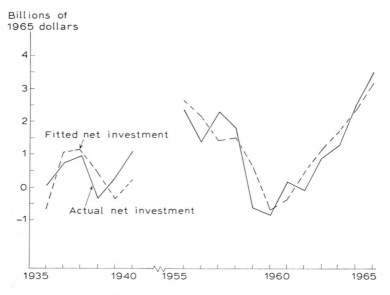

FIGURE 2-6. Net Investment in Manufacturing Structures, 1935–40 and 1954–65, Second Stage Regressions

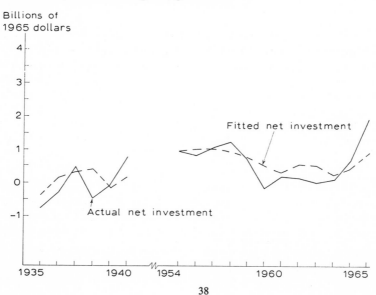

FIGURE 2-7. Net Investment in Nonfarm Nonmanufacturing Equipment, 1935–40 and 1954–65, Second Stage Regressions

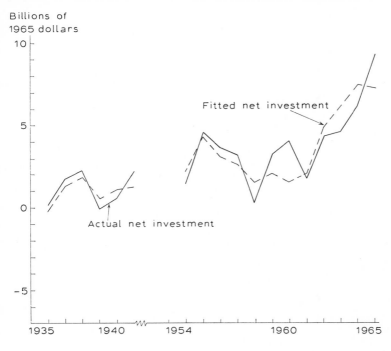

and that the coefficients of $\beta(S)$ lie along a second degree polynomial. Accordingly, we employ the second stage regressions for further analysis of the distributed lag function.

Also presented in Table 2-3 (column 2) are the results of testing the null hypothesis of no autocorrelation in the finite parabolic distributed lag model. The $\mathscr{F}$-statistic for this test is

$$\mathscr{F} = 14(\hat{\epsilon}_0' \hat{\epsilon}_0 - \hat{\epsilon}_1' \hat{\epsilon}_1)/(\hat{\epsilon}_1' \hat{\epsilon}_1),$$

where 14 is the number of degrees of freedom in the unconstrained regression, $\hat{\epsilon}_1' \hat{\epsilon}_1$ is the sum of squared residuals in that regression, and $\hat{\epsilon}_0' \hat{\epsilon}_0$ is the sum of squared residuals in the constrained regression. The unconstrained regressions are those reported in Table 2-2. The constrained regressions are of precisely the same form as those in Table 2-2 except that the variables have not been subjected to the autoregressive transformation. As can be seen, there is evidence of autocorrelation in all sectors except nonmanu-

FIGURE 2-8. Net Investment in Nonfarm Nonmanufacturing Structures, 1935–40 and 1954–65, Second Stage Regressions

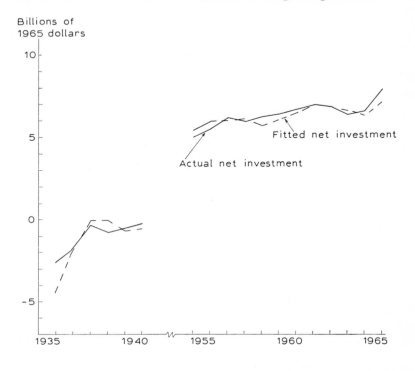

facturing equipment. The null hypothesis is rejected in both equations for structures. These results are exactly in accord with the regression results for the first stage regressions reported in Table 2-1. The very high autocorrelation in the equation for nonmanufacturing structures suggests the possibility of specification error.

Distributed lags

The parameters of the distributed lag function μ_τ may be estimated by employing the constraint that the sum of the coefficients of this function must be unity to estimate the parameter $\hat{\alpha}$.[47] The resulting estimates are given in Table 2-3. The derived estimates of the parameters of the distributed lag function are plotted in Figures 2-9–2-12. The mean lag for each function

[47] For detailed discussion of this restriction and its use in estimating the parameter α, see Jorgenson, "Rational Distributed Lag Functions," pp. 135 and 147–48.

is also given in Table 2-3. When these mean lags are compared with estimates from our earlier studies, the new estimates are found to be very similar for investment in equipment. The mean lag is now estimated to be slightly lower for manufacturing equipment and slightly higher for nonfarm nonmanufacturing equipment. For structures, however, the new estimates differ

FIGURE 2-9. Estimated Lag Function β_τ, for Manufacturing Equipment

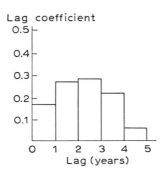

FIGURE 2-10. Estimated Lag Function β_τ, for Manufacturing Structures

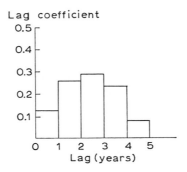

substantially from the old. The old estimate of the mean lag for manufacturing structures was 3.84 years, whereas the new estimate is 1.86; the old estimate of the mean lag for nonfarm nonmanufacturing structures was 7.49 years, while the new estimate is 1.92. For both sets of results the lags are estimated to be longer for structures than for equipment.

FIGURE 2-11. Estimated Lag Function β_τ for Nonfarm Nonmanufacturing Equipment

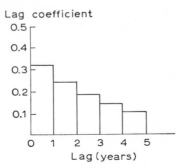

FIGURE 2-12. Estimated Lag Function β_τ for Nonfarm Nonmanufacturing Structures

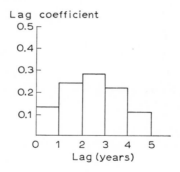

A disturbing feature of our earlier results is that the lag pattern fails to agree with the substantial body of evidence from studies by Jorgenson and Stephenson at the level of two-digit industries and by Jorgenson and Siebert at the level of the individual firm.[48] For manufacturing, Jorgenson and Stephenson estimate the average lag at about two years, while results from individual industries range from six to eleven quarters and cluster in the neighborhood of the overall average. The results for individual firms are characterized by more variability than the results for industries, as

[48] Dale W. Jorgenson and James A. Stephenson, "The Time Structure of Investment Behavior in United States Manufacturing, 1947–1960," *Review of Economics and Statistics*, Vol. 49 (February 1967), pp. 16–27; and Dale W. Jorgenson and Calvin D. Siebert, "Optimal Capital Accumulation and Corporate Investment Behavior," *Journal of Political Economy*, Vol. 76 (November–December 1968), pp. 1123–51.

would be expected. The average lags estimated by Jorgenson and Siebert range from less than a year to over three years, with values between one and two years predominating. Based on a survey he made, Mayer's estimate of the average lag from the decision to undertake investment to the completion of the project for manufacturing is seven quarters.[49] We conclude that our new estimates agree closely with Mayer's results and with estimates derived from investment functions for industry groups and for individual firms. Our previous estimates of the average lags for structures are evidently biased by specification errors in the underlying distributed lag functions and should be replaced by our new estimates.

Impact of Tax Policy on Investment Behavior

If desired capital stock is increased by a change in tax policy, through a consequent change in the rental price of capital services, additional net investment is generated; if the determinants of investment then remain at stationary levels, this net investment eventually brings actual capital stock up to the new desired level. The initial burst of net investment increases gross investment at first, but this effect gradually declines to zero as the gap between desired and actual capital stock is eliminated. However, gross investment is permanently increased by the higher levels of replacement associated with higher levels of capital stock. If desired capital stock is decreased by tax policy, these effects are precisely reversed.

The qualitative features of the response of investment to a change in tax policy are essentially the same for all changes. To evaluate the effects of particular tax measures, it is useful to assess the response of investment quantitatively. Accordingly, we calculate the effects of changes in tax policy that have taken place in the United States in the postwar period. The calculations are based on a partial equilibrium analysis of investment behavior. All determinants of investment expenditures except tax policy are held equal to their actual values. We then measure the impact of tax policy by substituting into our investment functions parameters of the tax structure—tax rate, depreciation formulas, tax credit, and depreciation lifetimes—appropriate to alternative tax policies. The difference between investment resulting from actual tax policy and investment that would have resulted from alternative tax policies is our measure of the impact of tax policy.

[49] Thomas Mayer, "Plant and Equipment Lead Times," *Journal of Business*, Vol. 33 (April 1960), pp. 127–32.

We present estimates of the impact of the adoption of accelerated depreciation in 1954 and of new lifetimes for depreciation of equipment and the investment tax credit in 1962, the tax cut of 1964, and the suspension of the tax credit for equipment and restriction of the use of accelerated depreciation for structures in 1966–67. The tax measure of 1964 reduced the corporate tax rate from 52 percent to 48 percent and also restored the tax credit to the depreciation base for tax purposes. In our earlier studies we presented calculations of the effects of all these changes in tax policy. In view of the substantial revisions in the underlying investment data and the alterations in our specification of the investment functions, we provide a complete set of estimates based on our new results.

In the new calculations both investment and capital stock are measured in 1965 prices. We estimate the impact of all changes in tax policy through 1970. In order to make these estimates, we employed a rough set of projections of the determinants of investment. No great precision was required in these projections, since the estimates of the differential impacts of alternative policies are not at all sensitive to the assumed level of investment. The projected levels of gross value added and the price deflators for investment goods are shown in Table 2-4.[50] Although the projections of gross value added are in current dollars and are likely to be serious underestimates because of the relatively rapid rate of inflation that has developed recently, this will not affect the results, since only the ratio of gross value added and the investment deflator enter the calculations. Finally, all tax variables were assumed to stay at their 1965 values, except for the brief suspension of the investment tax credit and accelerated depreciation in 1966–67; the treatment of this suspension is described in detail below.

As a basis for comparison with alternative tax policies, Table 2-5 presents data on the actual levels of gross investment, net investment, and capital stock, for 1950–65. Also included are extrapolated values calculated from the fitted investment functions for 1966–70 for plant and equipment, for both the manufacturing and nonfarm nonmanufacturing sectors.

Accelerated Depreciation, 1954

The first change in tax policy we attempt to evaluate is the adoption of accelerated methods of depreciation for tax purposes in 1954. As an alternative policy we suppose that only the straight-line formula was permitted from

---

[50] These are crude extrapolations of previous trends, modified by fragmentary data available in October 1967, the time of the computations.

TABLE 2-4. Projected Levels of Gross Value Added and Price Deflators for Manufacturing and Nonfarm Nonmanufacturing, 1966–70

	Gross value added (billions of current dollars)		Price deflators (1965=1.000)		
Year	Manufacturing	Nonfarm non-manufacturing	Manufacturing equipment	Nonfarm non-manufacturing equipment	Structures, both sectors
1966	198.4	363.6	1.031	1.031	1.043
1967	209.1	383.2	1.068	1.068	1.079
1968	221.6	406.2	1.103	1.095	1.100
1969	234.9	430.6	1.142	1.121	1.121
1970	249.0	456.4	1.183	1.150	1.144

Source: See text, p. 44.

1954 to 1970 and that all other determinants of investment are unchanged. The levels of the annual rental price of capital services, and the reduction brought about in 1955 (the first full year) through the adoption of accelerated methods of depreciation, were:

	Without accelerated depreciation	*With accelerated depreciation*	*Percentage decrease*
Manufacturing equipment	0.293	0.267	8.9
Manufacturing structures	0.229	0.208	9.2
Nonfarm nonmanufacturing equipment	0.375	0.341	9.1
Nonfarm nonmanufacturing structures	0.239	0.217	9.2

Estimates of the increase in gross investment, net investment, and capital stock resulting from the adoption of accelerated depreciation in 1954 are given in Table 2-6.

The effects of the adoption of accelerated depreciation are very substantial. Although the same pattern prevails in all four classes of assets, it is useful to trace out the quantitative impact of tax policy on net investment, gross investment, and capital stock for each class. The peak effect on net investment for manufacturing equipment is attained in 1956 with a level of $744 million, or 32 percent of net investment in that year. By 1959 the effect is essentially nil; however, the adoption in 1962 of new equipment lifetimes for tax purposes and of the investment tax credit provides an additional stimulus from the use of accelerated methods of depreciation.

TABLE 2-5. Gross Investment, Net Investment, and Capital Stock in Equipment and Structures, by Industrial Sector, Actual, 1950–65 and Projected, 1966–70

(In billions of 1965 dollars)

	Manufacturing						Nonfarm nonmanufacturing					
	Equipment			Structures			Equipment			Structures		
	Investment		Capital	Investment		Capital	Investment		Capital	Investment		Capital
Year	Gross	Net	stock	Gross	Net	stock	Gross	Net	stock	Gross	Net	stock
Actual												
1950	5.553	0.627	33.488	1.949	−0.252	35.220	14.469	4.079	54.028	9.323	3.986	76.903
1951	7.265	2.247	34.115	2.776	0.591	34.968	14.659	3.485	58.107	8.895	3.281	80.889
1952	8.291	2.942	36.362	2.888	0.666	35.558	14.421	2.577	61.592	8.775	2.934	84.170
1953	8.578	2.796	39.304	3.091	0.827	36.224	15.020	2.680	64.169	10.348	4.303	87.104
1954	8.544	2.351	42.100	3.276	0.960	37.051	14.327	1.472	66.849	11.345	5.001	91.407
1955	7.927	1.388	44.451	3.222	0.846	38.011	17.699	4.561	68.321	12.195	5.504	96.408
1956	9.034	2.291	45.840	3.526	1.097	38.858	17.714	3.699	72.882	13.264	6.191	101.912
1957	8.875	1.795	48.131	3.751	1.254	39.955	17.973	3.246	76.581	13.445	5.943	108.104
1958	6.726	−0.618	49.926	3.321	0.745	41.209	15.595	0.244	79.827	14.125	6.210	114.046
1959	6.423	−0.830	49.308	2.490	−0.132	41.954	18.671	3.273	80.072	14.740	6.394	120.256

1960	7.299	0.168	48.477	2.821	0.207	41.822	20.090	4.063	83.345	15.459	6.669	126.651
1961	7.067	—0.089	48.645	2.786	0.159	42.029	18.617	1.809	87.408	16.190	6.937	133.320
1962	8.040	0.897	48.557	2.681	0.044	42.188	21.475	4.319	89.216	16.563	6.829	140.258
1963	8.550	1.275	49.454	2.836	0.196	42.233	22.641	4.654	93.535	16.582	6.374	147.087
1964	9.941	2.479	50.729	3.353	0.701	42.429	25.175	6.293	98.189	17.251	6.601	153.461
1965	11.333	3.506	53.208	4.659	1.963	43.130	29.323	9.231	104.482	18.977	7.869	160.061
Projected												
1966	11.434	3.092	56.714	4.462	1.644	45.093	28.337	6.470	113.713	19.557	7.903	167.930
1967	11.259	2.462	59.806	4.306	1.385	46.737	28.149	5.038	120.183	20.127	7.924	175.833
1968	11.138	1.978	62.268	4.216	1.208	48.122	29.198	5.118	125.221	20.841	8.088	183.757
1969	11.044	1.593	64.246	4.165	1.082	49.330	29.598	4.534	130.339	21.610	8.296	191.845
1970	11.104	1.419	65.839	4.222	1.071	50.412	30.243	4.307	134.873	22.446	8.556	200.141

Source: Unpublished data from the 1966 capital goods study of the U.S. Department of Commerce, Office of Business Economics. The capital stock figures are derived from unrounded data and will not necessarily equal the sum of the preceding year's capital stock and net investment.

TABLE 2-6. Estimated Changes in Gross and Net Investment in Equipment and Structures, and in Capital Stock, Resulting from Accelerated Depreciation, 1954–70

(In millions of 1965 dollars)

	Manufacturing						Nonfarm nonmanufacturing					
	Equipment			Structures			Equipment			Structures		
	Investment		Capital stock	Investment		Capital stock	Investment		Capital stock	Investment		Capital stock
Year	Gross	Net		Gross	Net		Gross	Net		Gross	Net	
1954	209	209	0	79	79	0	847	847	0	204	204	0
1955	627	596	209	280	275	79	1,871	1,708	847	649	635	204
1956	862	744	805	432	410	354	1,756	1,265	2,555	944	886	839
1957	878	650	1,549	450	402	764	1,723	988	3,820	1,023	903	1,725
1958	621	298	2,199	323	250	1,166	1,662	737	4,808	867	684	2,628
1959	395	27	2,497	181	92	1,416	1,519	453	5,545	584	354	3,312
1960	369	— 2	2,524	153	59	1,508	1,294	141	5,998	448	194	3,666
1961	406	35	2,522	169	71	1,567	1,386	205	6,139	478	214	3,810
1962	487	111	2,557	180	78	1,638	1,573	353	6,344	430	201	4,024
1963	545	152	2,668	172	65	1,706	1,779	491	6,697	473	178	4,225
1964	660	245	2,820	165	53	1,771	2,090	708	7,188	440	134	4,403
1965	733	282	3,065	159	45	1,824	2,049	531	7,896	384	70	4,537
1966	727	235	3,347	93	— 24	1,869	2,067	446	8,427	206	—114	4,607
1967	696	170	3,582	41	— 74	1,845	2,068	362	8,873	113	—205	4,593
1968	682	131	3,752	97	— 14	1,771	2,213	437	9,235	258	— 46	4,388
1969	702	131	3,883	193	83	1,757	2,214	354	9,672	471	169	4,342
1970	728	138	4,014	287	172	1,840	2,309	377	10,049	675	362	4,511

48

We estimate that 17.5 percent of the net investment in manufacturing equipment over the period 1954–70 may be attributed to the change in methods for calculating depreciation. Similarly, the peak effect for nonfarm nonmanufacturing equipment is $1.708 billion in 1955, or 37.4 percent of the net investment that took place in that year. Over the seventeen-year period, 15.4 percent of the net investment in nonfarm nonmanufacturing equipment may be attributed to the change in depreciation rules in 1954.

Although the average lag in response of investment is longer for structures than for equipment, the effects of accelerated depreciation are broadly similar. For manufacturing structures the peak effect on net investment occurs in 1956 with $410 million, or 37.3 percent of the net investment that took place in that year. For the 1954–70 period the increase in net investment in manufacturing structures due to accelerated depreciation is estimated at 15.0 percent of the total. For nonfarm nonmanufacturing structures, the peak effect on investment occurs in 1957 with $903 million, or 15.2 percent of the net investment that took place in that year. Over the whole period, 4.5 percent of the net investment in nonfarm nonmanufacturing structures may be attributed to the adoption of accelerated methods for depreciation in 1954.

Capital stock is a cumulation of net investment so that its behavior is implied by that of net investment. For both manufacturing and nonfarm nonmanufacturing equipment, two phases in the response of capital stock can be distinguished. First, the immediate impact of adoption of accelerated depreciation was to raise desired capital substantially above actual capital. By 1957 more than half the gap resulting from accelerated depreciation was eliminated; by 1959 none remained. Second, adoption of accelerated depreciation in 1954 resulted in additional stimulus from subsequent changes in lifetimes for tax purposes and from adoption of the investment tax credit. Half the total rise in the stock of manufacturing equipment from 1954 to 1970 took place by 1958, while half the rise in nonfarm nonmanufacturing equipment took place by 1959. The patterns for structures in both the manufacturing and nonfarm nonmanufacturing sectors are qualitatively similar to those for equipment but without a clear demarcation between successive phases. As in equipment, half the total rise in the stock of manufacturing structures over the period as a whole took place by 1958, while half the rise in nonfarm nonmanufacturing structures took place by 1959.

Gross investment is the sum of net investment and replacement; further, replacement rises in proportion to capital stock. By 1958 replacement had become the dominant component in the response of gross investment in

equipment to the adoption of accelerated depreciation for both the manufacturing and nonfarm nonmanufacturing sectors. For manufacturing
the peak response of gross investment occurred in 1957 with a change of
$878 million. By 1970, added replacement requirements are expected to
maintain gross investment at near-peak levels of $728 million. Similarly,
gross investment in nonfarm nonmanufacturing equipment reached a peak
of $1.871 billion in 1955, declined for several years, and will rise to a new
peak of $2.309 billion by 1970, propelled by rising replacement requirements.
For manufacturing structures the high of $450 million was attained in
1957; by 1970 it is estimated the level will reach $288 million. The general
pattern of response for investment in nonfarm nonmanufacturing structures
is similar in timing but different in magnitude. The largest response of gross
investment was $1.023 billion in 1957; the level in 1970 is estimated at
$672 million.

The total effect of the adoption of accelerated depreciation in 1954 on
gross investment during the whole period from 1954 to 1970 may be assessed
by comparing investment resulting from the new methods of depreciation
with investment that would have taken place under the old methods. For
equipment, 6.7 percent of gross investment in manufacturing and 8.0 percent
of the gross investment in nonfarm nonmanufacturing may be attributed to
accelerated depreciation over the period in question. For structures, the
percentages are 5.7 for manufacturing and 3.0 for nonfarm nonmanufacturing. By 1970 we estimate that 6.6 percent of gross investment in
manufacturing equipment, and 7.7 percent of gross investment in nonfarm
nonmanufacturing equipment, will be due to the adoption of accelerated
depreciation in 1954. The corresponding percentages for structures are 6.8
for manufacturing and 3.0 for nonfarm nonmanufacturing.

Depreciation Life Guidelines, 1962

The adoption of new guidelines for the determination of lifetimes
allowable for tax purposes in 1962 [51] affected only equipment lifetimes.
The levels of the annual rental price of capital services, and the reductions
brought about through the adoption of the 1962 depreciation guidelines,
were:

	Without guidelines	With guidelines	Percentage decrease
Manufacturing equipment	0.315	0.307	2.5
Nonfarm nonmanufacturing equipment	0.384	0.374	2.6

[51] U.S. Treasury Department, Internal Revenue Service, *Depreciation Guidelines and Rules*, Publication No. 456 (July 1962).

Estimates of the increase in gross investment, net investment, and capital stock in equipment resulting from adoption of the new guidelines are given in Table 2-7.

Investment Tax Credit and Long Amendment, 1962

A second change in tax policy during 1962 was the adoption of an investment tax credit of 7 percent for equipment in the Revenue Act of 1962. As has been noted, various limitations on the applicability of the tax credit reduce the effective rate to 6 percent for manufacturing and 5.8 percent for nonfarm nonmanufacturing. Furthermore, the imposition and subsequent repeal of the Long amendment first eliminated the tax credit from the depreciation base in 1962 and 1963 and then restored it in 1964 and subsequent years. The levels of the annual rental price of capital services for 1963, and the reductions brought about by adoption of the tax credit with the Long amendment, were:

	Without credit	*With credit*	*Percentage decrease*
Manufacturing equipment	0.316	0.297	6.0
Nonfarm nonmanufacturing equipment	0.383	0.361	5.7

Estimates of the increase in gross investment, net investment, and capital stock in equipment resulting from the investment tax credit are given in Table 2-7. The impact of both of these policies is substantial, although the effect of the investment credit is several times larger than that of the depreciation guidelines. For the guidelines, the peak response in manufacturing industries of net investment in equipment took place in 1964, when they accounted for 12.5 percent of total net investment. The peak response to the investment credit took place a year later in 1965; in that year it accounted for 28.4 percent of net investment in equipment in the manufacturing sector. In nonmanufacturing industries, both peak responses took place earlier —17.2 percent for the guidelines in 1962 and 36.8 percent for the investment credit in 1964—reflecting the shorter lag in equipment investment in that sector.

The responses to the investment credit in both sectors show a dip resulting from its suspension in 1966–67. A smaller dip appears in the estimated effect of the depreciation guidelines during the same period, especially in the nonmanufacturing sector. This is explained by the fact that after the repeal of the Long amendment, investment credit and depreciation policies enhanced each other's effect. Thus the depreciation guidelines had a smaller

TABLE 2-7. Estimated Changes in Gross and Net Investment in Equipment, and in Capital Stock, Resulting from 1962 Depreciation Guidelines and Investment Tax Credit, by Industrial Sector, 1962–70

(In millions of 1965 dollars)

	Depreciation guidelines						Investment tax credit					
	Manufacturing equipment			Nonfarm nonmanufacturing equipment			Manufacturing equipment			Nonfarm nonmanufacturing equipment		
	Investment		Capital stock	Investment		Capital stock	Investment		Capital stock	Investment		Capital stock
Year	Gross	Net		Gross	Net		Gross	Net		Gross	Net	
1962	165	165	0	743	743	0	185	185	0	804	804	0
1963	292	268	165	770	627	743	527	500	185	1,711	1,556	804
1964	375	311	433	845	582	1,370	992	891	685	2,773	2,319	2,360
1965	369	260	744	816	441	1,952	1,229	997	1,576	2,726	1,826	4,679
1966	260	112	1,004	828	368	2,393	1,015	637	2,573	2,069	818	6,505
1967	215	51	1,116	641	110	2,761	724	252	3,210	2,017	609	7,323
1968	211	39	1,167	687	135	2,871	635	126	3,462	2,516	991	7,932
1969	218	41	1,206	687	109	3,006	723	195	3,588	2,283	567	8,923
1970	226	43	1,247	716	117	3,115	884	328	3,783	2,330	505	9,490

impact during the period of the suspension of the investment credit for equipment.

Corporate Tax Cut, 1964

In analyzing the effect of the reduction from 52 percent to 48 percent in the corporate tax rate in 1964, we assume that the before-tax rate of return was left unchanged. Under this condition the effect of a change in the tax rate on the rental price of capital services is neutral provided that depreciation for tax purposes is equal to economic depreciation.[52] Under the conditions actually prevailing in 1964, depreciation for tax purposes was in excess of economic depreciation for both plant and equipment in the manufacturing and nonfarm nonmanufacturing sectors. Accordingly, the rental price of capital services resulting from the tax cut was actually greater than the rental price before the cut. Following are the results for the annual rental prices for 1965, the first full year of the tax cut:

	Without tax cut	*With tax cut*	*Percentage increase*
Manufacturing equipment	0.296	0.299	1.0
Manufacturing structures	0.237	0.240	1.3
Nonfarm nonmanufacturing equipment	0.352	0.355	0.9
Nonfarm nonmanufacturing structures	0.247	0.250	1.2

Our estimates of the change in gross investment, net investment, and capital stock resulting from this change are given in Table 2-8. In general, the effects of the rate reduction are small and negative. It should be emphasized that these estimates depend on the level of output actually resulting from the tax cut; quite clearly the overall effect of the tax cut was to stimulate investment by increasing output.

Repeal of Long Amendment, 1964

A second, little-noticed change in tax policy in 1964 was the repeal of the Long amendment, which restored the tax credit to the depreciation base for tax purposes. Under the amendment, the effective rate of the tax credit

[52] For further discussion of tax-neutral depreciation, see pp. 17–18 above and Brown, "Business-Income Taxation and Investment Incentives"; Musgrave, *Theory of Public Finance*; Samuelson, "Tax Deductibility of Economic Depreciation To Insure Invariant Valuations"; and Smith, "Tax Depreciation Policy and Investment Theory."

TABLE 2-8. Estimated Changes in Gross and Net Investment in Equipment and Structures, and in Capital Stock, Resulting from the Tax Cut of 1964, by Industrial Sector, 1964–70

(In millions of 1965 dollars)

	Manufacturing						Nonfarm nonmanufacturing					
	Equipment			Structures			Equipment			Structures		
	Investment		Capital	Investment		Capital	Investment		Capital	Investment		Capital
Year	Gross	Net	stock	Gross	Net	stock	Gross	Net	stock	Gross	Net	stock
1964	— 49	— 49	0	—20	—20	0	—135	—135	0	— 44	— 44	0
1965	—136	—129	— 49	—62	—61	— 20	—267	—241	—135	—125	—123	— 44
1966	—181	—155	—178	—88	—83	— 81	—217	—145	—376	—167	—155	—167
1967	—186	—137	—333	—87	—77	—164	—223	—123	—521	—168	—146	—322
1968	—155	— 86	—470	—66	—51	—241	—274	—150	—644	—142	—110	—468
1969	—120	— 38	—556	—43	—25	—292	—245	— 92	—794	— 99	— 59	—578
1970	—119	— 32	—594	—43	—23	—317	—213	— 43	—886	— 88	— 44	—637

54

was approximately 6 percent; repeal raised it to almost 10 percent. The levels of the annual rental price of capital services, and the resulting reductions, are:

	With Long amendment	*Without Long amendment*	*Percentage decrease*
Manufacturing equipment	0.302	0.293	3.0
Nonfarm nonmanufacturing equipment	0.363	0.352	3.0

Estimates of the increase in gross investment, net investment, and capital stock resulting from this change are given in Table 2-9.

TABLE 2-9. Estimated Changes in Gross and Net Investment in Equipment, and in Capital Stock, Resulting from Repeal of the Long Amendment, 1964–70

(In millions of 1965 dollars)

Year	Manufacturing equipment			Nonfarm nonmanufacturing equipment		
	Investment		Capital stock	Investment		Capital stock
	Gross	Net		Gross	Net	
1964	238	238	0	1,042	1,042	0
1965	400	365	238	958	758	1,042
1966	412	329	567	706	360	1,800
1967	349	217	896	750	335	2,160
1968	229	67	1,113	1,021	541	2,495
1969	236	64	1,180	761	177	3,036
1970	297	115	1,244	792	174	3,213

These increases are quite substantial. The peak effect for manufacturing equipment took place in 1965, when the net investment in equipment attributable to the repeal was 10.4 percent of total net investment. In nonfarm nonmanufacturing, the peak effect for equipment came in 1964, accounting for over $1 billion and 16.6 percent of net investment in that sector. Once again, the diminution of the impact of this policy change can be seen in 1966 and one or two years after, resulting from the suspension of the investment credit. The lag structure in the nonmanufacturing sector makes the dip much more noticeable there than in the manufacturing sector.

TABLE 2-10. Estimated Changes in Gross and Net Investment in Equipment and Structures, and in Capital Stock, Resulting from Suspension of the Investment Tax Credit for Equipment and Accelerated Depreciation for Structures from October 10, 1966, through March 8, 1967, 1966–70

(In millions of 1965 dollars)

	Manufacturing						Nonfarm nonmanufacturing					
	Equipment			Structures			Equipment			Structures		
	Investment		Capital stock	Investment		Capital stock	Investment		Capital stock	Investment		Capital stock
Year	Gross	Net		Gross	Net		Gross	Net		Gross	Net	
1966	−177	−177	0	−46	−46	0	−762	−762	0	−119	−119	0
1967	−271	−245	−177	−89	−86	−46	−599	−452	−762	−200	−192	−119
1968	−153	−91	−422	−60	−52	−132	69	303	−1,214	−126	−104	−311
1969	−9	66	−513	11	12	−184	51	226	−911	−11	18	−415
1970	157	223	−447	74	75	−172	18	150	−685	111	139	−397

56

Investment Credit Suspension, 1966

In 1966 an important objective of economic policy was to restrain investment. After a number of alternative changes in tax policy were considered and rejected,[53] the investment tax credit for equipment was suspended beginning October 10, 1966; at the same time accelerated depreciation for structures was replaced by 150 percent declining-balance depreciation. Originally, the suspension was to remain in effect until the end of 1967, or almost fifteen months, but it was lifted on March 9, 1967, so that the period was a little less than five months. The effects of the suspension on the annual rental price of capital in 1967 were the following:

	Without suspension	With suspension	Percentage increase
Manufacturing equipment	0.320	0.351	9.7
Manufacturing structures	0.259	0.276	6.6
Nonfarm nonmanufacturing equipment	0.379	0.414	9.2
Nonfarm nonmanufacturing structures	0.270	0.287	6.3

Our estimates of the effects of the suspension on gross investment, net investment, and capital stock are given in Table 2-10.

For all categories of assets, the suspension had a restraining effect on the level of investment in 1967, which we estimate continued into 1968 except for nonfarm nonmanufacturing equipment. For both sectors the restoration of the original tax credit for equipment and accelerated depreciation for structures will result in a stimulus to investment in 1969 and 1970. For no class of assets is the level of capital stock as high at the end of 1970 as it would have been in the absence of the suspension. The total gross investment for the five-year period 1966–70 is considerably lower than it would have been in the absence of the five-month suspension.

If the suspension of the investment tax credit for equipment and accelerated depreciation for structures had continued for fifteen months, the impact on the level of investment would have been much more substantial, as our estimates in Table 2-11 reveal. For investment in structures the restraining effect of the suspension would have continued into 1969 in both sectors, although the impact would have been very slight in that year. For investment in equipment, as well as in structures, the magnitude of

---

[53] Policies under consideration during early 1966 and their potential impact on investment expenditures are discussed in Hall and Jorgenson, "Role of Taxation in Stabilizing Private Investment."

TABLE 2-11. Estimated Changes in Gross and Net Investment in Equipment and Structures, and in Capital Stock, Resulting from Hypothetical Suspension of the Investment Tax Credit for Equipment and Accelerated Depreciation for Structures from October 10, 1966, through December 31, 1967, by Industrial Sector, 1966–70

(In millions of 1965 dollars)

	Manufacturing						Nonfarm nonmanufacturing					
	Equipment			Structures			Equipment			Structures		
	Investment		Capital stock	Investment		Capital stock	Investment		Capital stock	Investment		Capital stock
Year	Gross	Net		Gross	Net		Gross	Net		Gross	Net	
1966	−177	−177	0	− 46	− 46	0	− 762	− 762	0	−119	−119	0
1967	−872	−846	− 177	−250	−247	− 46	−3,190	−3,043	− 762	−614	−606	− 119
1968	−567	−416	−1,023	−234	−216	−293	208	940	−3,805	−475	−425	− 725
1969	−181	31	−1,439	− 63	− 32	−509	171	722	−2,865	−154	− 74	−1,150
1970	270	477	−1,408	117	152	−541	093	505	−2,143	193	278	−1,224

the impact would have been much greater. As a result, the stimulus from restoration of the tax credit and accelerated depreciation would have been correspondingly increased.

Conclusion

The objective of this study is to assess the effects of tax policy on investment behavior. For this purpose we have presented an econometric model of investment behavior based on the neoclassical theory of optimal capital accumulation. This model differs from a version used in two earlier studies [54] mainly in the imposition of further restrictions on the parameters of the underlying distributed lag function. These restrictions enable us to improve our specification of the lag structure and to economize on the number of parameters to be estimated. The resulting numerical estimates of the unknown parameters of our econometric model reflect the alterations in our statistical technique and incorporate data that have become available since our earlier studies. The lag structure derived from our new estimates suggests that the average lag between changes in the determinants of investment and actual expenditures for structures is shorter than that derived from our previous estimates. The new results are in much better agreement with evidence on the lag structure from sample surveys and from econometric models of investment fitted to data for industry groups for individual firms.

Our overall conclusion is the same as that in our previous studies: Tax policy can be highly effective in changing the level and timing of investment expenditures. Qualitatively speaking, a change in tax policy that reduces the rental price of capital services will increase the desired level of capital stock. This increase will generate net investment that eventually brings actual capital up to the new desired level. Gross investment follows the course of net investment at first, but gradually replacement requirements resulting from the higher level of capital stock come to predominate. Even if all the determinants of desired capital remain stationary at their new levels, gross investment is permanently increased by the higher levels of replacement associated with higher levels of capital.

From a quantitative point of view the tax measures we consider have substantially different impacts. The investment tax credit, essentially a subsidy to the purchase of equipment, has had a greater impact than any of the other changes in tax policy during the postwar period, especially

---

[54] *Ibid.*, and Hall and Jorgenson, "Tax Policy and Investment Behavior."

after repeal of the Long amendment made it even more effective. The shortening of lifetimes used in calculating depreciation for tax purposes and the use of accelerated methods for depreciation have been very important determinants of levels of investment expenditure since 1954. Suspension of the investment tax credit and accelerated depreciation from late 1966 to early 1967 had an important restraining effect on the level of investment; if this suspension had been allowed to remain in force for fifteen months rather than five, the impact would have been substantially greater. Of all the tax measures, only the reduction of the corporate tax rate in 1964, in our view, has had little impact on the level of investment expenditures. The reason for this is that tax depreciation and economic depreciation were virtually equal by 1964 so that any change in the tax rate would have been neutral in its effects on the price of capital services. The much-acclaimed tax cut of 1964 affected investment, but its main direct impact was through the enhanced effectiveness of the investment tax credit; reduction in the tax rate had a small but clearly negative impact on the level of investment.

CHAPTER III

The Effect of Alternative
Lag Distributions

CHARLES W. BISCHOFF *Yale University*

FISCAL AND MONETARY POLICY MAKERS share the desire to influence the flow of business fixed investment. Their overall purposes may be for the short run (for example, to counteract a business cycle) or the long run (to affect the rate of growth of potential output). In the first case, it is desirable to apply a policy tool with prompt, highly concentrated impact, for the cyclical situation may have drastically changed by the time a policy with a long lag takes hold. In the second, it is desirable to affect the flow of investment more gradually, or else the policy itself may create short-run instability. In either case, as Griliches and Wallace have emphasized, "whether or not a particular stabilization or growth policy will actually do more harm than good depends crucially on the form of the lag function." [1]

Through tax changes in 1954, 1962, and 1964, the federal government has sought to encourage investment spending, presumably with long-run goals in mind. On the other hand, monetary changes since the Treasury-Federal Reserve accord in 1951 have presumably aimed at prompt and reversible influence. Without doubt, the 1966 and 1967 offsetting changes in the tax treatment of investment were explicitly designed to have short-run effects on investment.

---

[1] Zvi Griliches and Neil Wallace, "The Determinants of Investment Revisited," *International Economic Review*, Vol. 6 (September 1965), p. 328.

This chapter seeks to evaluate the direct effects of fiscal and monetary instruments, as well as other determinants, on expenditures for producers' durable equipment, the largest component of business fixed investment.[2] In particular, it is concerned not only with *how much* a particular policy affects investment, but also *when* the effect occurs. Jorgenson, in a series of papers with several colleagues, has drawn the striking conclusion that "any measures which result in a once-over change in demand for capital will result in a relatively short and sharp boom in investment demand followed by a lengthy period of steadily worsening stagnation induced by a decline in total investment expenditures relative to their peak levels."[3] This conclusion, if correct, has important policy implications. However, a controversial feature of the model from which it is derived is the assumption that all of the determinants of investment act with the same distributed lag. I have attempted to relax this restrictive assumption.

The model discussed in this chapter is heavily influenced by Jorgenson's neoclassical investment model, in the extended version developed by Hall and Jorgenson to study the effects of tax policy on investment. All fiscal and monetary parameters in their model affect investment by means of changes in the imputed rent on the services of capital goods. By assumption, in their model the elasticity of investment demand with respect to this rent is unity, and thus the elasticity of investment demand

---

[2] By the direct effect of a change in a policy parameter, I mean its effect with all other determinants of investment unchanged. A tax credit stimulates investment indirectly through feedbacks on the other determinants of investment, but the magnitude of these feedbacks can be discussed only in the context of a complete model.

[3] Dale W. Jorgenson, "Anticipations and Investment Behavior," in James S. Duesenberry, Gary Fromm, Lawrence R. Klein, and Edwin Kuh (eds.), *The Brookings Quarterly Econometric Model of the United States* (Chicago: Rand McNally and Co., 1965; Amsterdam: North-Holland, 1965), pp. 85–86. See also Dale W. Jorgenson, "Capital Theory and Investment Behavior," in American Economic Association, *Papers and Proceedings of the Seventh-fifth Annual Meeting, 1962* (*American Economic Review*, Vol. 53, May 1963), pp. 247–59; Dale W. Jorgenson and James A. Stephenson, "The Time Structure of Investment Behavior in United States Manufacturing, 1947–1960," *Review of Economics and Statistics*, Vol. 49 (February 1967), pp. 16–27; Dale W. Jorgenson and James A. Stephenson, "Investment Behavior in U.S. Manufacturing, 1947–1960," *Econometrica*, Vol. 35 (April 1967), pp. 169–220; Robert E. Hall and Dale W. Jorgenson, "Tax Policy and Investment Behavior," *American Economic Review*, Vol. 57 (June 1967), pp. 391–414; Robert E. Hall and Dale W. Jorgenson, "The Role of Taxation in Stabilizing Private Investment," in Vincent P. Rock (ed.), *Policymakers and Model Builders: Cases and Concepts* (Washington: Gordon and Breach, 1969); and Chap. 2 in this volume.

with respect to each of the determinants of the rent is an assumed, rather than estimated, value. In removing this second restrictive assumption, I provide estimates of the direct effects of various policy changes that are less dependent on the particular way the model is put together.

The next section sets forth a rationale for the estimation of separate lag distributions for different determinants of investment. The rationale is stated in terms of a neoclassical model in which factor proportions are variable only up to the point when new machines are installed.[4] With the addition of assumptions about how machines wear out and how expectations about future prices are formed, this model implies that the short-run elasticity of investment demand with respect to changes in the rent will never exceed the long-run elasticity. This rationale, while plausible, is not, however, the only way in which a divergence in lag distributions could be justified.

The model is used to explain quarterly data for aggregate expenditures on producers' durable equipment. The long-run price elasticity of demand for equipment is estimated to be very close to unity, with the short-run elasticity considerably smaller. At the same time, the short-run elasticity of equipment demand with respect to output substantially exceeds the long-run elasticity. Tax parameters, the interest rate, and the yield on equities all appear to be important determinants of the level of expenditures, although the quantitative impact of the investment tax credit, adopted in 1962, appears to be greater than that of any of the other policy measures studied.

Specification of a Distributed Lag Model

To provide policy makers with knowledge about the speed with which their actions can affect investment, it is necessary to estimate the parameters of a model of investment demand in which explicit attention is given to monetary and fiscal parameters. This section discusses the specification of

---

[4] For theoretical developments of this model, mostly in the context of long-run growth, see Leif Johansen, "Substitution versus Fixed Production Coefficients in the Theory of Economic Growth: A Synthesis," *Econometrica*, Vol. 27 (April 1959), pp. 157–76; Robert M. Solow, "Substitution and Fixed Proportions in the Theory of Capital," *Review of Economic Studies*, Vol. 29 (June 1962), pp. 207–18; Benton F. Massell, "Investment, Innovation, and Growth," *Econometrica*, Vol. 30 (April 1962), pp. 239–52; Edmund S. Phelps, "Substitution, Fixed Proportions, Growth and Distribution," *International Economic Review*, Vol. 4 (September 1963), pp. 265–88; and Murray C. Kemp and Pham Chí Thành, "On a Class of Growth Models," *Econometrica*, Vol. 34 (April 1966), pp. 257–82.

such a model, in which a number of terms, reflecting relative prices, capital costs, and the effects of taxes, are combined into a single expression for the imputed rent on a piece of equipment. In the long run, it is assumed that the demand for equipment is a log-linear function of this rent, which is identified with the price of the services provided by a unit of equipment. In addition, the demand for equipment is assumed to be proportional to the sum of (a) desired changes in capacity and (b) replacement of capacity.

A crucial feature of this model is the assumption that changes in the determinants of the rent may affect investment expenditures with a lag distribution different from that which exists for changes in the determinants of desired capacity. Given the current state of knowledge about possibilities in the real world for changes in factor proportions, it cannot be assumed a priori that all of the determinants of investment affect expenditures with the same time pattern.

The stylized world on which the model of investment behavior is based is one in which a firm, at time t, must make investment decisions η periods ahead. Any equipment that is ordered in period t is delivered in period $t+\eta$ and can be put immediately into production. From the vantage point of period t, the firm knows that even if it orders no new equipment in period $t+\eta$ it will have a certain amount of equipment on hand. This equipment includes the machinery available in period t, plus the equipment previously ordered that will be delivered between t and $t+\eta$, less the equipment that will be retired during this same period. The factor proportions on all of this equipment are assumed to be fixed, although in general they will differ from machine to machine. Each machine, if operated for a period by the appropriate amounts of the cooperating factors, can produce a certain amount of output,[5] which is defined as the capacity of the machine.[6] The aggregate capacity of all the machines that will be in existence at the beginning of period $t+\eta$, with no new investment, is Q_{K_0}.

With the assumption that the firm's objective in fixing factor proportions is the minimization of cost, it must decide (a) how much new capacity to order for delivery η periods later, and (b) what blueprint should be used to specify the factor proportions on the new capacity. I assume that the two

[5] For the present it is assumed there is only a single homogeneous output.

[6] In fact, unless fixed capital is used on a twenty-four-hour basis, there is still no unique measure of capacity. It does not seem unreasonable, however, to assume that institutional patterns set a "normal" degree of utilization that can be altered only by incurring higher costs.

decisions are separable, and, given the amount of new capacity to be ordered, consider first the question of the blueprint.

Choice of Factor Proportions

In a situation in which relative prices will change over the lifetime of the capacity, it will be impossible, in general, to choose proportions that use the optimal amount of all factors at all times. In order to simplify the problem of choice, it is assumed that starting from an initial rent $c(0)$ earned by a new machine, the flow of rent is expected to decline exponentially, so that $c(t) = c(0)e^{-\delta t}$. This decline may result from physical deterioration of the capacity so that the flow of output it can produce becomes less over time, from rises in the wages or rents on nonfixed factors, from changes in the price of the output produced, or from other causes. This assumption is a very crude approximation, and may compromise the results.[7] If it is granted, however, the present value of the stream of rents earned (after deduction of income taxes) by a unit of new capacity over its lifetime may be written (ignoring subscripts)

$$\int_0^\infty e^{-rt}(1-u)c(0)e^{-\delta t}dt + kq + q(1-k')u\int_0^T e^{-rs}D(s)ds, \qquad (3.1)$$

in which

q = the price of the ith capital good (when new)
k = the rate of tax credit on investment in the ith good
k' = the rate of tax credit that must be deducted from the depreciation base
r = the appropriate discount rate (including adjustment for risk)
u = the rate of direct taxation of business income
T = the lifetime of the ith good prescribed for tax purposes
$D(s)$ = the proportion of the depreciation base for an asset of age s that may be deducted from taxable income
δ = the exponential rate of decline in the value of services provided by a unit of the ith good.

The first term in (3.1) is the discounted stream of quasi-rents, after deduction

---

[7] This assumption, in particular, implies that the quasi-rent will approach zero only asymptotically. However, if the reason for the expected decline in quasi-rent is, for example, an expected rise in all wages at a constant rate $\dot{w}$, then $c(t) = c(0)(1 - w_0 e^{\dot{w}t})$ (where w_0 is the initial wage share), and this function declines at an increasing rate and reaches zero in finite time.

of direct taxes. The second term allows for tax credits of a certain proportion of the cost of the machine. The third term is the discounted value of the stream of taxes saved as a result of a deduction of depreciation expenses from taxable income.

If this present value is equated to q, the price of a new machine, it is possible to solve for $c(0)^*$, the quasi-rent that must be earned by a new machine to justify its purchase. If z denotes $\int_0^T e^{-rs}D(s)ds$, the present value of the depreciation deduction, the equality is

$$q(1-k-uz+uzk') = \int_0^\infty e^{-(\delta+r)t}c(0)^*(1-u)dt; \qquad (3.2)$$

integrating the right-hand side leads to [8]

$$c(0)^* = \frac{q(r+\delta)(1-k-uz+uzk')}{1-u}. \qquad (3.3)$$

The blueprints tell how much of the malleable output must be molded into each of the models of machinery that are available. In order to proceed further, it is assumed that at any particular point of time, the available blueprints correspond to a neoclassical production function of the special constant elasticity of substitution (CES) class [9] (in the first degree homogeneous version as originally developed by Arrow, Chenery, Minhas, and Solow).[10] With m factors, this function, with suitable normalization,[11] may be written

$$Q = \left[\sum_{i=1}^m \alpha_i X_i^{(\sigma-1)/\sigma} \right]^{\sigma/(\sigma-1)}, \qquad (3.4)$$

[8] This derivation closely follows that of Hall and Jorgenson in "Tax Policy and Investment Behavior," and the formula arrived at differs from theirs only because I have distinguished between k and k'.

[9] This m-factor constant-elasticity-of-substitution function, though itself a special case, is still relatively general compared with the two most popular alternatives, the Cobb-Douglas and Leontief production functions, both of which are special cases of the class of CES functions.

[10] Kenneth J. Arrow, Hollis B. Chenery, B. S. Minhas, and Robert M. Solow, "Capital-Labor Substitution and Economic Efficiency," *Review of Economics and Statistics*, Vol. 43 (August 1961), pp. 225–50.

[11] As originally written by Arrow, Chenery, Minhas, and Solow, the right-hand side was multiplied by a scaling (or so-called efficiency) parameter v, with the sum of the α's set equal (normalized) to unity. With no loss of generality, the efficiency parameter may be set equal to unity. If the alternative normalization is adopted, the sum of all the distribution parameters (the α's) is then equal to $v^{(\sigma-1)/\sigma}$.

in which

Q = output in physical terms
X_i = the input of the ith factor [12]
σ = the elasticity of substitution
α_i = the distribution parameter for the ith factor (as noted below, these parameters may change over time).

Suppose, for the moment, that no factor price is expected to vary over the lifetime of the capacity to be installed. In this case, the assumed decline in rent could come about if, for example, a certain portion of the capacity disappeared each period, thus reducing both the output and the costs by exactly the same proportion. For this special case, a single set of factor proportions will minimize costs at all times. Given knowledge of prices for a unit of the services of each of the factors $(c_i, i = 1, \ldots m)$, conditions for cost minimization subject to the production constraint (3.4) may be derived by forming the Lagrangian expression

$$COST = \sum_{i=1}^{m} c_i X_i + \Lambda \left[Q - \left(\sum_{i=1}^{m} \alpha_i X_i^{(\sigma-1)/\sigma} \right)^{\sigma/(\sigma-1)} \right], \qquad (3.5)$$

and, as necessary conditions, setting the m first derivatives with respect to the X_i equal to zero. This leads to the equations

$$c_i - \Lambda \alpha_i (Q/X_i)^{1/\sigma} = 0, \qquad i = 1, \ldots m. \qquad (3.6)$$

From (3.6) it would be possible to derive $m-1$ equations expressing the cost-minimizing ratios of each of the other $m-1$ factors to X_1 (numbering the factors so that equipment, the factor being studied, is the first);

$$X_i/X_1 = \alpha_i^{\sigma} c_1^{\sigma} / \alpha_1^{\sigma} c_i^{\sigma}, \quad i = 2, \ldots m. \qquad (3.7)$$

Substituting these ratios into the production function leads to the expression

$$X_1/Q = \left[\alpha_1 + \sum_{i=2}^{m} \frac{\alpha_i^{\sigma} c_1^{\sigma-1}}{\alpha_1^{\sigma-1} c_i^{\sigma-1}} \right]^{\sigma/(\sigma-1)} \qquad (3.8)$$

---

[12] This input may be thought of as a flow of services per unit of time, or, without loss of generality, as a stock of fixed factor that provides a flow of services proportional to the stock, with the proportionality factor normalized to unity by appropriate choice of units. Changes in units will, of course, change the distribution parameter for the factor in question, but as long as σ does not change over time, this will not cause any difficulty. The input of the factor "machinery" in what follows is the number of units of the homogeneous output that are frozen into the machine of the particular blueprint chosen.

for the amount of the first factor to be embodied in (or needed to cooperate with) each unit of new capacity.

Not only is (3.8) very awkward, especially if the number of factors is greater than two, but also it is necessary to make assumptions about the time paths of each of the α_i in order to use it to derive the demand for a factor. Unless it is assumed that each of the distribution parameters is constant over time, or that each changes according to some exponential time pattern, (3.8) leads to hopeless difficulties. In addition, the choice of units in which to measure each of the other factors presents problems. In computing a wage rate, for example, should labor be measured in man-hours, or man-hours adjusted for education, or some other unit? Although it will certainly prove necessary to make arbitrary assumptions about smoothness with regard to technical changes in the distribution parameter for equipment, it seems desirable to make as few as possible.

Fortunately, the number of such assumptions can be decreased by using the economic interpretation of the Lagrangian multiplier Λ, and adding one plausible behavioral assumption. Note first that Λ represents the minimum average total cost of output produced with the newest technology. If the firm is investing in new equipment, this average cost must represent its marginal cost as well.[13] The interpretation of Λ as a minimum average cost may be verified by rewriting equation (3.6) in the form

$$c_i = \Lambda \alpha_i X_i^{-(1/\sigma)} \left[\sum_{i=1}^{m} \alpha_i X_i^{(\sigma-1)/\sigma} \right]^{1/(\sigma-1)}, \quad i = 1, \ldots m, \quad (3.9)$$

multiplying both sides of each equation by X_i, and summing all m equations, to get

$$\sum_{i=1}^{m} c_i X_i = \Lambda \left[\sum_{i=1}^{m} \alpha_i X_i^{(\sigma-1)/\sigma} \right] \left[\sum_{i=1}^{m} \alpha_i X_i^{(\sigma-1)/\sigma} \right]^{1/(\sigma-1)}$$

$$= \Lambda \left[\sum_{i=1}^{m} \alpha_i X_i^{(\sigma-1)/\sigma} \right]^{\sigma/(\sigma-1)} \quad (3.10)$$

$$= \Lambda Q.$$

[13] When the firm is investing in new machinery, the average *variable* costs on the oldest machinery in use cannot exceed the appropriate calculated average *total* cost using new machinery. The trick lies in calculating average total cost, which must include allowance for expected decreases in value of new machinery, without knowledge about expectations of future prices. The simplified rules of thumb I have assumed make the calculation easy, but they may not be at all appropriate.

Thus

$$\Lambda = \frac{\sum_{i=1}^{m} c_i X_i}{Q}, \tag{3.11}$$

the average cost with the latest technology, assuming that static cost-minimizing factor proportions are used.

With the addition of the behavioral assumption that price p is set as a constant markup factor M on marginal or minimum average cost, so that

$$p = M\Lambda, \qquad M \geq 1, \tag{3.12}$$

it is possible to use observed output price as a proxy for minimum average cost. If (3.12) is substituted into (3.6), only this one equation is required to write the demand for the first factor per unit of new capacity as a function of its rental, its distribution parameter, the price of output, and M. Thus

$$X_1/Q = [\alpha_1 p/c_1 M]^{\sigma}. \tag{3.13}$$

The derivation of (3.13) has proceeded under the assumption of a static world, with no changes in prices or technology. In a time series analysis, it is unrealistic to assume that the underlying production function will not change over time. As long as technical change is factor-augmenting only with respect to factors other than machinery, the marginal product of machinery will not, however, be changed.

Factor augmentation, in the sense used here, may be defined as follows. A change in one of the distribution parameters α_i cannot be distinguished from a change in the units in which the factor X_i is measured. Thus the production function (3.4), governing additions to capacity at time t, may be written with unchanged distribution parameters, but with scale factors that multiply the quantities of each factor when these quantities are measured in time-invariant units. These scale factors are functions of time, and thus the production function may be written

$$Q_t = \left[\alpha_1\{h_{1_t} X_{1_t}\}^{(\sigma-1)/\sigma} + \sum_{i=2}^{m} \alpha_i\{h_{i_t} X_{i_t}\}^{(\sigma-1)/\sigma}\right]^{\sigma/(\sigma-1)}, \tag{3.4.1}$$

where the first factor is equipment. In (3.4.1) technical change that increases h_{i_t} is factor-augmenting with respect to the ith factor; a single unit of that factor goes further. Each of the derivatives of (3.4.1) with respect to any factor involves only the scaling of that particular factor, so that

$$\partial Q_t / \partial X_{1_t} = \alpha_1 h_{1_t} (Q_t / h_{1_t} X_{1_t})^{1/\sigma}. \qquad (3.14)$$

For equipment, therefore, a change in h_{i_t} $(i = 2, m)$ is Harrod-neutral.[14]

If, however, there is a change in h_{i_t} (including a Hicks-neutral technical change, in which all the h_{i_t} rise by the same proportion), the marginal product of a unit of equipment will change over time.[15] Without loss of generality, all equipment-augmenting technical progress may be treated as embodied in new equipment, for Hall has shown that "given rates of embodied and disembodied technical change and a given deterioration function cannot be distinguished from a lower rate of embodied technical change, a higher rate of disembodied change, and a higher rate of deterioration."[16] This means that the rate of disembodied equipment-augmenting change can be arbitrarily normalized to zero; ways to make old equipment more productive will simply show up as slower deterioration of the capacity embodied in that equipment.

As soon as the possibility of technical change is admitted, the assumption that relative prices and factor costs do not change becomes untenable. In addition, if the model is to be applied empirically, there must be some recognition that prices are, in fact, constantly changing. If the production function and the costs of time t were to persist forever, the factor proportions that would minimize costs would be

$$X_{1_t} / Q_t = (1/h_{1_t})(h_{1_t} \alpha_1 p_t / c_{1_t} M)^\sigma \equiv V_t, \qquad (3.13.1)$$

but these will generally be the wrong proportions in a world of changing prices.

For purposes of estimation, it is assumed that entrepreneurs choose their factor proportions by a simple suboptimal rule of thumb. This rule involves factor proportions V_t^* which are calculated as a distributed lag

[14] Technical change is said to be Harrod-neutral if, at a constant rate of interest, technical change leaves the capital-output ratio unchanged. This condition will be satisfied if the marginal product of capital, as a function of the capital-output ratio, is unaffected by the technical change.

[15] Technical change is said to be Hicks-neutral if, for a given set of factor proportions, the technical change does not affect the ratio of the marginal products of any pair of factors. Since the marginal product of the jth factor includes h_{j_t} raised to the power $(\sigma-1)/\sigma$, equal proportional changes in h_{i_t} and h_{j_t} will not affect the ratio of the marginal product of the ith factor to the marginal product of the jth factor.

[16] Robert E. Hall, "Technical Change and Capital from the Point of View of the Dual," *Review of Economic Studies*, Vol. 35 (January 1968), p. 38.

function of past values of V, the *static* optimum amount of equipment per unit of capacity defined in output terms. Thus,

$$V_t^* = \sum_{k=0}^{\infty} \chi_k V_{t-k}. \tag{3.15}$$

There is no particular reason why the weights χ should add up to one.

This rule is undoubtedly a vast oversimplification. It would be desirable to consider explicitly the ways in which expectations about interest rates, equipment prices, and prices of other factors are formed, and the choice of optimum proportions in the face of such expectations. However, such an explicit model would require many more specific assumptions than I have been willing to make.

Gross Additions to Capacity

The decision as to how much capacity to order at time t for delivery η periods later depends on how much is needed for replacement, and how much is desired for net additions. Replacement temporarily aside, desired net additions to capacity should equal the difference between the capacity the firm desired to have, and placed orders to achieve, in period $t+\eta-1$ and the capacity desired in period $t+\eta$. Desired capacity Q_K^* is assumed to be a roughly constant [17] multiple ($\zeta^* \geq 1$) of output planned for period $t+\eta$, $Q_{t+\eta}^*$, that is,

$$Q_{K_{t+\eta}}^* = \zeta^* Q_{t+\eta}^*. \tag{3.16}$$

Furthermore, Q^* may, it is assumed, be approximated by a function of past outputs

$$Q_{t+\eta}^* = \sum_{i=0}^{\infty} \xi_i Q_{t-i}. \tag{3.17}$$

[17] With fixed proportions prevailing ex post, there will be an optimal degree of excess capacity which depends on the certainty with which demand expectations are held, the costs, due to lost sales or overtime work, of not having enough capacity, and the cost of holding excess capacity. Thus, in general the desired capacity-output ratio ζ will be a function of relative prices, among other things, but for simplicity I assume it is approximately constant. For approaches to the problem of the optimal degree of excess capacity for relatively special cases, see Alan S. Manne, "Capacity Expansion and Probabilistic Growth," *Econometrica*, Vol. 29 (October 1961), pp. 632–49, and Kenneth R. Smith, "The Determinants of Excess Capacity," paper presented to the North American Regional Conference of the Econometric Society, Washington, 1967.

Then net additions to desired capacity are

$$Q^*_{K_{t+\eta}} - Q^*_{K_{t+\eta-1}} = \zeta^* \left[\sum_{i=0}^{\infty} \xi_i (Q_{t-i} - Q_{t-i-1}) \right]. \tag{3.18}$$

For different firms, and for different types of equipment within a firm, the lead time η will vary. Therefore, in deriving an aggregate model, it is desirable to specify that actual net additions to capacity are a distributed lag function of past desired net additions, with the weights adding up to one and with each particular weight ψ_j indicating the proportion of the capacity ordered in period t that is installed in period $t+j$. In other words, ψ_j represents the proportion of the equipment aggregate for which the waiting period η is equal to j. Thus an aggregate equation for actual net additions to capacity would be

$$Q_{K_t} - Q_{K_{t-1}} = \zeta^* \left[\sum_{j=0}^{\infty} \sum_{i=0}^{\infty} \psi_j \xi_i (Q_{t-i-j} - Q_{t-i-j-1}) \right]. \tag{3.19}$$

This equation can be written in general form as

$$Q_{K_t} - Q_{K_{t-1}} = \zeta^* \left[\sum_{k=0}^{\infty} \varphi_k (Q_{t-k} - Q_{t-k-1}) \right].$$

The above equation, however, is nothing but a first-order difference equation with a very simple solution,

$$Q_{K_t} = \zeta^* \sum_{k=0}^{\infty} \varphi_k Q_{t-k} + Constant, \tag{3.20}$$

where the constant is arbitrary and must be zero if actual capacity is to equal desired capacity in a steady state.

If net additions to capacity actually follow such a pattern (either without error, or with very small, serially independent errors), current capacity can be adequately approximated as a function of past output levels. This approximation is not likely to be very good in the case of an individual firm or industry, or even in the aggregate in the face of a substantial downswing, for the lag between desired and actual net decreases in capacity cannot be expected to resemble the lag for net increases.[18] Nevertheless,

---

[18] This is the well-known problem of asymmetry in the operation of the acceleration principle. Aggregation, of course, does not solve the problem, except to the extent that some firms can sell their excess capacity to others. Nevertheless, the declines in aggregate net new orders for machinery in the post-Korean period, even in the worst recessions, have been moderate enough to encourage the feeling that the bias from this source will not be serious.

in the absence of any direct measures of capacity or capacity utilization for the economy as a whole, an approximation of this sort is perhaps the best available measure.

The conceptual stock of capacity specified in equation (3.20) is the analogue in this model to the stock of capital that ordinarily appears in investment functions. The crucial difference is that in this model the amount of investment necessary to replace a unit of capacity that wears out or becomes obsolete will depend on recent relative prices rather than on the amount of investment that originally took place.

As to replacement demand, by far the simplest assumption is that the flow of services from a unit of capacity declines exponentially from the time the capacity is installed. Under static conditions, such a pattern would imply exponential decline in the prices of used machinery. Since existing evidence suggests that exponential decline may be an adequate approximation to the true pattern,[19] this assumption can be rationalized, and leads to the conclusion that the proportion of existing capacity to be replaced in a given time period may be adequately approximated by a constant (δ).[20] Then gross additions to capacity, or gross investment in capacity units I_{QK}, may be written as

$$I_{QK_t} = \zeta^* \sum_{k=0}^{\infty} \varphi_k (Q_{t-k} - Q_{t-k-1}) + \delta \zeta^* \sum_{k=0}^{\infty} \varphi_k Q_{t-k-1}, \qquad (3.21)$$

using (3.20) to express the net stock of capacity at the end of period $t-1$ (the beginning of period t).

---

[19] See, for example, George Terborgh, *Realistic Depreciation Policy* (Machinery and Allied Products Institute, 1954), Chaps. 4 and 5; Zvi Griliches, "Capital Stock in Investment Functions: Some Problems of Concept and Measurement," in Carl F. Christ and others, *Measurement in Economics: Studies in Mathematical Economics and Econometrics in Memory of Yehuda Grunfeld* (Stanford University Press, 1963), pp. 121–23; and Gregory C. Chow, *Demand for Automobiles in the United States: A Study in Consumer Durables* (Amsterdam: North-Holland, 1957).

[20] A simplification of this sort may not be tenable, however, in a model with ex post fixed proportions, to the extent that rising variable costs eliminate the quasi-rents on old equipment even before it is physically worn out. In such circumstances, the proportion of capacity retired in any given period would be a function of relative prices, among other things. On the other hand, if there is some possibility of choosing the durability of machinery, and more durable machines cost more, one would expect that market forces would lead to the manufacture of capital goods in which the physical life is normally *less* than the economic life.

Equipment Expenditures

To derive an investment function, gross additions to capacity must be scaled by a factor that represents the incremental ratio of equipment to capacity considered optimal at the time the plans are made final. The rule of thumb for choosing this marginal ratio is given in (3.15). As given in (3.15), V_t^* must be multiplied by net additions to desired capacity in period $t+\eta$, as given by (3.17), and also by the amount of replacement to take place in period $t+\eta$, which will be $\delta\zeta^*$ times the output planned for $t+\eta$. Thus, desired gross additions to capacity I_{QK}^* are given by

$$
\begin{aligned}
I_{QK_{t+\eta}}^* &= \zeta^* \sum_{i=0}^{\infty} \xi_i(Q_{t-i}-Q_{t-i-1}) + \delta\zeta^* \sum_{i=0}^{\infty} \xi_i Q_{t-i-1} \\
&= \zeta^* \sum_{i=0}^{\infty} \xi_i[Q_{t-i}-(1-\delta)Q_{t-i-1}],
\end{aligned}
\tag{3.22}
$$

and planned expenditure $I_{t+\eta}^*$ is

$$
I_{t+\eta}^* = \zeta^* \sum_{k=0}^{\infty} \chi_k V_{t-k} \sum_{i=0}^{\infty} \xi_i[Q_{t-i}-(1-\delta)Q_{t-i-1}].
\tag{3.23}
$$

If a lag is introduced between plans and expenditures, as before, *aggregate* equipment expenditures in period t are expressed in terms of past output levels and relative price ratios as

$$
I_t = \zeta^* \sum_{j=0}^{\infty} \sum_{k=0}^{\infty} \sum_{i=0}^{\infty} \psi_j \chi_k \xi_i V_{t-k-j}[Q_{t-i-j}-(1-\delta)Q_{t-i-j-1}].
\tag{3.24}
$$

This expression may be thought of as a special case of the general form

$$
I_t = \zeta^* \sum_{j=0}^{\infty} \sum_{i=0}^{\infty} \beta_{ij} V_{t-i} Q_{t-j}.
\tag{3.25}
$$

The relationship between the coefficients β_{ij} in equation (3.25) and the coefficients of the equation that immediately precedes it is as follows:

$$
\beta_{ij} = \sum_{k=0}^{\min[i,j]} \psi_k \chi_{i-k}[\xi_{j-k}-(1-\delta)\xi_{j-k-1}].
\tag{3.26}
$$

Equation (3.25) involves a large—indeed, in principle, infinite—matrix of coefficients β_{ij} of relative price and output terms. Unrestricted estimation of the matrix, however, is neither possible nor desirable.

The common-sense interpretation of (3.25) is that equipment spending is a complex weighted sum of the effects of lagged relative prices and output levels, interacting multiplicatively. But if quarterly changes in V and Q are small relative to their levels, (3.25) is approximately proportional to

$$I_t \approx \zeta^* \sum_{i=0}^{n} \lambda_i V_{t-i} \tilde{Q}_t + \zeta^* \sum_{j=0}^{n} \mu_j Q_{t-j} \tilde{V}_t, \tag{3.27}$$

in which $\tilde{Q}_t$ and $\tilde{V}_t$ are approximations to the levels of Q and V over the period $t-n, t$. On this interpretation

$$\lambda_i \approx \sum_{j} \beta_{ij} = \sum_{k=0}^{i} \delta \psi_k \chi_{i-k} \tag{3.28}$$

and

$$\mu_j \approx \sum_{i} \beta_{ij} = \sum_{k=0}^{j} \psi_k [\xi_{j-k} - (1-\delta)\xi_{j-k-1}]; \tag{3.29}$$

that is, the λ's represent row sums of the β_{ij} coefficient matrix and the μ's represent column sums. Since all of the ψ's and χ's are assumed positive, the λ's should all be positive.[21] With respect to the μ's, only the first nonzero μ_j weight can be specified a priori to be positive; nevertheless it seems likely that the first few μ_j would be positive, while the weights applied to more distant output effects would be negative. In other words, both recent and distant relative prices are expected to enter the equation with the same sign, but recent output levels are expected to have a positive effect on investment while past levels should have a negative effect. This simply reflects the familiar acceleration principle; for a given level of current output a higher level of past output means a smaller output rise and hence less investment. The distinction between the expected pattern of λ's and the μ's arises because without ex post substitution, investment reacts not to a change in relative prices but only to the level of the ratio.[22] In this model there is no acceleration effect with respect to relative prices.

Using (3.26), Table 3-1 sets out a numerical example of what the full coefficient matrix β would be, with δ arbitrarily set at 0.10, and given the

[21] This statement requires amplification. The χ weights, which partly represent expectations about future relative prices, might conceivably contain negative terms. The assumption that they should all be positive implies that V_t^* is a positively weighted sum of past values of V_t, which may not be true.

[22] To the extent that more capacity is replaced when V is rising, because old capacity (put in place when V was low) becomes uneconomical, I might react to changes in V even when ex post substitution does not exist. As noted earlier, the assumption of exponential retirement patterns excludes this possibility, but the assumption may not be valid.

arbitrarily chosen sets of weights [23]

$$[\xi_0 \ \xi_1 \ \xi_2] = [0.5 \ 0.4 \ 0.15]$$
$$[\chi_0 \ \chi_1 \ \chi_2 \ \chi_3] = [0.4 \ 0.3 \ 0.2 \ 0.1]$$
$$[\psi_0 \ \psi_1 \ \psi_2] = [0.25 \ 0.5 \ 0.25]. \tag{3.30}$$

In the example, the row sums are all positive, while the column sums are first positive and then negative. The same pattern is evident in each row across; the coefficients are first positive and then negative.

The Standard Neoclassical Model

The functional forms (3.25) and (3.27) are particularly appropriate for testing the hypothesis that a more general functional form is needed than is provided by the standard neoclassical model, because the standard model can also be fitted into these forms. I identify the "standard" model with the path-breaking work of Jorgenson, mentioned in the introduction to this study; [24] the most important particular in which it differs from the model I have specified is that in it factor proportions are assumed to be freely variable at all times. In this case, (3.13.1) would give the appropriate

TABLE 3-1. Example of Beta Matrix with Ex Post Fixed Proportions

Number of periods factor proportions are lagged	Number of periods output is lagged						Total [a] λ_j
	0	1	2	3	4	5	
0	0.050	—0.005	—0.021	—0.014	0.000	0.000	0.010
1	0.038	0.096	—0.026	—0.052	—0.027	0.000	0.029
2	0.025	0.072	0.032	—0.043	—0.041	—0.014	0.032
3	0.012	0.049	0.027	—0.028	—0.029	—0.010	0.021
4	0.000	0.025	0.022	—0.013	—0.017	—0.007	0.010
5	0.000	0.000	0.012	—0.001	—0.006	—0.003	0.003
Total μ_i [a]	0.125	0.237	0.048	—0.151	—0.120	—0.034	0.105

Source: Equation (3.26).
[a] Details may not add to totals due to rounding.

[23] These weights imply (a) that output planned at $t+\eta$ is one-half of output at t, plus 40 percent of output at $t—1$, plus 15 percent of output at $t—2$; (b) that $V_t^* = 0.4V_t + 0.3V_{t-1} + 0.2V_{t-2} + 0.1V_{t-3}$; and (c) that 25 percent of orders placed in period t are filled in that period, 50 percent in period $t+1$, and 25 percent in period $t+2$.

[24] See note 3, p. 62.

conditional operating rule for the cost-minimizing ratio of capital stock to output.[25]

Jorgenson recognizes, however, that there exists a lag—or series of lags—between the making of plans and the delivery of equipment. In the most rigid form of this model, plans are made without regard to this lag; one interpretation of this assumption would be that expectations are static,[26] that is,

$$Q^*_{t+\eta} = Q_t \tag{3.31}$$

and

$$V^*_t = V_t. \tag{3.32}$$

A desired stock of equipment K^* is computed as

$$K^*_t = V^*_t Q^*_{t+\eta} = V_t Q_t. \tag{3.33}$$

If equipment is ordered to cover any change in desired capital stock, and a proportion ψ_j of the aggregate total of equipment ordered in period t is delivered in period $t+j$, then

$$K_t - K_{t-1} = \sum_{j=0}^{\infty} \psi_j (V_{t-j} Q_{t-j} - V_{t-j-1} Q_{t-j-1}) \tag{3.34}$$

and

$$K_t = \sum_{j=0}^{\infty} \psi_j V_{t-j} Q_{t-j}, \tag{3.34.1}$$

where K_t is the aggregate stock at the end of period t.

Then, since (3.34) provides an expression for net investment in period t, and replacement in that same period will be δK_{t-1} if exponential retirement is assumed, this means

$$I_t = \sum_{j=0}^{\infty} \psi_i (V_{t-j} Q_{t-j} - V_{t-j-1} Q_{t-j-1}) + \delta K_{t-1}. \tag{3.35}$$

[25] I am also assuming that the standard model includes enough assumptions to assure the existence of an aggregate capital stock. See Franklin M. Fisher, "Embodied Technical Change and the Existence of an Aggregate Capital Stock," *Review of Economic Studies*, Vol. 32 (October 1965), pp. 263–88. The operating rule does not, however, specify how the optimum output is chosen.

[26] Nothing would be changed if expectations embodied some sort of constant trend so that, for example, expected output Q^* was a constant multiple of current output. The constant trend factor could not, in the estimation, be untangled from the other coefficients.

If (3.35) is substituted for K_{t-1}, then

$$
\begin{aligned}
I_t &= \sum_{j=0}^{\infty} \psi_j (V_{t-j} Q_{t-j} - V_{t-j-1} Q_{t-j-1}) + \delta \sum_{j=0}^{\infty} \psi_j V_{t-j-1} Q_{t-j-1} \\
&= \sum_{j=0}^{\infty} \psi_j (V_{t-j} Q_{t-j} - [1-\delta] V_{t-j-1} Q_{t-j-1}).
\end{aligned} \tag{3.36}
$$

This corresponds to (3.25) with the matrix β simply

$$
\begin{bmatrix}
\psi_0 & 0 & 0 & \cdots \\
0 & \psi_1 - (1-\delta)\psi_0 & 0 & \\
0 & 0 & \psi_2 - (1-\delta)\psi_1 & \\
\cdot & & & \cdot \\
\cdot & & & \cdot \\
\cdot & & & \cdot
\end{bmatrix}.
$$

The row and column sums are obviously identical. The expected sign pattern of the weights on the main diagonal would be $\beta_{11} > 0$, $\beta_{22} \gtrless 0$, depending on whether or not $\psi_1 > (1-\delta)\psi_0$. All the weights could be positive if $\psi_{i+1} \geq (1-\delta)\psi_i$ for all i. But this would appear unlikely, for this restriction implies that the mean lag between orders and deliveries of equipment would have to be at least $1/\delta$ periods (that is, six to twelve years for plausible values of δ).

The lag pattern derived above depends not only on ex post variability of factor proportions but also on the existence of static expectations. There is no reason why the two assumptions should be connected, and relaxing the assumption of static expectations leads to a much different lag pattern. If, for example, price and output expectations are generated by processes of the form

$$
Q_{t+\eta}^* = \sum_{i=0}^{\infty} \xi_i Q_{t-i}, \tag{3.37}
$$

and

$$
V_{t+\eta}^* = \sum_{k=0}^{\infty} \chi_k V_{t-k}, \tag{3.38}
$$

then an argument precisely analogous to the one just given leads to the expression

$$
I_t = \sum_{j=0}^{\infty} \sum_{k=0}^{\infty} \sum_{i=0}^{\infty} \psi_j \chi_k \xi_i [V_{t-k-j} Q_{t-i-j} - (1-\delta) V_{t-k-j-1} Q_{t-i-j-1}]. \tag{3.39}
$$

If equation (3.39) is also considered a special case of

$$I_t = \sum_{j=0}^{\infty} \sum_{i=0}^{\infty} \beta_{ij} V_{t-i} Q_{t-j},$$ (3.39.1)

the correspondence between the coefficients β_{ij} and the coefficients of (3.39) is

$$\beta_{ij} = \sum_{k=0}^{\min[i,j]} \psi_k [\chi_{i-k} \xi_{j-k} - (1-\delta)\chi_{i-k-1} \xi_{j-k-1}].$$ (3.40)

In this case the row and column sums of the β matrix will not be identical unless the coefficients χ_k are identical with the coefficients ξ_i. A condition that is sufficient, though not necessary, to guarantee that all the row sums in the β matrix corresponding to (3.39) will be positive is that $\chi_{i+1} \geq (1-\delta)\chi_i$ for all i.

Table 3-2 gives a numerical example of a β matrix derived from equation (3.40) using the same sets of ψ, χ, and ξ weights that were used in deriving Table 3-1. In this example, both the row sums and the column sums are first positive and then negative, which would be the normal case.

TABLE 3-2. Example of Beta Matrix for Standard Neoclassical Model with Nonstatic Expectations

Number of periods factor proportions are lagged	Number of periods output is lagged						Total [a] λ_j
	0	1	2	3	4	5	
0	0.050	0.040	0.015	0.000	0.000	0.000	0.105
1	0.038	0.085	0.055	0.016	0.000	0.000	0.194
2	0.025	0.061	0.000	—0.020	—0.012	0.000	0.055
3	0.012	0.038	—0.004	—0.061	—0.045	—0.014	—0.074
4	0.000	0.014	—0.009	—0.045	—0.033	—0.010	—0.083
5	0.000	0.000	—0.010	—0.030	—0.021	—0.007	—0.068
6	0.000	0.000	0.000	—0.011	—0.009	—0.003	—0.024
Total [a] μ_i	0.125	0.237	0.048	—0.151	—0.120	—0.034	0.105

Source: Equation (3.40).
[a] Details may not add to totals due to rounding.

To summarize, I have shown that in the most extreme form of the standard model (with the implicit assumption of static expectations) the jth row sum of the coefficient matrix of equation (3.25) would be identical to the jth column sum. In the less restrictive case in which expectations about both V and Q are formed as weighted averages of past observations on V and Q, with all the weights having positive signs, the presumption is that both the row sums and the column sums would be positive at first and then negative. This contrasts to the hypothesized sign pattern of row sums derived from a theoretical model in which ex post substitution is not possible. In that case, all the row sums would be positive.[27]

As noted in the introduction, policy makers should be concerned with whether a measure that affects the implicit rent on equipment sets off a short-lived investment boom. Thus, for the purposes of short-run policy, the most important thing is to be able to estimate the parameters of (3.25) or (3.27), and to derive a qualitative (and quantitative) description of the λ weights. It would also, however, be desirable to be able to interpret the estimates and to draw conclusions about the sort of capital-theoretic model that generated the data. I have noted that an unambiguous interpretation will not generally be possible. All that can be said is that, if all the λ weights turn out to have the same sign, if only a few of them are negative, or if they differ very significantly from the distribution of the μ weights, then these results are not inconsistent with a model in which ex post substitution is not possible. In addition, this pattern would seem improbable in a model in which factor proportions could be easily altered even after fixed equipment was in place.

Estimation of the Parameters of the Model

This section describes an attempt to use the model specified in equations (3.3), (3.13.1), and (3.25) to explain the U.S. Department of Commerce's quarterly series of expenditures for producers' durable equipment in the United States (see Appendix Table 3-A-1, pages 128–30). This aggregate is the most comprehensive series available on equipment expenditures by American firms; it is also the only quarterly series available that separates expenditures for equipment from expenditures for new construction. In a sense, the estimation of the lag distributions corresponding to the model provides a test of the putty-clay hypothesis that choice of technique is possible only up to the point at which new machinery is put into place.[28]

---

[27] This is true, at least given the assumptions that V_t^* is a positively weighted average of past values of V, and that the amount of capacity desired is not a function of V.

[28] Models of this sort have become known as "putty-clay" models because, in one stylized version, machinery is assumed to be made of "putty," which can be shaped into any given form until it is put into place, after which it becomes hard-baked "clay."

Choice of Variables and Parameters

In the development of the model, a single homogeneous output was assumed. For empirical applications, however, it may be more realistic to think of the production function (3.4) as an aggregate approximation, entailing a summation over many products for each of which there exists at any moment several blueprints defining the feasible methods of production.[29] The approximation will be useful if the demand for investment goods, as a function of relative prices and gross additions to capacity, behaves as predicted by (3.13.1). In particular, the separate estimation of σ, which represents the long-run elasticity of equipment demand with respect to the inverse of product rent, will provide an important test of the degree to which the demand for equipment is sensitive to the price of a unit of equipment services, and thus to fiscal and monetary parameters that affect the rent.

The central hypothesis of this analysis is contained in the equation

$$I_t = \zeta^* \sum_{j=0}^{\infty} \sum_{i=0}^{\infty} \beta_{ij} V_{t-i} Q_{t-j} + \varepsilon_t. \tag{3.41}$$

For the estimation, the variables in (3.41) are defined as follows:

I_t = deflated expenditures for producers' durable equipment (in 1958 dollars, seasonally adjusted quarterly totals at annual rates)[30]

Q_t = business gross product (gross national product less the gross product of government, households and institutions, and rest of world, in 1958 dollars, seasonally adjusted at annual rates)

V_t = a variable that is proportional to the equilibrium ratio of equipment to output, given the prices and technology of period t

ε_t = an independently distributed random error.

As specified in equations (3.13) and (3.13.1),

$$V_t = h_{1_t}^{\sigma-1}(\alpha_1 \, p_t)^{\sigma}(c_{1_t} M)^{-\sigma}. \tag{3.13.2}$$

Two of the parameters, α_1 and M, are constants independent of time; α_1 is the distribution parameter for equipment in the production function and M is the markup proportion over minimum average cost. In the estimation these parameters are absorbed into the coefficients β, and it is not possible to identify them separately. Thus for purposes of estimation, a new

---

[29] Of course, all of the usual problems associated with index numbers arise.

[30] Unless otherwise stated, all seasonally adjusted variables are used as provided by the U.S. Department of Commerce. The basic data are given in App. Table 3-A-1, pp. 128–30.

variable V' is defined as follows[31]

$$V_t' = h_{1_t}^{\sigma-1} p_t^\sigma c_{1_t}^{-\sigma}. \tag{3.42}$$

In this expression

> σ = the price elasticity of demand for equipment
> h_{1_t} = the technical change parameter for equipment
> p_t = the implicit price deflator for business gross product (seasonally adjusted)
> c_{1_t} = the imputed rent per unit of new equipment.

The technical change parameter h_{1_t} is assumed to follow a smooth trend.[32] A parameter h' is defined such that

$$h_{1_t}^{\sigma-1} = e^{h'\text{TIME}}, \tag{3.43}$$

with TIME equal to zero at the midpoint of 1958 and incremented by one each quarter. The rate (per year) of equipment-augmenting technical change is then

$$4h'/(\sigma-1), \tag{3.44}$$

since

$$h_{1_t} = e^{h'\text{TIME}/(\sigma-1)}. \tag{3.45}$$

The expression for the imputed rent on new equipment is derived from (3.3),

$$c_{1_t} = \frac{q_t(r_t+\delta)(1-k_t-u_t z_t+u_t z_t k_t')}{1-u_t}. \tag{3.46}$$

In this expression

> δ = annual rate of decline of value of the services provided by a unit of fixed equipment
> q_t = implicit price deflator for producers' durable equipment (seasonally adjusted)
> r_t = discount rate (per year)
> u_t = general rate of income taxation for corporations

[31] After V' has been substituted for V in equation (3.41), the sum of all the distributed lag weights $(\Sigma_j \Sigma_i \beta_{ij})$ will correspond to $\delta(\alpha_1/M)^\sigma (\Sigma_j \psi_j)(\Sigma_k \chi_k)(\Sigma_i \xi_i)$, whereas in the examples shown in Tables 3-1 and 3-2, $\Sigma_j \Sigma_i \beta_{ij} = \delta(\Sigma_j \psi_j)(\Sigma_k \chi_k)(\Sigma_i \xi_i)$. The parameter ζ^* is also assumed constant and cannot be estimated separately; it is subsumed in the estimated values of the β_{ij} weights.

[32] Unless some such assumption about the smoothness of technical change is made, there is no possible way to distinguish between the effects of technical change and those of relative prices.

z_t = present value of the depreciation deduction
k_t = effective rate of tax credit against equipment purchases
k_t' = rate of tax credit deducted from depreciation base.

Although it was initially my intention to estimate δ, this did not prove feasible, and it was specified to be 0.16 (see below). The choice of measures for r_t, z_t, and k_t requires more extensive comment.

The appropriate empirical measure of the discount rate is subject to a great deal of disagreement, but from the point of view of policy the choice is crucial. The discount rate implicit in investment decisions made in an uncertain world might not be highly correlated with any observed market yields. It might be beyond even slight influence by the monetary authorities.

In a riskless world, the market rate of interest would provide an adequate approximation to the unobservable discount rate appropriate to investment decisions.[33] Yields on equities might differ from the interest rate, but only to the extent that growth in earnings (either in real terms or because of inflation) was anticipated. The risk factor, however, cannot be ignored, and inasmuch as the discount rate fluctuates cyclically due to changing market interpretations of the risk involved, the yield on equity may be more closely correlated with the discount rate. As a very rough approximation, the discount rate might be represented by a weighted sum of Moody's industrial bond yield RM_{MBCIND}, Moody's industrial dividend-price ratio $DIV/PRICE$,[34] the corporate income tax rate u, and a time trend $TIME$ (equal to zero at mid-1958—see Appendix Table 3-A-1, pages 128–30). Thus,

$$r_t = (r_0 + r_1\, RM_{\text{MBCIND}} + r_2\, DIV/PRICE + r_3\, TIME)(1 - r_4 u_t). \quad (3.47)$$

The general formula for z_t, the present value of the depreciation deduction, is

$$z_t = \int_0^T e^{-rs} D(s)\,ds. \quad (3.48)$$

[33] In their most recent study of the electric utility industry, Miller and Modigliani found that, for the three years studied (1954, 1956, 1957), the long-term interest rate seemed to be the variable most closely related to their measure of the cost of capital. See Merton H. Miller and Franco Modigliani, "Some Estimates of the Cost of Capital to the Electric Utility Industry, 1954–57," *American Economic Review*, Vol. 56 (June 1966), pp. 333–91.

[34] If dividend payouts are an approximately constant proportion of expected earnings (when earnings have been adjusted for overstatement of depreciation) but adjust only slowly to earnings fluctuations, the dividend-price ratio will be a more accurate representation of actual market discounting of expected earnings than the more volatile ratio of actual earnings to price.

In this formula,

> r = the discount rate
>
> $D(s)$ = the proportion of the cost basis for an asset of age s that may be deducted from income for tax purposes
>
> T = the lifetime of the asset for tax purposes.

Until the end of 1953, the dominant method of depreciation in the United States was the straight-line method, for which

$$D(s) = \begin{cases} 1/T \text{ for } 0 \leq s \leq T, \\ 0 \quad \text{otherwise.} \end{cases} \tag{3.49}$$

According to Hall and Jorgenson, the present value of the deduction for straight-line depreciation is

$$z_{SL_t} = (1 - e^{-r_t T_t})/(r_t T_t) \tag{3.50}$$

if the current discount rate is expected to persist.[35]

Starting in 1954, two accelerated depreciation methods were permitted by law, the sum-of-the-years-digits method, and the double-declining-balance method. The sum-of-the-years-digits method, as Hall and Jorgenson show, "dominates the double-declining-balance and straight-line formulas in the range of discount rates and lifetimes with which we are concerned."[36] The advantage over the double-declining-balance method, however, is small, especially for assets with relatively short lives, and this factor, along with the computational ease of the double-declining-balance method, may account for the fact that the latter has been preferred. Because the present values for the two accelerated methods are close together for the relevant range of lifetimes and discount rates, with the sum-of-the-years-digits method dominant, I have chosen to use the sum-of-the-years-digits formula to represent all depreciation taken by accelerated methods. A continuous approximation to the formula for the deduction is

$$D(s) = \begin{cases} 2(T-s)/T^2 \text{ for } 0 \leq s \leq T, \\ 0 \qquad\qquad \text{otherwise,} \end{cases} \tag{3.51}$$

and the present value of the deduction according to the sum-of-the-years-digits method is

$$z_{SYD_t} = [2/(r_t T_t)][1 - (1 - e^{-r_t T_t})/(r_t T_t)]. \tag{3.52}$$

[35] Hall and Jorgenson, "Tax Policy and Investment Behavior," p. 394.
[36] *Ibid.*, p. 395.

The present values of the depreciation deduction for the two methods for selected lifetimes and discount rates, as calculated by Hall and Jorgenson, are given in Table 3-3.[37]

TABLE 3-3. Present Values of Depreciation Deduction for Selected Depreciation Methods, Lifetimes, and Discount Rates

Lifetime (years)	Discount rate	Present values	
		Straight-line	Sum-of-the-years-digits
5	0.06	0.864	0.907
5	0.12	0.752	0.827
10	0.06	0.752	0.827
10	0.12	0.582	0.696
25	0.06	0.518	0.643
25	0.12	0.317	0.456

Information about the extent to which accelerated methods have actually been adopted is given by Ture.[38] He found that, according to the U.S. Treasury Department's special compilation, "Life of Depreciable Assets," for taxable year 1959, 29.3 percent of the production machinery, transportation vehicles and equipment, and furniture and office machinery and related equipment that had been acquired since 1953 was being depreciated by the double-declining-balance method, and 23.1 percent was being depreciated by the sum-of-the-years-digits method. On the basis of this information, I have chosen to represent the present value of the depreciation deduction (per dollar of equipment purchased) as

$$z_t = \varsigma z_{\mathrm{SYD}_t} + (1 - \varsigma) z_{\mathrm{SL}_t}, \qquad (3.53)$$

with ς, equal to 0.524 starting in the first quarter of 1954. As Figure 3-1 shows, there is apparently no trend (or learning curve) associated with the adoption of accelerated depreciation by corporations. From this evidence, the assumption that ς was zero before 1954 and then rose immediately to some constant value does not seem unreasonable. It should be noted, however,

---

[37] *Ibid.*

[38] Norman B. Ture, *Accelerated Depreciation in the United States, 1954–60* (Columbia University Press for the National Bureau of Economic Research, 1967), Table A-12, pp. 147–55.

FIGURE 3-1. Proportion of Depreciable Assets of Corporations Depreciated by Accelerated Methods, by Year of Purchase, 1954–60

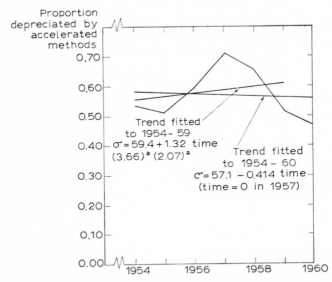

Source: Norman B. Ture, *Accelerated Depreciation in the United States, 1954–60* (Columbia University Press for the National Bureau of Economic Research, 1967), Table A-8, p. 133.
    a Standard error.

that the sample for this part of the Treasury survey was rather small, and also that this conclusion is quite the opposite of the one reached by Wales, using different data and methods.[39] Further work is needed to clear up the inconsistency.

Equipment lifetimes, represented by T, have been adjusted to take account both of changes in guideline lives and of what is known about actual practice. These adjustments accord with those of Hall and Jorgenson;[40] it is assumed that the new depreciation guidelines shortened average tax lifetimes from 15.1 to 13.1 years, starting in the third quarter of 1962.

The Long amendment to the initial 1962 tax credit legislation provided that any credit claimed had to be deducted from the depreciation base, but it was repealed by the Revenue Act of 1964; starting in the first quarter of 1964, k' is assumed to be zero.

[39] Terence J. Wales, "Estimation of an Accelerated Depreciation Learning Function," *Journal of the American Statistical Association*, Vol. 61 (December 1966), pp. 995–1009.

[40] Hall and Jorgenson, "Tax Policy and Investment Behavior," p. 400.

Although business confidence that a credit would be passed must have built up after passage by the House on March 29, 1962, substantial assurance about the effective date and terms of the credit could not have existed before the bill was reported by the Senate Finance Committee in August.[41] The parameter k, representing the effective rate of tax credit, is arbitrarily assumed to be zero until the third quarter of 1962, and to be equal to 5 percent for later periods.

The estimated effective rate is lower than the maximum statutory rate, 7 percent, for several reasons: (a) restrictions on the applicability of the credit to short-lived equipment; (b) confinement of the maximum credit for public utility companies to 3 percent; and (c) restrictions on the amount of credit taken in any one year. The limitations on the credit taken in any one year have now been amended, but there remains applicable the most important restriction in the original law, which provided that the amount of the credit taken in any one year could not exceed the first $25,000 of tax liability plus one-fourth of any remaining tax liability.

My estimate of the actual effective rate is based on information for 1963, the only year for which the tax credit was fully in effect and for which relatively complete data have been published. Expenditures for producers' durable equipment in 1963 amounted to $34.8 billion (current dollars). When all the figures for "cost of eligible property" that can be found in the 1963 Treasury data reported in *Statistics of Income*[42] are added together and allowance is made for some double counting of partnerships and small corporations, the total is about $32.98 billion. Considering that the Treasury data are not quite complete, and more important, that they are based on the bookkeeping years of the taxpaying units, the two numbers are remarkably close. For practical purposes it seems unlikely that identifying producers' durable equipment and cost of eligible property as one and the same thing will lead to serious error.

Adding up all the tentative credits for corporations, sole proprietorships, and partnerships (again adjusting for double counting) results in a total of $1.917 billion.[43] This is 5.5 percent of $34.8 billion, and can be called the

[41] This summary of events is based on U.S. Treasury Department, Office of Tax Analysis, "Investment Credit: Log of Actions and Events" (mimeograph; February 1, 1967), supplied by Melvin I. White.

[42] U.S. Treasury Department, Internal Revenue Service, *Statistics of Income—1963, U.S. Business Tax Returns* (1967).

[43] The tentative credit is the amount that could be claimed if there were no restrictions on amounts claimed.

"effective rate of tentative credit." It is lower than 7 percent because (a) about 20 percent of the equipment was purchased by public utilities, which could claim only 3 percent credit, thus lowering the effective rate by 12 percent; and (b) for corporations (the only unit for which the two figures are available) qualified investment is only about 90 percent of cost of eligible property, since much of the eligible property has a tax life of less than eight years.[44] These two adjustments account for virtually all of the difference between 7 percent and 5.5 percent.

Restrictions on the maximum credit that could be claimed mean that actual credits taken amounted to only about $1.39 billion, or 4.0 percent of spending for producers' durable equipment. The difference, however, was not lost. Because of carry-back and carry-forward provisions, it seems likely that most of this credit could eventually be claimed, although the delay would make the present value of a dollar's credit amount to less than a dollar. Furthermore, it must be assumed that corporations, when planning their investments, *expect* to make profits in the relatively near future. It is very hard to derive an expression to introduce correctly the portion of the tentative credit not immediately claimed. But it will not do to ignore it completely. On a priori grounds the true effective rate of tax credit should be at least as close to the rate of tentative credit as it is to the rate of actual credit. I have chosen 5 percent as a compromise between 4 percent and 5.5 percent.

Restrictions on Lag Distributions

At the close of the first section, it was argued that the interesting parameters in equation (3.41) are the row and column sums of the β matrix —the λ and μ weights. One feasible method of approximation involves estimating two coefficients out of each row and column of the coefficient matrix β to act as proxies for all the rest of the coefficients in the row or column. Experimentation with various patterns reveals that the results are insensitive to the choice of coefficients to be estimated, as long as at least two coefficients in each row are estimated.[45] The practice of estimating two diagonal sets of coefficients $\beta_{i,i}$ and $\beta_{i,i-1}$ for $i = 2, \ldots, n$ has been adopted for all regressions that are reported here. The maximum lag n has been chosen equal to 12, implying that the estimated value of equipment

---

[44] Qualified investment differs from cost of eligible property because assets with short lives receive weights of less than one in determining qualified investment.

[45] Estimating more than two coefficients in each row and column produced negligible improvements in the unadjusted coefficient of determination and reduced the adjusted coefficient of determination in all cases in which it was tried.

spending is based on values of V' and Q for the preceding three years.[46] Since $\mu_j = \beta_{jj} + \beta_{j+1,j}$ and $\lambda_k = \beta_{kk} + \beta_{k,k-1}$, the coefficients to be estimated determine μ_j for $j = 1, 12$, and λ_k for $k = 2, 12$.[47] Thus, the equation to be estimated, referred to as the expenditures equation, is

$$I_t = \sum_{i=2}^{12} \beta_{i,i-1} V'_{t-i} Q_{t-i+1} + \sum_{i=2}^{12} \beta_{i,i} V'_{t-i} Q_{t-i} + \varepsilon_t. \tag{3.54}$$

Multicollinearity would not permit the estimation of all twenty-two of the $\beta_{i,i-1}$ and $\beta_{i,i}$ coefficients, and to overcome this difficulty, I have used the technique developed by Shirley Almon.[48] The $\beta_{i,i-1}$ coefficients are constrained to be values of a third-degree polynomial in i, with the additional constraint that the value of the polynomial for $i = 13$ should be zero. This last constraint has the effect of forcing the $\beta_{i,i-1}$ coefficients to approach zero as the index approaches 13. In mathematical form the constraints applied amount to

$$\beta_{i,i-1} = A_3(i^3 - 2197) + A_2(i^2 - 169) + A_1(i - 13) \text{ for } 2 \leq i \leq 13.$$

A similar constraint has been applied to the estimated $\beta_{i,i}$ coefficients:

$$\beta_{i,i} = B_3(i^3 - 2197) + B_2(i^2 - 169) + B_1(i - 13) \text{ for } 2 \leq i \leq 13.$$

With the insertion of these constraints into (3.54) all but six of the linear coefficients may be eliminated. The coefficients A_1, A_2, A_3, and B_1, B_2, B_3 could be estimated, or, as I have done, the constraints could be applied

[46] In the theoretical development, all lag weights were specified to extend over the infinite past. For the purposes of estimation, an infinite lag specification could have been adopted. In this case, finite lags are more convenient, especially because there are several different lag distributions to be estimated. A priori, it is at least as plausible to assume that the effects of a change in a particular variable will become negligible after a finite period as it is to assume that the effects will continue forever. In addition, even though only a finite number of lagged values of Q enter equation (3.54), it is shown in the section beginning on p. 109 that this does not generally imply that the *complete* adjustment of capacity to a change in output takes place within a finite period (see Table 3-12).

[47] This estimation procedure requires the first row sum λ_1 to be zero. Alternative regressions in which this requirement was removed produced no evidence that λ_1, the row sum representing the effects of V' lagged only one quarter, was significantly different from zero. The regressions reported below show estimated values of λ_2 as well which are essentially zero; no significant effects of variations in relative prices are found until the third quarter after the change.

[48] Shirley Almon, "The Distributed Lag between Capital Appropriations and Expenditures," *Econometrica*, Vol. 33 (January 1965), pp. 178–96.

by making use of Lagrangian interpolation weights.[49] The six coefficients actually estimated, A_1', A_2', A_3', and B_1', B_2', B_3', are linear functions of, respectively, A_1, A_2, A_3, and B_1, B_2, B_3.

Preliminary Exploration of the Parameter Space

Even with these simplifications, estimation of the parameters of (3.54) presents a complicated nonlinear problem. The variable V' is a nonlinear function of σ, δ, r_0, r_1, r_2, r_3, r_4, and h'. If it is assumed that the error term ε in equation (3.54) is normally distributed with zero mean, constant variance, no serial correlation, and independent of all the right-hand variables, then maximum likelihood estimates of the parameters of (3.54) may be obtained by minimizing the sum of squared residuals with respect to all eight nonlinear parameters and the six linear A' and B' parameters. The next section describes the simultaneous nonlinear estimation of all these parameters (with the exception of r_3, r_4, and δ).

It is a considerably simpler task to obtain maximum likelihood estimates of the lag parameters alone, conditional on some assumed values of the nonlinear parameters. This estimation involves only linear methods. Because there is no guarantee that the nonlinear maximization technique will produce a global maximum of the likelihood function, it is generally a good idea to conduct some preliminary exploration of the parameter space. With so many nonlinear parameters, a systematic search of the parameter space is not feasible. The discussion of the nonsystematic preliminary search which follows is useful because it provides an impression of the sensitivity of the estimated error variance to the various parameters. It is possible that more can be learned in this way about the role and interactions of each of the variables than from reference only to a final set of estimates (complete with asymptotic standard errors whose interpretation is not at all clear).

Twelve preliminary trials have been carried out. For each trial, particular values of all the nonlinear parameters except σ have been guessed, and then an exhaustive search has been made in the interval (0, 2) for the value of σ that maximized the unadjusted coefficient of determination. The parameter values assumed in the various preliminary trials are indicated in Table 3-4. The assumption that h' is equal to zero implies that all technical change is other-factor augmenting. It should be noted that there is no particular

---

[49] For a more extensive discussion of the use of these weights, see Almon, "The Distributed Lag between Capital Appropriations and Expenditures." Except for rounding error in computation, the alternative methods for eliminating all but six coefficients will produce identical results.

reason why the weights r_1 and r_2 should sum to one, or any other specific value. Trials 1 and 2 represent constant after-tax discount rates. Trial 3 corresponds to the assumption Hall and Jorgenson made originally that the before-tax rate of return was constant at 0.14 throughout the period.[50] In the other trials, the assumed value for r_4 of 0.2 is an approximation to the desired proportion of debt in capital structure, included in the cost of capital in the manner suggested by the Modigliani-Miller theory.[51] Trials 7 and 12 use a discount rate based only on Moody's industrial bond yield, but the constants r_0 (the intercept) and r_3 (the time trend in the discount rate) are adjusted so that the discount rate actually used in the calculations has no trend, and has a mean value of 6 percent.[52] Similar adjustments have been made in the constants for trial 8, in which the discount rate is based only on the dividend-price ratio.

In all of the preliminary trials, the accelerated depreciation proportion parameter ς is assumed to be equal to 0.4, while the effective rate of tax credit k is assumed to be 7 percent. As several experiments discussed on pages 123–24 below make clear, the model is not at all sensitive to the assumed value of the proportion of accelerated depreciation. Only the estimated value of the elasticity of substitution σ is sensitive to the assumption about k; the experiments suggest that if, in the preliminary trials, k had been assumed equal to 5 percent instead of 7 percent, the estimated values of σ would have been about 20 percent higher.

For all of the trials, the sample period includes quarterly data from the third quarter of 1951 through the fourth quarter of 1965 (a total of fifty-seven observations; the third quarter of 1952 was eliminated because of abnormalities caused by the steel strike and seizure by the federal government).[53] For the same sample period, two of the most popular alternative models of investment behavior have also been used to explain equipment spending. The first of these models is an extension of the acceleration principle, with investment specified to be a function of net capital stock and changes in output. The model

[50] Hall and Jorgenson, "Tax Policy and Investment Behavior," p. 400.

[51] Miller and Modigliani, "Some Estimates of the Cost of Capital."

[52] This formulation might be interpreted as implying that the trend in RM_{MBCIND} does not affect the discount rate, but is instead offset by an opposite trend in the risk adjustment, and thus that only deviations about the trend are of significance.

[53] Observations on all the variables were available from 1947, but the equation could be fitted only for periods for which n lagged values were available. The time period starting in 1951 was chosen because some preliminary experiments were carried out assuming values for n as high as 18, but the right-hand variables with very long lags turned out to have insignificant coefficients.

TABLE 3-4. Trial Values of Parameters for Preliminary Estimates, Assuming a Depreciation Rate of 0.16 and No Technical Change

Trial number	r_0	r_1	r_2	r_3	r_4
1	0.07	0	0	0	0
2	0.04	0	0	0	0
3	0.14	0	0	0	1.0
4	0	1.0	0.5	0	0.2
5	0	0.75	0.75	0	0.2
6	0	0.5	1.0	0	0.2
7	0.01907	1.0	0	—0.0003178	0
8	0.03202	0	1.0	0.0004180	0
9	0	0.667	0.333	0	0.2
10	0.03	0.667	0.333	0	0.2
11	—0.03	1.5	0.5	0	0.2
12	0.01907	1.0	0	—0.0003178	0.2

Note: See p. 83 for definition and use of symbols.

estimated is

$$I_t = \alpha' \sum_{i=1}^{17} \beta_i \Delta Q_{t-i} + \delta K_{t-1} + \varepsilon_t. \tag{3.55}$$

The second alternative model corresponds to the standard neoclassical model with static expectations (see pages 76–80). In this model desired capital stock is assumed to be the product of V_t' and Q_t, and investment expenditures are assumed to be the sum of (a) a distributed lag function of changes in desired capital stock, and (b) replacement. The relationship is specified to be

$$I_t = \alpha' \sum_{i=1}^{17} \beta_i (V_{t-i}' Q_{t-i} - V_{t-i-1}' Q_{t-i-1}) + \delta K_{t-1} + \varepsilon_t. \tag{3.56}$$

In calculating V' for use in equation (3.56), nonlinear parameter values have been chosen to make it correspond as closely as possible to the model of Hall and Jorgenson. These parameters are the same as those used in trial 3, except that the proportion of depreciation by accelerated methods ς in equation (3.53) is set equal to 1 after 1954, in accordance with the assumption made by Hall and Jorgenson that the best proxy for the present value of depreciation deductions taken after 1954 is the present value for the sum-of-the-years-digits pattern. The assumed value of δ, 0.16, is between the value Hall and Jorgenson used for manufacturing equipment (0.1471) and the value they used for nonfarm nonmanufacturing equipment (0.1923).[54]

Both (3.55) and (3.56) are simply special cases of the more general model I have presented (except for the addition of the net capital stock as a right-hand variable).[55] In (3.55), σ is zero, and all of the terms involving relative prices drop out of the equation. In (3.56), σ is 1.0, and all of the elements of the β matrix not on the main diagonal are assumed to be zero. The more general form of the standard neoclassical model (with nonstatic expectations) can best be represented by estimating the lag distributions in equation (3.54). It is possible for the sign pattern of the estimated row sums to conform either to the predictions of the putty-clay model (with all of the row sums positive, as in Table 3-1) or to the general form of the standard neoclassical model (with the row sums positive for short lags and negative for long lags, as in Table 3-2).

In estimating both (3.55) and (3.56), the Almon polynomial technique has been used to restrict the lag weights; the restriction involves a fourth degree polynomial, according to the equation

$$\beta_i = C_4(i^4 - 104976) + C_3(i^3 - 5832) + C_2(i^2 - 324) + C_1(i - 18)$$

for $1 \leq i \leq 18$.

Table 3-5 reveals that it is possible to explain equipment spending quite well under a number of different discount rate assumptions, including the assumption that nothing can affect the discount rate used in investment decisions. However, the best fitting trials (4, 7, 9, 10, and 12) are those that emphasize the bond yield as the most important indicator of the prevailing discount rate. The best of these (trial 9) explains 35 percent of the variance left unexplained by the best constant rate equation (trial 3). It is also the

[54] Despite these similarities, the results are not comparable to the original results of Hall and Jorgenson because they used the consumer durables deflator and estimated the lag by a considerably different method, and because they carried out the estimation on net rather than gross investment. In a more recent paper, they present more comparable results, in terms of both the deflator used and the way in which the lag distributions are estimated. See Chap. 2 in this volume.

[55] The argument in the section beginning on p. 76 suggests that if either (3.55) or (3.56) were the correct specification, and if the errors were not autocorrelated, the net capital stock term would not add anything to the equation. In fact, it proved highly significant in both (3.55) and (3.56) and the errors were still autocorrelated. Several different net capital stocks, developed from historical data going back to 1909, were used; those calculated on the basis of an assumed δ equal to 0.16 provided the best fits. This same capital stock, when added to the better fitting versions of (3.54), added virtually nothing to the explanatory power of the equation.

best trial from the point of view of serial correlation, which is undesirably high for most of the cases. Given the crudeness of the linear formulation and the fact that no systematic method of choosing the weights for the discount rate estimate has been used, the improvement is surprisingly large.

Inclusion of the dividend-price ratio in the cost of capital seems to produce a slight improvement over formulations based solely on the trend-adjusted bond yield (compare trials 4 and 9 with trials 7 and 12); but the results are hardly conclusive. When the cost of capital is based heavily on

TABLE 3-5. Elasticities of Substitution and Goodness of Fit Statistics Derived from Preliminary Trials

Model and trial	Elasticity of substitution	Coefficient of multiple determination[a]	Adjusted standard error of estimate[b] (in millions of 1958 dollars)	Coefficient of varia-tion[c]	Durbin-Watson statistic
Expenditures equation (3.54)					
1	0.87	0.97936	$ 804.9	0.027	0.97
2	0.94	0.98286	732.7	0.024	1.17
3	0.98	0.98370	714.4	0.024	1.24
4	0.85	0.98859	597.7	0.020	1.74
5	0.65[d]	0.97356	910.0	0.030	0.79
6	0.35[d]	0.95406	1,199.4	0.040	0.50
7	0.74	0.98737	628.8	0.021	1.58
8	0.65[d]	0.96359	1,067.7	0.036	0.56
9	0.90	0.98936	577.1	0.019	1.88
10	0.89	0.98739	628.4	0.021	1.57
11	0.60[d]	0.98039	783.5	0.026	1.10
12	0.77	0.98793	614.8	0.020	1.66
Accelerator model (equation 3.55)					
...	(0.00)[e]	0.95233	1,218.0	0.041	0.46
Standard neoclassical model with static expectations (equation 3.56)					
...	(1.00)[e]	0.92269	1,541.0	0.051	0.43

Source: Statistics for trials 1–12 are computed using the model given in equation (3.54), with trial values of various parameters as specified in Table 3-4. The specification for the accelerator model is given in equation (3.55) and the specification for the standard neoclassical model is given in equation (3.56).

[a] Unadjusted.

[b] Square root of sum of squared residuals divided by the number of observations minus the number of estimated parameters, equal to 7 for trials 1–12 and 5 for the accelerator model and the standard neoclassical model.

[c] Adjusted standard error of estimate divided by the mean of the dependent variable.

[d] Price elasticity of demand is estimated only to the nearest 0.05; other estimates are to the nearest 0.01.

[e] By assumption.

stock market yields, however, not only does the statistical fit worsen markedly, but also the estimates of the price elasticity of demand are much lower. This implies that many of the fluctuations in the stock market (which are reflected in the denominator of the dividend-price ratio) produce no corresponding change in investment; the only way the model permits less weight to be given to these fluctuations is through a lower estimate of the elasticity of substitution σ.

The possibility that the role of the stock market has been fundamentally misspecified in this equation cannot, however, be ruled out. It could be that movements in the dividend-price ratio are primarily reflections of expectations, or confidence, in which case it is a mistake to include them as part of the user cost of capital. Such an expectational variable might well have great effect on investment in the short run but little in the long run; but if it is included with relative price variables, the impact of which is the reverse, the various lag distributions will be muddled.

Some support for such a hypothesis may be found in the residuals for trial 9. There was, for example, a deceleration in equipment spending in late 1962 and early 1963. Because the dividend-price ratio in the equation is constrained to act with the same lag as all the other user cost variables, the sharp (20 percent) rise in dividend yields as a result of the market break in prices in 1962 does not help much in explaining this investment dip. At this time, allowing for more than two lag distributions does not seem fruitful, but it might be explored at some later date.

The improvement of trial 9 over the two alternative models is due to many factors. However, the difference between trial 3 and the standard neoclassical model can be accounted for almost completely by the additional flexibility in the lag structure allowed by the estimation of more elements in the β matrix, for the nonlinear parameters in both trials are virtually identical.[56] Nearly 80 percent of the variance left unexplained by the standard neoclassical model is explained when the more general lag structure is allowed.

Allowing for substitution significantly improves the explanation, as is demonstrated by a comparison of trial 3—in which tax parameters and the price of equipment relative to that of output are the only relative price varia-

[56] The only difference is in the accelerated depreciation proportion parameter ς which affects the fit hardly at all. The addition of the net capital stock to trial 3 does not improve its explanatory power. The superior fit in trial 3 cannot be attributed to the free estimation of σ; the estimated value (0.98) is very close to 1, with an asymptotic standard error of about 0.07.

FIGURE 3-2. Equipment Expenditures, Third Quarter 1951 through Fourth Quarter 1965, Actual, and Predicted Using Accelerator Model

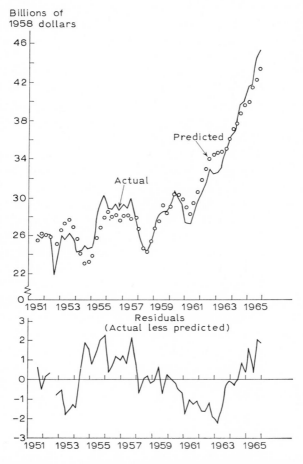

Sources: App. Table 3-A-1, pp. 128–30, for actual data, and equation (3.55) for predicted values. A predicted value for the third quarter of 1952 is omitted because of the effects of the steel strike.

bles—with the accelerator model—in which the equipment-output ratio is constant. This is true even without any consideration of monetary variables. But the improvement occurs only if the relative price variable V' is allowed a lag structure distinct from that for output Q. The standard neoclassical model as stated in equation (3.56), which does not allow this freedom, explains less of the variance of investment than does the accelerator model.[57]

Fitted and actual values of expenditures, as predicted by the accelerator model and the standard neoclassical model, are given in Figures 3-2 and 3-3. As the Durbin-Watson ratios confirm, the errors are highly serially correlated. Although the accelerator model based on output alone explains the major qualitative movements of the investment series, Figure 3-2 shows that, without relative price effects, the investment booms of the mid-fifties and mid-sixties are underpredicted and the investment slowdown of the early sixties is not sufficiently reflected. Figure 3-3 demonstrates that the introduction of relative price effects without a separate lag smooths out the peaks and troughs in the series of estimated values even more. An explanation for this pattern can be derived from a comparison of the estimated lag structures for equations (3.55) and (3.56). When relative price effects are added without a separate lag structure, the apparent misspecification seems to bias the estimated accelerator coefficients downward in the first few periods. The mean lag is increased as the lag structure lengthens, and the sensitivity of predicted investment to changes in output is considerably reduced.

The lag distributions estimated for the various trials with the general lag specification are of particular interest. In every case they conform to the qualitative pattern represented in Table 3-1 and suggested by the putty-clay model, as opposed to the pattern represented in Table 3-2 and suggested by the standard neoclassical model with nonstatic expectations. For all trials, the row sums (λ weights) are all either positive or insignificantly different from zero, while the column sums (μ weights) are first positive and then negative. For trials 1, 2, 3, 5, and 7, the first λ weight has the wrong sign; otherwise the estimated row sums are all positive. The lag distributions are discussed at greater length below; clearly, however, the results of the preliminary estimation strongly support the hypothesis that, no matter how the discount rate is specified, the lag structure between changes in relative prices

---

[57] This striking result does not hold, however, when the two alternative models are reestimated using the consumer durables deflator as the deflator for investment expenditures and as the price index for equipment in calculating the rent. The coefficient of variation for the accelerator model was virtually unchanged when this deflator was used, but the fit for the standard neoclassical model improved markedly, so that it provided a slightly better explanation than the accelerator model. The sum of squared residuals, however, was still nearly four times the residual sum of squares for a version of trial 9 using the same deflator. These suggestive results were not explored further, but one interpretation is that the rigid form of the standard neoclassical model is much more sensitive to precise specification than the other equations.

FIGURE 3-3. Equipment Expenditures, Third Quarter 1951 through Fourth Quarter 1965, Actual, and Predicted Using Standard Neoclassical Model

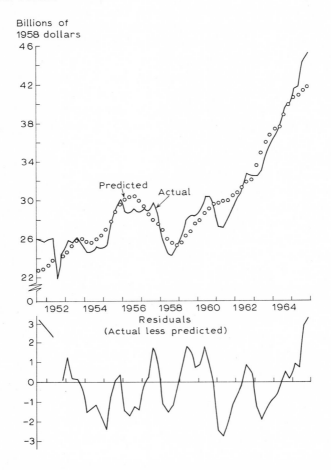

Sources: App. Table 3-A-1, pp. 128–30, for actual data, and equation (3.56) for predicted values. A predicted value for the third quarter of 1952 is omitted because of the effects of the steel strike.

V' and equipment spending is significantly different from the lag structure leading from changes in output Q.

The reason for the insensitivity of the estimated lag structures to the way in which the discount rate is specified seems to be that changes in V' are dominated by changes in tax policy (see Figure 3-5 below) that affect all of the trials in the same way. The lag distributions estimated for trial 9 may be taken as typical. Table 3-6 gives the $\beta_{i,\,i-1}$ and $\beta_{i,\,i}$ coefficients and standard errors estimated for trial 9; in Table 3-7 the estimated weights are arranged in the form of a β matrix (but it should be recalled that the coefficients that are estimated are simply proxies for the complete set of coefficients in each row and column).

TABLE 3-6. Estimates of Lag Coefficients and Standard Errors for Trial 9

Coefficient	Estimate	Standard error
$\beta_{2,1}$	0.0363	(0.0032)
$\beta_{3,2}$	0.0334	(0.0024)
$\beta_{4,3}$	0.0300	(0.0023)
$\beta_{5,4}$	0.0262	(0.0024)
$\beta_{6,5}$	0.0223	(0.0025)
$\beta_{7,6}$	0.0182	(0.0025)
$\beta_{8,7}$	0.0142	(0.0025)
$\beta_{9,8}$	0.0104	(0.0025)
$\beta_{10,9}$	0.0069	(0.0024)
$\beta_{11,10}$	0.0040	(0.0020)
$\beta_{12,11}$	0.0016	(0.0013)
$\beta_{2,2}$	—0.0356	(0.0039)
$\beta_{3,3}$	—0.0315	(0.0027)
$\beta_{4,4}$	—0.0274	(0.0025)
$\beta_{5,5}$	—0.0234	(0.0027)
$\beta_{6,6}$	—0.0195	(0.0028)
$\beta_{7,7}$	—0.0158	(0.0028)
$\beta_{8,8}$	—0.0123	(0.0026)
$\beta_{9,9}$	—0.0091	(0.0024)
$\beta_{10,10}$	—0.0062	(0.0021)
$\beta_{11,11}$	—0.0037	(0.0017)
$\beta_{12,12}$	—0.0016	(0.0010)

Source: Data are derived from parameter estimates for equation (3.54) using trial values of certain parameters listed for trial 9, Table 3-4.

Nonlinear Estimates of the Model

An iterative technique has been used to obtain estimates of the parameters of the nonlinear version of the expenditures equation that maximize the likelihood function, at least locally. Because there may be several maxima, and because the iterative technique used cannot guarantee a global

TABLE 3-7. Estimates of Coefficients of $V'_{t-i}Q_{t-j}$ for Trial 9

i/j	1	2	3	4	5	6	7	8	9	10	11	12	$\lambda_i = \Sigma_j \beta_{ij}$
1													0.0000
2	0.0363	−0.0356											0.0007
3		0.0334	−0.0315										0.0019
4			0.0300	−0.0274									0.0026
5				0.0262	−0.0234								0.0028
6					0.0223	−0.0195							0.0028
7						0.0182	−0.0158						0.0024
8							0.0142	−0.0123					0.0019
9								0.0104	−0.0091				0.0013
10									0.0069	−0.0062			0.0007
11										0.0040	−0.0037		0.0003
12											0.0016	−0.0016	0.0000
Total[a]	0.0363	−0.0022	−0.0015	−0.0012	−0.0011	−0.0013	−0.0016	−0.0019	−0.0022	−0.0022	−0.0021	−0.0016	0.0174[b]

Source: Lag distributions are derived from parameter estimates for equation (3.54) using trial values of certain parameters listed in trial 9 of Table 3-4.

[a] $\mu_j = \Sigma_i \beta_{ij}$.

[b] $\Sigma_i \lambda_i = \Sigma_j \mu_j = 0.0174$.

maximum, the process has been started from a number of initial sets of estimates, including all of the sets of parameters used in the preliminary trials. All have led to the same local maximum.

The technique used is called the "maximum neighborhood" method by its originator, Donald Marquardt.[58] It combines the favorable features of two better-known techniques for solving nonlinear equations, Gauss's method and the method of steepest ascent. Gauss's method involves linearization of the model by expanding it in a Taylor series about the initial guesses of the parameters (and truncating after the first order terms). The normal equations for the linearized model can be solved, and they provide a new set of parameter estimates which usually give a larger value for the likelihood function when they are inserted into the original model. The method can break down, however, if the linear approximation is not sufficiently good in the neighborhood of the "corrected" parameter estimates: the new estimates may actually give a smaller value of the likelihood function.[59]

With the method of steepest ascent, however, it is always possible to improve the parameter estimates in such a way as to increase the likelihood function (except at a local maximum or a saddle point). The difficulty is that convergence may be extremely slow. Marquardt's method "in effect, performs an optimum interpolation between the Taylor series method and the gradient method, the interpolation being based upon the maximum neighborhood in which the truncated Taylor series gives an adequate representation of the nonlinear model."[60]

Convergence to a local maximum has been considered complete only when every one of the corrections estimated from the linearized model has passed the test

$$\frac{|b_i^{q+} - b_i^q|}{0.001 + |b_i^q|} < 0.00005,$$

where

b_i^q = the value of the ith parameter on the qth iteration

[58] Donald W. Marquardt, "An Algorithm for Least-Squares Estimation of Nonlinear Parameters," *Journal of the Society for Industrial and Applied Mathematics*, Vol. 11 (June 1963), pp. 431–41.

[59] In this case, Hartley recommends correcting the parameter estimates by only a fraction of the vector of corrections provided by the linearized model. See H. O. Hartley, "The Modified Gauss-Newton Method for the Fitting of Non-Linear Regression Functions by Least Squares," *Technometrics*, Vol. 3 (May 1961), pp. 269–80.

[60] Marquardt, "An Algorithm for Least-Squares Estimation of Nonlinear Parameters," p. 431. The program I used embodies the Marquardt algorithm and is a slight revision of IBM Share Program No. SDA-3094-01.

b_i^{q+} = the corrected value of the parameter.

Depending on the initial guesses, convergence for the model has involved as few as three iterations or as many as sixty.

Parameter Constraints and Estimates

In practice, it appears that convergence cannot be achieved if both the coefficient of the rate of technical change h' and the coefficient on the time trend in the discount rate equation r_3 are allowed to vary. Since both represent trend terms, the linearized model is too nearly singular to get meaningful results. Thus r_3 has been arbitrarily set at zero. Similarly, it has seemed necessary arbitrarily to normalize either the depreciation rate δ, the coefficient

TABLE 3-8. Nonlinear Estimates of Parameters, Asymptotic Standard Errors, and Summary Statistics for Expenditures Equation

Parameters and summary statistics	Value	Asymptotic standard error
Parameters		
r_0	—0.008	(0.002)
r_1 (bond yield)	0.535	(0.096)
r_2 (stock yield)	0.098	(0.028)
σ	1.022	(0.069)
h'	0.00182	(0.00030)
A_1'	0.0254	(0.0053)
A_2'	0.0184	(0.0032)
A_3'	0.0069	(0.0022)
B_1'	—0.0263	(0.0061)
B_2'	—0.0161	(0.0030)
B_3'	—0.0058	(0.0020)
Summary statistics		
Coefficient of multiple determination[a]	0.98954	
Adjusted standard error of estimate[b]	0.597×10^9	
Coefficient of variation[c]	2.00%	
Durbin-Watson statistic	1.95	
Sum of squared residuals	16.37×10^{18}	
Mean of dependent variable	29.89×10^9	
Number of observations	57	

Source: Expenditures equation (3.54).
[a] Unadjusted.
[b] Square root of sum of squared residuals divided by number of observations minus 11.
[c] Adjusted standard error of estimate divided by mean of dependent variable.

on the industrial bond yield r_1, or the coefficient on the dividend-price ratio r_2, and to estimate, in effect, only the ratios r_1/δ, r_2/δ, and r_1/r_2. The parameter δ has therefore been set at 0.16 in all cases (some rough tests indicate that the results are not at all sensitive to the absolute value of δ, within the range $0.10-0.20$). No attempt has been made to estimate the coefficient of the tax rate r_4 in the discount rate equation, which plays a very small role in the model in any case. Instead, this parameter has been set at 0.2 on the basis of rather casual examination of movements in debt-equity ratios at market value and book value.

Nonlinear solution of the model thus has involved obtaining least squares estimates of the parameters r_0, r_1, r_2, σ, and h', and of the A' and B' parameters. Asymptotic standard errors have been computed, but they are in fact only the standard errors of the parameter estimates as computed from the linearized model. The Taylor series model can be written

$$\hat{I} = f(Q, V'; \hat{\beta}) + \partial(\beta - \hat{\beta}), \qquad (3.57)$$

in which $f(Q, V'; \hat{\beta})$ is the $m_2 \times 1$ vector of predicted values of I as a nonlinear function of the matrix of right-hand variables Q, V', and the $m_3 \times 1$ vector of final parameter estimates $\hat{\beta}$; $(\beta - \hat{\beta})$ is an $m_3 \times 1$ vector; and ∂ is the $m_2 \times m_3$ matrix of partial derivatives of the estimated values of I with

TABLE 3-9. Estimates of Long-run Elasticities of Equipment Expenditures for Selected Determinants, at Selected Price Levels, 1953–65

Determinant	1953 : 1 prices	1958 : 1 prices	1963 : 1 prices	1965 : 4 prices
Output[a]	1.00	1.00	1.00	1.00
Price of output	1.02	1.02	1.02	1.02
Price of equipment	—1.02	—1.02	—1.02	—1.02
Bond yield	—0.20	—0.21	—0.22	—0.23
Dividend-price ratio	—0.07	—0.05	—0.04	—0.02
Corporate tax rate	—0.20	—0.18	—0.17	—0.06
Proportion of depreciation by accelerated methods	—	0.02	0.02	0.02
Service lifetime for tax purposes	—0.10	—0.09	—0.09	—0.09
Rate of tax credit	—	—	0.05	0.10
Time[b]	0.01	0.01	0.01	0.01

Source: Data are derived from nonlinear parameter estimates for expenditures equation (3.54).

[a] By assumption.

[b] Since the origin of the variable time is completely arbitrary, these elasticities have been calculated as $(\partial I/\partial t) \cdot (1/I)$ instead of $(\partial I/\partial t) \cdot (t/I)$. For the purposes of these calculations, time is measured in years, although for the other calculations it is measured in quarters.

respect to each of the parameters, evaluated at $\hat{\beta}$, that is,

$$\partial_{ij} = \frac{\partial f_i}{\partial \beta_{j_{\hat{\beta}}}} . \qquad (3.58)$$

In this case,

$$\frac{\sum\limits_{t=1}^{m}(I_t - \hat{I}_t)^2}{m_2 - m_3} (\partial'\partial)^{-1}$$

FIGURE 3-4. Equipment Expenditures, Third Quarter 1951 through Fourth Quarter 1965, Actual, and Predicted Using Expenditures Equation

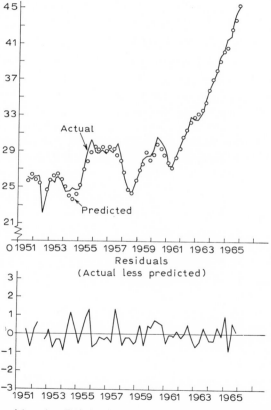

Sources: For actual data, App. Table 3-A-1, pp. 128–30; for predicted values, expenditures equation (3.54), using nonlinear estimates of the parameters. A value for the third quarter of 1952 is omitted because of the effects of the steel strike.

is the asymptotic variance-covariance matrix of the parameter estimates from which the asymptotic standard errors have been derived.

The fruits of the nonlinear estimation are given in (a) Table 3-8, which presents the estimated parameters and various summary statistics; (b) Table 3-9, which shows the estimated long-run elasticities of equipment spending with respect to all of the important variables and policy parameters in the model; and (c) Figure 3-4, in which the fitted and actual values and the residuals are plotted. The unadjusted coefficient of variation is improved hardly at all over trial 9, and the adjusted standard error is actually slightly larger. The Durbin-Watson statistic, however, is slightly closer to 2.0.

CAPITAL COST. The estimated values of both r_1 and r_2 are large compared with their asymptotic standard errors, but this is misleading, for these coefficients were quite unstable when small changes were made in the model or sample. The estimate of r_0 is negative, and if equation (3.47) is taken as an estimate of the discount rate, the predicted result seems unreasonably low. But examination of the underlying model indicates that, of the two places in which the discount rate enters, its absolute level matters only when it is used to discount depreciation patterns in computing the present value of the depreciation deduction. In this role, a low discount rate may act primarily as an ad hoc adjustment to weaken the influence of changes in depreciation rules as a determinant of investment.[61] Thus, it decreases the elasticity of investment demand with respect to, for example, a change in guideline lives.

TECHNICAL CHANGE. The estimated trend term h' is positive, and indicates that with all other variables held constant, the ratio of equipment spending to output is estimated to rise at a rate of about 0.73 percent per year. Although h' was included in the equation to allow for technical change, it would not be proper to interpret this parameter as a reliable measure of the degree to which technical change is capital-augmenting or capital-using.

Instead, the estimate of h' seems to reflect primarily an offset to trends in other variables. For example, the higher the estimate of r_1, the greater the weight given to the bond yield, which has a very definite uptrend, in the determination of the discount rate. Other things equal, then, the rent will become higher over time and the equilibrium equipment-output ratio lower. But if this ratio is not to fall over time (and Figure 3-5 indicates that it was about as high in 1965 as it was in 1948) then the estimate of h' must be higher, as can be seen by substituting equation (3.43) into equation (3.42), other things

[61] At a discount rate of zero, all depreciation patterns have the same present value.

being equal, whenever r_1 is higher. If a high estimate of r_1 results from a high cyclical partial correlation between investment orders and the bond yield, the equilibrium effects are offset by an algebraically larger estimate of h'.

The relationship of all this to technical change seems rather remote. Despite the fact that it cannot be interpreted, it still seems useful to allow for a trend in order to minimize the danger of accepting one of the other variables as significant when it is really acting as a proxy for the trend.

PRICE ELASTICITY. The estimated price elasticity is close to 1, and also close to the preliminary estimates. The estimated effect of the tax credit is relatively large; with repeal of the Long amendment, the elasticities in Table 3-9 indicate that repeal of the investment tax credit would lead eventually to a permanent reduction of about 10 percent in equipment spending. Accelerated depreciation is estimated to have an effect that, while substantial, is considerably smaller than that of the tax credit. The impact of variations in guideline lives within the range that has been contemplated is also relatively small.[62]

The very large change over time in the elasticity with respect to the corporate tax rate requires some comment. This elasticity is proportional to the derivative of the rent with respect to u. From (3.3), the expression for the rent, the relevant derivative is

$$\frac{q(r+\delta)(1-k-z+zk')}{(1-u)^2}.$$

Thus the elasticity is proportional to $1-k-z+zk'$, and when z, the present value of the depreciation deduction, is close to 1, the elasticity is quite sensitive to the value of k, the rate of tax credit. For a piece of equipment on which the whole credit of 7 percent can be claimed, if z is greater than 0.93 and with k' equal to zero after repeal of the Long amendment, an increase in the tax rate should increase investment, for the discounted depreciation deductions exceed the cost of the machine (net of credit), and the higher the investment, the greater the savings on the excess deductions.

Relative Factor Proportions and Lag Distributions

The time path of V', which summarizes all of the relative price and trend effects, is plotted in Figure 3-5. Apart from the general downtrend of V' through most of the period, attributable to rising equipment prices (relative to the

---

[62] The simulations reported in pp. 116–21 give considerably more information about the estimated effects of tax policies.

FIGURE 3-5. Time Series of Conglomerate Relative Prices V' as Estimated from Expenditures Equation, 1948–66

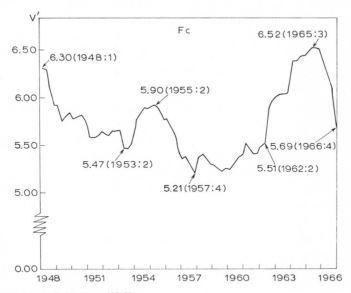

Source: App. Table 3-A-1, pp. 128–30.

rest of output) and to rising interest rates, there are three major movements in the series, all primarily the results of changes in tax laws. In 1954–55, the adoption of accelerated depreciation provided a significant additional investment incentive. In the last half of 1962, adoption of the tax credit, along with liberalization of depreciation guidelines, provided another significant offset to rising costs; the repeal of the Long amendment in 1964, restoring the tax credit to the depreciation base, added to the value of this incentive. Finally, temporary repeal of the tax credit in late 1966 created a situation in which the indicated equilibrium ratio of equipment per unit of capacity was only slightly above its low levels of the late fifties and early sixties (with the improvement due to the relative stability of equipment prices since 1958).

Figure 3-5 is of particular interest in light of Bert Hickman's conclusion, based on investment functions fitted for the period 1949–60, that the capital-output ratio in the United States was declining.[63] If true, this proposition might

[63] Bert G. Hickman, *Investment Demand and U.S. Economic Growth* (Brookings nstitution, 1965).

mean that private investment demand would be insufficient to sustain full employment. Figure 3-5 indicates that the marginal capital-output ratio might well have declined during the period studied by Hickman, although not necessarily for technological reasons. But it also indicates that at least the desired ratio of equipment to output has been substantially affected by government policy since that time. Hickman did not allow for this effect (which was less important for his sample period), but it has played a significant part in the revival of investment demand since 1963.

LAG DISTRIBUTIONS. Table 3-10 gives estimates of the lag parameters derived from the nonlinear estimates of the $\beta_{i,\, i-1}$ and $\beta_{i,\, i}$ parameters. As suggested by the putty-clay model, and as illustrated in the example in Table 3-1, all of the row sums are either positive or insignificantly different from zero (the asymptotic standard error for the one row sum that is negative is 0.0012). Only the first column sum is positive while all the others are negative. One might have expected the first two or three column sums to be pos-

TABLE 3-10. Lag Distributions Obtained from Nonlinear Estimation of Expenditures Equation

Period i	Coefficients of $V'_{t-i}Q_{t-i+1}$ $\hat\beta_{i,\, i-1}$	Coefficients of $V'_{t-i}Q_{t-i}$ $\hat\beta_{i,\, i}$	Column sums of β matrix $\hat\mu_i$	Row sums of β matrix $\hat\lambda_j$
0	—	—	—	—
1	—	—	0.0254	—
2	0.0254	—0.0263	—0.0019	—0.0009
3	0.0245	—0.0238	—0.0011	0.0007
4	0.0227	—0.0210	—0.0007	0.0017
5	0.0203	—0.0181	—0.0007	0.0022
6	0.0174	—0.0151	—0.0009	0.0023
7	0.0143	—0.0121	—0.0011	0.0021
8	0.0110	—0.0093	—0.0014	0.0017
9	0.0079	—0.0067	—0.0016	0.0012
10	0.0050	—0.0043	—0.0017	0.0007
11	0.0026	—0.0024	—0.0015	0.0003
12	0.0009	—0.0009	—0.0009	0.0000
Total[a]	0.1520	—0.1400	0.0120	0.0120

Source: Data are derived from nonlinear parameter estimates for expenditures equation (3.54).
Note: $\Sigma\Sigma\hat\beta_{ij} = \Sigma\hat\beta_{i,\, i-1} + \Sigma\hat\beta_{i,\, i} = \Sigma\hat\mu_j = \Sigma\hat\lambda_i = 0.01197$.

[a] Details may not add to totals due to rounding.

itive, but the result may be occasioned by the particular approximating technique that was used.

Impact of Changes in Output and Factor Proportions

The sum of all the coefficients shows that a rise in output of $1 billion (1958 value) will eventually increase the flow of expenditures for producers' durable equipment by V' times $11.97 million, or, at the level of V' in the fourth quarter of 1965 (6.494), by roughly $78 million.[64] Due to the accelerator effect, this response will be exceeded as capacity is initially adjusted upward, and only after three years will the response die down to the steady-state effect, which is replacement on the equipment needed to produce $1 billion of output. Table 3-11 gives the increments in spending for producers' durable equipment that would stem from a sustained rise in output, as percentages of the steady-state increment.

The most disturbing lag coefficient is the relatively large response of investment in the first quarter following a change in output. Some investment functions have specified a priori that no stimulus lagged less than two quarters can have *any* effect, in view of the supposed accuracy of investment anticipations. But Eisner and Evans and Green have found that unexpected rises in sales, or simply changes in sales occurring *after* anticipations have been reported, can enhance explanations based on anticipations alone.[65] In principle, changes in output might well be reflected very rapidly in changes in orders (especially cancellations) and at least some of these orders could be promptly translated into expenditures. Although the elasticity of I_t with respect to Q_{t-1} seems too large to be reconciled with Eisner's estimates of the elasticity of I_t with respect to sales in period $t-1$, the constraint of this lag

---

[64] If the depreciation rate δ is 0.16, this would correspond to an equipment-output ratio of about 0.49; if δ is 0.10, the ratio would be 0.78. The Commerce Department data on net stocks of equipment in 1966 (in 1958 dollars, with straight-line depreciation) show $221 billion, compared with private business product of $579 billion in that year, a ratio of 0.38.

[65] Robert Eisner, "Realization of Investment Anticipations," in Duesenberry and others (eds.), *Brookings Quarterly Econometric Model*; and Michael K. Evans and Edward W. Green, "The Relative Efficacy of Investment Anticipations," *Journal of the American Statistical Association*, Vol. 61 (March 1966), pp. 104–16. Eisner's conclusions were tempered by the relatively unsuccessful results of tests based on extrapolation beyond the sample period. But extrapolations with the functions estimated by Evans and Green generally produced better predictions than the anticipations did.

TABLE 3-11. Effects of Sustained Rise in Output and Changes in Relative Prices on Equipment Expenditures during Next Twelve Quarters

(Percentage of steady-state response)

Quarter after change	Effect of change in physical output[a]	Effect of change relative prices[b]
0	—	—
1	212	—
2	197	—5
3	188	2
4	182	17
5	176	35
6	169	53
7	159	70
8	148	83
9	134	92
10	120	98
11	108	100
12	100	100

Source: Simulation of equation (3.54), using the nonlinear parameter estimates shown in Tables 3-9 and 3-10.

[a] Assuming no change in static optimum equipment per unit of capacity.

[b] Assuming constant 4 percent growth in physical output.

coefficient to zero, which is the principal feasible alternative, does not seem theoretically justifiable. In fact, even the requirement that changes in output cannot affect investment in the same quarter is hard to defend; this specification was adopted largely to minimize statistical problems resulting from simultaneous determination.

The distinction between output and sales should not, however, be overlooked. It is possible that changes in output (which, unlike sales, are under the control of the producer) are in fact correctly anticipated, and that their high correlation with nearly simultaneous investment is a result of this correct anticipation. Viewed in a slightly different way, changes in output may result from some external cause (say, changes in orders) which stimulates investment demand as well. If this is the case, orders themselves should be studied (though this can be done only on an industry level), but as a first approximation the linkage from aggregate demand (via orders) to output and then to investment may not be seriously misspecified if the intermediate orders stage is suppressed.

A less optimistic interpretation would point out that if serial correlation is present, lagging the endogenous output variable will not remove problems brought about by failure to consider all of the simultaneous equations in the underlying economic system. The presence of serial correlation in the empirical results must still be suspected because the Durbin-Watson test is not designed for use in equations that contain lagged endogenous variables. The difficulties may be compounded by the fact that the lagged output variable includes the dependent variable, equipment spending, as one of its components. Although estimation of a more complete system is not feasible in this study, a cautious interpretation of the lag distributions is certainly advisable.

Given relative prices, it is possible to compute the equilibrium increment to an imaginary net stock of equipment that will be brought about by a sustained unit change in output.[66] The lag weights, when combined with an a priori value of the depreciation rate, can be used to derive an expression for the proportion of the adjustment from one equilibrium stock to another that will be completed within n quarters after the change in output. For the estimated weights, the results, as a function of the assumed δ, are shown in Table 3-12. For reasonable values of δ, in the range from 0.08 to 0.16, the adjustment seems relatively slow; only 42 percent to 68 percent of the adjustment takes place within the first five years, and it is more than ten years before the adjustment even approaches 90 percent completion. Long lags in capital-stock adjustment models, of course, are nothing new, but it is these long lags that have led to criticism of many of the simpler versions of such models.

The speed of response of equipment spending to a change in V' varies with the rate of growth in output; the faster output grows, the faster substitution will take place. With investment running at a level of around $50 billion and with a 4 percent growth in real output, a 1 percent change in the interest rate (from the fourth quarter 1965 level of 4.72 percent) would eventually change the flow of spending for producers' durable equipment by about 5 percent (or $2.5 billion), but a year after the interest rate change, less than 20 percent of the eventual effect would have been felt. If the change were

---

[66] If both relative prices and technical change are held constant, it is possible to speak of a stock of equipment, since all machines are of the same model.

TABLE 3-12. Proportion of Adjustment of Stock of Equipment to Change in Physical Output Completed after Selected Number of Quarters, by Selected Depreciation Rates

(Percentage of adjustment)

Number of quarters	Depreciation rate				
	0.04	*0.08*	*0.12*	*0.16*	*0.20*
4	8	15	22	29	36
8	13	25	36	46	55
12	17	32	45	56	66
16	20	37	51	63	72
20	23	42	57	68	77
40	37	61	76	86	92

Source: Expenditures equation (3.54).

then reversed,[67] the effects of the original change would continue to build up and it would be more than a year after an equal deviation of interest rates in the opposite direction (from the normal level) before spending on equipment would return to the level that would have obtained had no changes taken place.[68] Table 3-13 gives the time pattern of effects for the sequence of

[67] In case the reversal merely restored interest rates to the original level (as in a sequence 4 percent—5 percent—4 percent, as opposed to 4 percent—5 percent—3 percent), it would take over a year for the second change simply to offset the effects of the first change sufficiently to restore spending to the level that existed when the second change took place. Such lag effects may not be reasonable, but they could result from the lag of shipments behind orders and also from a process in which steps once taken to adopt a new technique result in the old technique being "forgotten." Note must also be taken of the lag between the application of policy instruments and the effect on those factors directly determining investment. In the case of tax changes, the lag may be negligible, but in the case of interest rates, it may be substantial.

[68] This research contributes to a larger project on monetary policy, the FRB-MIT quarterly econometric model, described in more detail in Frank de Leeuw and Edward Gramlich, "The Federal Reserve-MIT Econometric Model," *Federal Reserve Bulletin*, Vol. 54 (January 1968), pp. 11–40, and in Robert H. Rasche and Harold T. Shapiro, "The F.R.B.-M.I.T. Econometric Model: Its Special Features," in American Economic Association, *Papers and Proceedings of the Eightieth Annual Meeting, 1967 (American Economic Review*, Vol. 58, May 1968), pp. 123–49. I have also, consequently, been concerned with the possibility that the effects of rationing, or availability of credit, might lead to more rapid monetary influences on investment. A variety of variables which have been suggested as likely to reflect such effects have been experimentally introduced into the model with very short lags, but none has come close to making a significant contribution to the explanation.

TABLE 3-13. Effect on Equipment Spending of a Change in Relative Prices Followed after One Year by a Change in the Opposite Direction of Twice the Magnitude of the Original Change

(Percentage of steady-state effect of the original change)

Quarters after first change	Change in equipment spending[a]
1	—
2	—5
3	2
4	17
5	35
6	63
7	66
8	49
9	22
10	—8

Source: Based on Table 3-11.
[a] Assuming a constant 4 percent growth in output.

interest rate changes assumed in this particular case; similar patterns can be computed from Table 3-11 for any desired sequence of changes.

Figure 3-6 compares the estimated short- and long-run responses of equipment spending to changes in V' and Q, based on the nonlinear estimates, to some previous estimates of lags in the investment process. The results are not comparable, especially inasmuch as the Jorgenson and Griliches and Wallace models included structures as well as equipment.[69] The most recent estimates by Hall and Jorgenson, based on yearly data for equipment spending, conform only relatively well to my estimates of the lag for changes in output. But they exclude any possibility of interest rate effects; only changes in tax policy and the relative price of new equipment influence V' in their model. Their results are not inconsistent with the view that the rela-

[69] Jorgenson, "Capital Theory and Investment Behavior"; Griliches and Wallace, "The Determinants of Investment Revisited." In view, however, of the small proportion of construction in the total investment of manufacturers, the short-run response of construction to relative price changes would have to exceed the long-run response by a factor of ten or more to produce lag patterns for *total* investment like those implicit in the models cited. This seems unlikely.

FIGURE 3-6. Selected Lag Distributions for Capital Expenditures

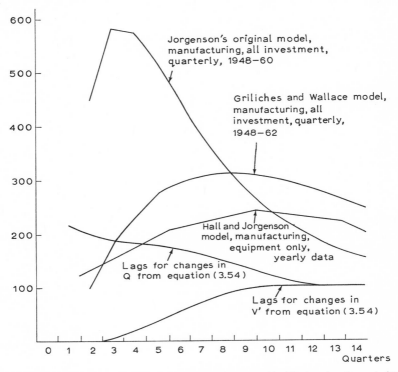

Sources: Dale W. Jorgenson, "Capital Theory and Investment Behavior," in American Economic Association, *Papers and Proceedings of the Seventy-fifth Annual Meeting, 1962 (American Economic Review*, Vol. 53, May 1963), Table 4, p. 259; Zvi Griliches and Neil Wallace, "The Determinants of Investment Revisited," *International Economic Review*, Vol. 6 (September 1965), Table 4, p. 321; and Robert E. Hall and Dale W. Jorgenson, this volume, Table 2-2, p. 36.

tively larger and more frequent fluctuations in output exerted a dominant influence in the estimation of the lag pattern. Granting this possibility, because no separate lag pattern was allowed for tax changes it would seem dangerous to base policy conclusions on the apparently large and rapid effects of tax policy found in their study.

Another way to judge the reasonableness of the estimates is to examine the equilibrium ratios of equipment stock (under idealized circumstances where such stocks make sense) to output, and also to compare the equilibrium shares of equipment spending in output. Both of these pairs of statistics are functions of the estimated values of V', and thus change over time.

The formula for the equilibrium ratio of equipment to capacity output, given the relative prices and technology of period t, is

$$V_t'(\sum_i \sum_j \beta_{ij})/\delta.$$

The estimate of $\Sigma\Sigma\beta_{ij}$ is 0.01197. Neither the absolute value of this sum nor the absolute value of the estimate of V' has any independent importance, but the product of V' and $\Sigma\Sigma\beta_{ij}$ represents the steady-state stream of replacements on the capacity needed to produce a unit of output. Thus for any assumed value of the rate of replacement δ, a certain ratio of the stock of equipment to output is implied.

TABLE 3-14. Equilibrium Equipment-Output Ratios, at Selected Price Levels

Period of price level	Ratio
1955 : 1	0.4406
1960 : 1	0.3961
1965 : 1	0.4837

Source: Data are derived from nonlinear parameter estimates for expenditures equation (3.54).

The implied ratios for $\delta = 0.16$ are given in Table 3-14.[70] In a stationary state with no growth in output, the proportion of equipment spending in gross business product, as estimated from the expenditures equation, would range between 5.7 percent and 7.0 percent for the range of values of V' observed during the sample period. With output growing at a steady 4 percent, the range would be about 7.5 percent to 9 percent. By comparison, the actual share of spending for equipment was 9.6 percent in the first quarter of 1948, then fell to 6.5 percent as a result of the steel crisis in 1952, and rose to 7.7 percent in the capital goods boom of 1955. At the low point in 1961, the ratio was only 6.3 percent, but it rose to 8.0 percent by the end of 1965.

[70] The actual ratio of the constant dollar net stock of equipment, consistent with exponential depreciation at 16 percent per year, was in the range of 35 percent of output throughout this period. But this ratio is not really comparable to the equilibrium ratios, which assume the existence of a steady state without growth in output. If output is growing, so that desired capital stock is greater than actual capital stock, equilibrium ratios will be higher than actual ratios, which is the result observed above.

Policy Simulations and Sensitivity Analysis of Tax Parameters

In order to evaluate more fully the effect of changes in tax policy, monetary policy, and relative prices, I have used the model, with the parameter estimates reported in Table 3-8, to simulate the time path of equipment expenditures under a number of alternative assumptions about tax parameters and other variables that affect V'. The simulated time paths of predicted equipment spending may be compared to the predicted values, given the actual policy parameters (or independent variables), in order to compute a measure of the direct effects of a policy such as accelerated depreciation or the investment tax credit. Without a complete model of national income determination, these computations are of limited meaning, for the path of output, as well as the paths of the other determinants of investment in equipment, must certainly be altered by induced changes in investment. Nevertheless, these computations might be conceived as the outcomes of controlled experiments in which the government sought to provide the same level of aggregate demand in two ways: (a) by direct government purchases of equipment, and (b) by indirect actions, such as tax incentives to encourage private equipment purchases, interest rate manipulations, and the like.

Policy Simulations

Seven sets of simulations have been carried out to represent the direct effects of the various combinations of tax policies that have been adopted since 1954. The results are tabulated in terms of constant dollar effects and proportions of actual expenditures in Table 3-15. The policies include the adoption of accelerated depreciation methods in 1954, the promulgation of new depreciation guidelines in 1962, adoption of an investment tax credit in 1962, the repeal of the Long amendment in 1964, and the reduction of general income tax rates for corporations in 1964 and 1965. There are interactions among the various policies—the depreciation guidelines would have induced slightly more investment if accelerated depreciation had not already been in effect, for example—and thus the effect of all of them is not the sum of the effects of each policy alone.

All of the policies taken together are estimated to have induced directly over $17 billion (1958 value) of gross expenditures between 1954 and 1966, with the largest effects coming in 1964–66. The most important single policy is the tax credit. Even with the restriction imposed by the Long amendment, it would have directly induced over $6 billion of gross investment by the end of 1966; with the Long amendment repealed, the effects add up to more

TABLE 3-15. Estimates of Direct Effects of Tax Policies on Equipment Expenditures, Dollar Amounts and Percentages of Actual Expenditures, 1954–66

Year	Accelerated depreciation	Depreciation guidelines	Investment tax credit with Long amendment	Repeal of Long amendment	Investment tax credit without Long amendment	Corporate income tax reductions of 1964–65	Total, all policies[a]
			Dollar amounts (in billions of 1958 dollars)				
1954	—0.01						—0.01
1955	0.22						0.22
1956	0.43						0.43
1957	0.44						0.44
1958	0.43						0.43
1959	0.51						0.51
1960	0.55						0.55
1961	0.57						0.57
1962	0.64						0.64
1963	0.67	0.05	0.22		0.22		0.95
1964	0.70	0.36	1.51	*	1.51	*	2.57
1965	0.77	0.54	2.14	0.90	3.04	0.05	4.41
1966	0.84	0.59	2.35	1.96	4.31	0.16	6.06
Total, 1954–66[a]	6.76	1.55	6.22	2.85	9.07	0.21	17.77
			Percentages of actual expenditures				
1954	*						*
1955	0.8						0.8
1956	1.5						1.5
1957	1.5						1.5
1958	1.7						1.7
1959	1.8						1.8
1960	1.8						1.8
1961	2.0						2.0
1962	2.0						2.0
1963	2.0	0.2	0.6		0.6		2.8
1964	1.8	1.0	3.9	*	3.9	*	6.7
1965	1.8	1.2	5.0	2.1	7.0	0.1	10.2
1966	1.7	1.2	4.8	4.0	8.8	0.3	12.4

Source: Estimated dollar effects of a policy are calculated as $(\hat{I}-\hat{I}_i{}^B)$ and estimated percentage effects are $(\hat{I}-\hat{I}_i{}^B)/I$, where I is the fitted value of $\hat{I}$ in equation (3.54), $\hat{I}_i{}^B$ is the value of $\hat{I}$ in a simulation in which the indicated policy is not carried out, and I is the actual value of equipment spending.
[a] Details may not add to totals due to rounding and interactions.
* Less than $5 million, or less than 0.05 percent.

117

than $9 billion. The directly induced investment is smaller than the losses in tax revenue for 1962 and 1963, approximately equal to the reductions in 1964, and considerably in excess of the reductions for 1965 and 1966.[71] Accelerated depreciation policies are estimated to have had disappointingly small effects (amounting to roughly a 2 percent increase above what expenditures would otherwise have been for each year after 1955). The depreciation guidelines apparently increased expenditures by about 1 percent in each year after 1963.

The magnitude of the impact attributed to the tax credit from 1962:3 to 1965:4 is revealed in the seasonally adjusted quarterly breakdown of the estimated effects given in Table 3-16.

TABLE 3-16. Estimates of Direct Effects of Investment Tax Credit on Equipment Expenditures, by Quarters, 1962–65

(In billions of 1958 dollars, seasonally adjusted at annual rates)

Year and quarter	Increment to equipment spending
1962 : 3	0
4	0
1963 : 1	—0.09
2	0.02
3	0.29
4	0.66
1964 : 1	1.04
2	1.39
3	1.62
4	1.97
1965 : 1	2.33
2	2.86
3	3.27
4	3.69

Source: Expenditures equation (3.54).

The assumptions built into the model make it inappropriate for use in evaluating a change in tax law widely publicized as, and believed to be, temporary. One such assumption is equation (3.15), which states that entre-

[71] It should be recalled that the estimated effective rate of tax credit for 1963 is 4.0 percent; for later years it might be higher, but probably not much more than 5.0 percent.

preneurs average up past values of relative prices as embodied in V to form V^*, the capital intensity to be used in new capacity. If the tax change is temporary, it is unlikely that it will be given much weight in planning capital intensity. Second, and perhaps more important, there is likely to be a speculative acceleration of orders in response to a temporary tax benefit and a similar postponement effect in situations like the suspension of the investment tax credit in late 1966 and early 1967. This sort of behavior would violate the assumption that $Q_K^* - Q$, the desired degree of overcapacity, is not a function of relative prices. For these reasons there has been no attempt to simulate the effects of the tax credit suspension.

Two additional simulations have been made to predict what equipment expenditures might have been if (a) the bond yield had remained constant at 3.75 percent and the dividend-price ratio had remained constant at 4.39 percent throughout the postwar period, and (b) if V' had remained constant

TABLE 3-17. Estimates of Net Direct Effects of Variations in Interest Rates on Equipment Expenditures, 1950–66

(Percentage of actual expenditures)

Year	First quarter	Second quarter	Third quarter	Fourth quarter	Annual average
1950	2.6	2.2	2.0	2.3	2.3
1951	2.6	2.8	2.8	3.1	2.8
1952	2.9	2.8	3.0	2.6	2.8
1953	2.5	2.6	2.6	2.7	2.6
1954	2.8	2.3	1.7	1.4	2.1
1955	1.4	1.6	1.9	2.2	1.8
1956	2.7	3.0	3.0	3.1	3.0
1957	3.0	2.9	2.4	1.8	2.5
1958	1.4	0.8	—0.4	—1.2	0.2
1959	—1.6	—1.7	—1.8	—1.7	—1.7
1960	—1.7	—2.0	—2.4	—2.9	—2.3
1961	—3.6	—4.0	—4.2	—4.2	—4.0
1962	—4.1	—4.0	—3.8	—3.8	—3.9
1963	—3.8	—3.8	—3.6	—3.6	—3.7
1964	—3.4	—3.3	—3.1	—3.1	—3.3
1965	—3.0	—3.2	—3.2	—3.2	—3.2
1966	—3.3	—3.3	—3.2	—3.4	—3.3

Source: Estimated effects of interest rates are calculated as $(\hat{I}-\hat{I}^r)/I$ where $\hat{I}$ is the predicted value of I in expenditures equation (3.54), $\hat{I}^r$ is the value of I in a simulation in which the bond yield is held constant at 3.75 percent and the dividend-price ratio is held constant at 4.39 percent, and I is the actual value of equipment spending.

TABLE 3-18. Estimates of Net Direct Effects of Variation in Conglomerate Relative Prices V' on Equipment Expenditures, 1950–66

(Percentage of actual expenditures)

Year	First quarter	Second quarter	Third quarter	Fourth quarter	Annual average
1950	12.2	10.2	8.2	7.7	9.4
1951	7.4	6.8	6.4	6.1	6.6
1952	5.2	4.4	4.2	3.1	4.2
1953	2.4	2.1	1.8	2.1	2.1
1954	2.0	1.4	0.5	0.1	1.0
1955	0.3	1.0	1.7	2.5	1.4
1956	3.4	4.0	4.0	3.9	3.8
1957	3.3	2.6	1.4	—0.1	1.8
1958	—1.4	—2.5	—4.6	—6.2	—3.6
1959	—7.1	—7.3	—8.0	—7.8	—7.6
1960	—8.2	—8.6	—9.1	—9.7	—8.9
1961	—10.7	—10.9	—10.0	—10.3	—10.7
1962	—9.8	—9.2	—8.8	—8.8	—9.2
1963	—9.2	—8.6	—7.2	—5.6	—7.6
1964	—3.9	—2.4	—1.3	—0.1	—1.9
1965	1.0	2.4	3.3	4.2	2.8
1966	5.1	5.6	5.8	5.9	5.6

Source: Estimated effects of relative prices are calculated as $(\hat{I}-\hat{I}^{v'})/I$ where $\hat{I}$ is the predicted value of I in expenditures equation (3.54), $\hat{I}^{v'}$ is the value of I in a simulation in which V' is held constant at 5.79, its average value during the period 1947–66, and I is the actual value of equipment spending.

at its mean value throughout the sample period. These simulations are reported in Tables 3-17 and 3-18. In both cases, of course, the estimated effects are only partial: Total output is assumed to follow its actual time path.

The most striking characteristic of the interest rate simulation is the large negative stimulus arising between 1956 and 1961, apparently associated with the movement of the bond yield from a relatively low level before 1955 to a relatively high plateau after 1960.[72] If an attempt is made to match up turning points in the interest rate series with those in the estimated effect on equipment spending, the lags vary from two to eight quarters, with the aver-

[72] For the thirty-eight quarters from the first quarter of 1947 to the second quarter of 1956 inclusive, quarterly averages of Moody's industrial bond yield all fell in the range of 2.60 percent to 3.39 percent. The yield rose sharply between the second quarter of 1956 and the third quarter of 1959; for the twenty-six quarters starting with the third quarter of 1959, the quarterly averages remained in the range from 4.38 percent to 4.72 percent.

age about six quarters. The result of adding the lag between monetary changes and movements in long-term interest rates certainly does not encourage the use of monetary policy as a countercyclical influence on investment.

Sensitivity Analysis of Tax Parameters

Because tax policy—especially the tax credit—plays such an important role in the explanation of equipment spending, I have attempted to assess the sensitivity of the results to the assumed values of the parameters k and ς. The model has been completely reestimated with assumed values of k—the effective rate of the tax credit—varying all the way from 0 to 20 percent. The somewhat surprising result, recorded in Table 3-19, is that the estimated

TABLE 3-19. Summary Statistics for Selected Assumed Effective Rates of Investment Tax Credit

Assumed effective rate of tax credit (percent)	R^2	Standard error of estimate	Durbin-Watson statistic	Estimate of price elasticity of demand	Estimated direct effect of tax credit (billions of 1958 dollars)		
					1963	1964	1965
0	0.98682	669.71	1.55	1.112	0.00	0.00	0.00
1	0.98772	646.48	1.67	1.319	—$0.03	$0.29	$0.68
2	0.98848	626.13	1.78	1.305	—0.04	0.60	1.39
3	0.98898	612.37	1.85	1.224	0.035	0.94	2.05
4	0.98932	602.96	1.91	1.125	0.131	1.25	2.61
5	0.98954	599.63	1.95	1.022	0.219	1.50	3.04
6	0.98969	592.49	1.97	0.959	0.334	1.77	3.50
7	0.98978	589.89	1.98	0.879	0.409	1.95	3.80
8	0.98983	588.37	1.99	0.808	0.477	2.11	4.05
9	0.98986	587.57	2.00	0.740	0.519	2.21	4.20
10	0.98987	587.22	2.00	0.676	0.541	2.29	4.30
11	0.98987	587.16	2.00	0.619	0.554	2.34	4.36
12	0.98987	587.28	2.00	0.573	0.570	2.39	4.43
13	0.98986	587.52	2.00	0.533	0.582	2.44	4.47
14	0.98985	587.83	2.00	0.498	0.596	2.48	4.53
15	0.98984	588.18	2.00	0.470	0.614	2.53	4.59
16	0.98982	588.54	2.00	0.440	0.612	2.55	4.61
17	0.98981	588.93	2.00	0.415	0.618	2.57	4.62
18	0.98980	589.31	1.99	0.394	0.625	2.59	4.65
19	0.98978	589.70	1.99	0.374	0.633	2.62	4.68
20	0.98977	590.08	1.99	0.356	0.637	2.64	4.70

Source: See text.

price elasticity adjusts so as largely to offset even very extreme assumed values of k. The best explanation apparently is achieved with k assumed to be 11 percent, but the improvement in fit is quite small.

Because of the offsetting variations in the estimate of σ, the estimated direct stimulation of equipment spending due to the credit varies much less than the variations in k. Thus even if k is assumed to be 10 percent rather than 5 percent, a 100 percent increase, the estimated direct impact on equipment spending in 1965 increases by only 41 percent, from $3.04 billion to $4.30 billion.

It would be nice if the statistics in Table 3-19 could be used to construct a confidence interval for k (and for direct effects of the credit). But because of the nonlinearities in the model none of the standard tests for linear models is applicable. However, for large samples a likelihood ratio test can be used, and asymptotically this is equivalent to using a standard $\mathscr{F}$ test. To give some indication of the size of the reduction in error variance that comes as a result of relaxing the assumption $k = k^*$ (where k^* is an a priori value specified for k), I have tabulated values of the ratio

$$\mathscr{F}' = \frac{\Sigma(\hat{\varepsilon}_{k*}^2 - \hat{\varepsilon}_k^2)}{\Sigma\hat{\varepsilon}_k^2/45}, \tag{3.59}$$

where $\hat{\varepsilon}_k$ are the residuals when k is estimated along with the other parameters, and $\hat{\varepsilon}_{k*}$ are the residuals conditional on k equals k^*. I have labeled this ratio $\mathscr{F}'$ because it is computed in the same way as a statistic that would have an $\mathscr{F}$-distribution under the null hypothesis that k equals k^*, in the general linear model.[73] The ratio $\mathscr{F}'$ for various values of k^* is found in Table 3-20. Since little improvement in fit results from relaxing the prior assumption—that k is approximately 5 percent—I have adopted it. At the same time, Tables 3-19 and 3-20 show quite clearly that the time series examined provides little support for the hypothesis that k^* equals 0 (meaning that the tax credit has no effect at all). A substantial reduction in error variance can be achieved by adopting almost any hypothesis that implies that k is greater than 0.

The results suggest that the estimated price elasticity is not very sensitive to assumptions about k. But it should be noted that other regres-

---

[73] If the model were completely linear, this is exactly the ratio that would be computed, with fifty-seven observations, to test the hypothesis that one of twelve coefficients took a specified value, while the other eleven were estimated without restriction. See Franklin A. Graybill, *An Introduction to Linear Statistical Models*, Vol. 1 (McGraw-Hill, 1961), pp. 133–40.

TABLE 3-20. $\mathscr{F}'$ **Statistics for Alternative Assumed Effective Rates of Investment Tax Credit**

Assumed effective rate of tax credit (percent)	$\mathscr{F}'$	Assumed effective rate of tax credit (percent)	$\mathscr{F}'$
0	13.54	10	0.01
1	9.55	11	0.00
2	6.17	12	0.02
3	3.95	13	0.05
4	2.45	14	0.10
5	1.46	15	0.16
5.5	1.03	16	0.21
6	0.82	17	0.27
7	0.42	18	0.33
8	0.19	19	0.39
9	0.06	20	0.45

Source: Equation (3.59).

sions (not reported here) fitted to samples that did not include post-1962 data all produced estimates of σ, the relative price elasticity of equipment demand, that were close to 1. Still, on the basis of this evidence the possibility that highly visible policies such as the tax credit may have larger effects than would be produced by an equivalent reduction in equipment prices cannot be ruled out. The key factor is the effect on expectations about eventual factor price changes, and this effect could occur in many ways.

Similar experiments with the parameter ς, the proportion of depreciation taken under accelerated methods, have revealed that the model is almost totally insensitive to this parameter within the entire admissible range (0 to 1). With k set at 5 percent and ς varied from 0 to 1, the maximum variation in the sum of squared residuals is only 1.3 percent. The best fit is for ς equals 0, while the worst is for ς equals 1. None of the estimates of the other parameters changes by more than a few percent as ς is varied.

The sensitivity of the likelihood function to ς is so slight that no firm conclusions about even the direct effects of accelerated depreciation can be derived from the data. Trying to estimate ς empirically would be futile; no significant results could be obtained. But this also means that, in this model, the data give no support to the hypothesis that accelerated depreciation has any effect at all on investment! Of course, the data do not deny the hypothesis either; they simply shed no light. Since my prior value for ç, derived from analysis of Ture's data,[74] is about 0.5, I cannot reject this hypothesis, and it remains a part of the model. Some other researcher, whose null hypothesis was ç equals 0, could not reject that either. This result on the statistically insignificant effects of accelerated depreciation in a neoclassical aggregative model is very disturbing. All of the reported effects of accelerated depreciation are conditional on the assumption that a given change in the imputed rent on equipment has the same effect whether it comes about via changes in the depreciation rules or a change in some other component of the rent. However, the results with respect to the tax credit are by no means so ambiguous. Given the evidence that *some* tax incentives matter, this only strengthens my view that the presumption should be that tax incentives make a difference, even where the evidence is ambiguous. But it should be made clear that, in the case of accelerated depreciation, the conclusion is drawn on the basis of presumptions, not empirical evidence.

Conclusions

The principal conclusions drawn from the empirical work presented in this study may be summarized as follows:

The value and efficacy of the neoclassical approach—the inclusion of relative prices in the investment function—are substantially confirmed. Relative prices appear to have a statistically significant effect on equipment expenditures. At least one tax measure, the investment tax credit, is independently shown to have a statistically significant effect on equipment expenditures.[75]

The general neoclassical model provides an explanation of aggregate equipment expenditures superior to that given by either of the two most popular alternatives—the standard neoclassical model and

---

[74] As discussed on p. 85, Ture, *Accelerated Depreciation in the United States*, indicates that 52.4 percent of the equipment purchased by American corporations between 1954 and 1959 was being depreciated, in 1959, by accelerated methods.

[75] These statements are based on likelihood ratio tests, which are only approximate and apply only for large samples, and in no way depend on the reported asymptotic standard errors. In research carried out after this chapter was already in proof, it has become apparent that the asymptotic standard errors reported in Table 3-8 are subject to a great deal of rounding error. Alternative, but not necessarily better, methods of

the flexible accelerator model. As suggested by the putty-clay hypothesis, relative prices (including tax credits, interest rates, depreciation rules, and so forth) apparently affect equipment spending with a much longer lag than do changes in output.

The long-run elasticity of equipment spending with respect to the rental price of equipment services is estimated to be very close to unity, but this elasticity cannot be estimated with any great precision.

The investment tax credit adopted in 1962 has probably directly stimulated more investment spending than the policy has cost the government in taxes.

Variations in measures of the cost of capital seem to have the negative partial effect on equipment spending suggested by standard theory, but stable estimates of the effects of these variables have not been obtained.

The marginal ratio of equipment spending to output is apparently sensitive to direct fiscal and monetary policy measures, and there is no evidence pointing to a secular decline in this ratio. Attempts to manipulate this ratio for short-run purposes may, however, prove difficult to implement, due to lags in the response to the policy measures.

---

computing the asymptotic standard errors have led to estimates as much as six times the size of those reported. In any case, the standard errors cannot and should not be used for making inferences or testing hypotheses, for there is no accepted statistical theory of inference in nonlinear models based on asymptotic errors computed according to the formula on p. 104.

Data Estimates

TABLE 3-A-1. Equipment Expenditures, Output, and Components of Conglomerate Relative Price Term, First Quarter 1947 through Fourth Quarter 1966

Year and quarter	Expenditures for producers' durable equipment[a] (billions of 1958 dollars, seasonally adjusted annual rate)	Business gross product[a] (billions of 1958 dollars, seasonally adjusted annual rate)	Conglomerate relative price term[b]	Implicit price deflator for business gross product[a] (1958=1.000)	Imputed rent per unit of new equipment[c] (1958=1.000)	Implicit price deflator for producers' durable equipment[a] (1958=1.000)	Moody's composite industrial bond yield[d],[e] (percent)	Moody's industrial dividend-price ratio[d],[e] (percent)	Effective rate of tax credit against equipment purchases[c],[f] (percent)	Effective rate of tax credit to be deducted from depreciation base[c],[g] (percent)	General corporate income tax rate[c],[h] (percent)	Assumed lifetime of equipment for tax purposes[i] (years)	Proportion of equipment depreciated by accelerated methods[j] (percent)	Present value of depreciation deduction: Straight-line basis[k]	Present value of depreciation deduction: Sum-of-the-years-digits basis[l]	Basis used for tax purposes[m]
1947: 1	25.1	268.4	6.4950	0.7473	0.1106	0.619	2.62	4.57	0	0	38	17.5	0	0.9173	0.9441	0.9173
2	24.5	271.4	6.2984	0.7538	0.1151	0.642	2.60	5.10	0	0	38	17.5	0	0.9143	0.9420	0.9143
3	23.8	272.6	6.3156	0.7692	0.1174	0.654	2.64	4.97	0	0	38	17.5	0	0.9137	0.9416	0.9137
4	25.0	278.4	6.2633	0.7887	0.1216	0.668	2.84	5.35	0	0	38	17.5	0	0.9034	0.9345	0.9034
1948: 1	26.8	280.4	6.3026	0.8034	0.1233	0.673	2.90	5.74	0	0	38	17.5	0	0.8984	0.9311	0.8984
2	25.3	285.5	6.2916	0.8133	0.1252	0.689	2.82	5.34	0	0	38	17.5	0	0.9042	0.9351	0.9042
3	24.9	287.6	6.0861	0.8275	0.1319	0.721	2.87	5.73	0	0	38	17.5	0	0.8996	0.9319	0.8996
4	25.8	290.0	5.9347	0.8227	0.1346	0.730	2.88	6.56	0	0	38	17.5	0	0.8935	0.9277	0.8935
1949: 1	24.2	285.1	5.9195	0.8162	0.1341	0.728	2.79	6.95	0	0	38	17.5	0	0.8942	0.9282	0.8942
2	22.9	282.8	5.7539	0.8101	0.1371	0.743	2.78	7.18	0	0	38	17.5	0	0.8930	0.9273	0.8930
3	21.8	286.7	5.8172	0.8046	0.1350	0.738	2.71	6.59	0	0	38	17.5	0	0.8997	0.9319	0.8997
4	21.4	283.9	5.8528	0.8027	0.1341	0.735	2.67	6.54	0	0	38	17.5	0	0.9015	0.9332	0.9015
1950: 1	21.7	300.6	5.7810	0.7944	0.1346	0.733	2.63	6.46	0	0	42	17.5	0	0.9044	0.9352	0.9044
2	24.2	309.0	5.8024	0.8031	0.1358	0.741	2.65	6.17	0	0	42	17.5	0	0.9056	0.9360	0.9056
3	26.9	321.1	5.8216	0.8234	0.1390	0.755	2.68	6.49	0	0	42	17.5	0	0.9023	0.9337	0.9023
4	26.4	326.0	5.7659	0.8392	0.1433	0.774	2.70	6.92	0	0	42	17.5	0	0.8986	0.9312	0.8986
1951: 1	25.0	327.8	5.5861	0.8691	0.1533	0.809	2.73	6.59	0	0	50.75	17.5	0	0.9015	0.9332	0.9015
2	25.4	332.7	5.5774	0.8740	0.1547	0.807	2.92	6.56	0	0	50.75	17.5	0	0.8948	0.9286	0.8948
3	26.0	339.0	5.6081	0.8734	0.1540	0.807	2.93	6.13	0	0	50.75	17.5	0	0.8973	0.9303	0.8973
4	25.7	338.5	5.6351	0.8841	0.1555	0.815	2.97	5.86	0	0	50.75	17.5	0	0.8977	0.9306	0.8977
1952: 1	26.0	339.9	5.6345	0.8852	0.1560	0.815	2.99	5.64	0	0	52	17.5	0	0.8987	0.9313	0.8987
2	26.1	338.0	5.6086	0.8866	0.1572	0.822	2.97	5.69	0	0	52	17.5	0	0.8991	0.9315	0.8991
3	22.1	341.7	5.6493	0.8934	0.1576	0.824	3.00	5.52	0	0	52	17.5	0	0.8992	0.9316	0.8992
4	24.3	353.2	5.6627	0.8983	0.1583	0.827	3.05	5.36	0	0	52	17.5	0	0.8984	0.9311	0.8984

Period																		
1953:1	25.9	360.0	5.6603	0.8988	0.1588	0.827	3.11	5.27	0	0	52	17.5		0	0.8968	0.9300	0.8968	0.8968
2	25.5	364.1	5.4694	0.8959	0.1639	0.837	3.38	5.55	0	0	52	17.5		0	0.8853	0.9220	0.8853	0.8853
3	26.1	361.5	5.4699	0.8982	0.1646	0.839	3.39	5.66	0	0	52	17.5		0	0.8842	0.9212	0.8842	0.8842
4	25.6	357.2	5.5292	0.8952	0.1627	0.835	3.29	5.56	0	0	52	17.5		0	0.8884	0.9242	0.8884	0.8884
1954:1	24.2	351.6	5.7668	0.9089	0.1588	0.842	3.13	5.21	0	0	52	17.2	52.4	0	0.8982	0.9309	0.8982	0.9153
2	24.3	350.8	5.8327	0.9084	0.1572	0.841	3.07	4.80	0	0	52	17.0	52.4	0	0.9041	0.9350	0.9041	0.9203
3	24.8	355.7	5.8946	0.9061	0.1555	0.835	3.08	4.50	0	0	52	16.7	52.4	0	0.9073	0.9372	0.9073	0.9229
4	24.6	363.3	5.8918	0.9083	0.1562	0.843	3.06	4.27	0	0	52	16.4	52.4	0	0.9110	0.9397	0.9110	0.9260
1955:1	24.7	376.0	5.8959	0.9111	0.1569	0.846	3.11	4.14	0	0	52	16.2	52.4	0	0.9111	0.9398	0.9111	0.9262
2	27.1	383.4	5.9030	0.9121	0.1571	0.848	3.16	3.93	0	0	52	15.9	52.4	0	0.9123	0.9406	0.9123	0.9271
3	28.9	389.2	5.8463	0.9172	0.1598	0.862	3.23	3.72	0	0	52	15.6	52.4	0	0.9128	0.9410	0.9128	0.9276
4	30.1	392.9	5.7673	0.9221	0.1631	0.878	3.24	3.95	0	0	52	15.4	52.4	0	0.9121	0.9405	0.9121	0.9270
1956:1	28.8	390.1	5.7768	0.9318	0.1648	0.890	3.22	3.90	0	0	52	15.1	52.4	0	0.9147	0.9423	0.9147	0.9291
2	28.7	391.9	5.6692	0.9397	0.1696	0.908	3.39	3.83	0	0	52	15.1	52.4	0	0.9097	0.9388	0.9097	0.9249
3	29.2	390.4	5.5872	0.9515	0.1745	0.926	3.55	3.85	0	0	52	15.1	52.4	0	0.9045	0.9352	0.9045	0.9206
4	28.7	396.0	5.4187	0.9588	0.1815	0.947	3.84	3.99	0	0	52	15.1	52.4	0	0.8946	0.9284	0.8946	0.9123
1957:1	29.2	398.7	5.3675	0.9691	0.1855	0.961	3.94	4.17	0	0	52	15.1	52.4	0	0.8904	0.9255	0.8904	0.9088
2	28.9	398.0	5.3773	0.9753	0.1867	0.967	4.00	3.86	0	0	52	15.1	52.4	0	0.8903	0.9255	0.8903	0.9087
3	29.8	399.8	5.3046	0.9844	0.1913	0.976	4.26	4.01	0	0	52	15.1	52.4	0	0.8815	0.9193	0.8815	0.9013
4	28.5	393.6	5.2139	0.9883	0.1957	0.994	4.26	4.46	0	0	52	15.1	52.4	0	0.8790	0.9176	0.8790	0.8992
1958:1	26.0	382.8	5.3838	0.9955	0.1914	0.990	3.92	4.41	0	0	52	15.1	52.4	0	0.8897	0.9250	0.8897	0.9082
2	24.6	383.8	5.4144	0.9979	0.1911	0.998	3.80	4.10	0	0	52	15.1	52.4	0	0.8952	0.9288	0.8952	0.9128
3	24.3	394.7	5.3762	1.0007	0.1933	1.003	4.00	3.68	0	0	52	15.1	52.4	0	0.8914	0.9262	0.8914	0.9096
4	25.2	405.5	5.3191	1.0046	0.1964	1.010	4.24	3.32	0	0	52	15.1	52.4	0	0.8860	0.9225	0.8860	0.9051
1959:1	26.5	412.6	5.3023	1.0096	0.1984	1.018	4.29	3.25	0	0	52	15.1	52.4	0	0.8849	0.9217	0.8849	0.9042
2	28.1	423.7	5.2641	1.0115	0.2005	1.022	4.45	3.09	0	0	52	15.1	52.4	0	0.8809	0.9189	0.8809	0.9008
3	28.4	418.5	5.2342	1.0160	0.2029	1.022	4.69	3.02	0	0	52	15.1	52.4	0	0.8740	0.9141	0.8740	0.8950
4	28.5	423.2	5.2606	1.0167	0.2024	1.018	4.70	3.12	0	0	52	15.1	52.4	0	0.8731	0.9135	0.8731	0.8943
1960:1	29.0	432.9	5.2512	1.0210	0.2040	1.023	4.70	3.42	0	0	52	15.1	52.4	0	0.8715	0.9123	0.8715	0.8929
2	30.5	431.3	5.2998	1.0252	0.2033	1.023	4.63	3.47	0	0	52	15.1	52.4	0	0.8733	0.9136	0.8733	0.8944
3	29.9	428.9	5.3505	1.0265	0.2021	1.022	4.52	3.51	0	0	52	15.1	52.4	0	0.8764	0.9158	0.8764	0.8970
4	29.2	425.0	5.3870	1.0308	0.2019	1.021	4.52	3.54	0	0	52	15.1	52.4	0	0.8762	0.9157	0.8762	0.8969
1961:1	27.3	423.0	5.5178	1.0340	0.1982	1.009	4.46	3.16	0	0	52	15.1	52.4	0	0.8802	0.9184	0.8802	0.9002
2	27.2	433.4	5.4723	1.0339	0.2002	1.018	4.49	3.09	0	0	52	15.1	52.4	0	0.8797	0.9181	0.8797	0.8998
3	28.3	441.3	5.4149	1.0333	0.2025	1.025	4.60	2.98	0	0	52	15.1	52.4	0	0.8769	0.9162	0.8769	0.8975
4	29.4	450.5	5.4280	1.0379	0.2033	1.030	4.59	2.93	0	0	52	15.1	52.4	0	0.8775	0.9166	0.8775	0.8980
1962:1	30.3	457.1	5.4949	1.0422	0.2020	1.025	4.55	3.02	0	0	52	15.1	52.4	0	0.8782	0.9171	0.8782	0.8986
2	31.3	464.8	5.5105	1.0432	0.2020	1.026	4.44	3.51	0	5	52	15.1	52.4	5.0	0.8788	0.9175	0.8788	0.8991
3	32.8	470.0	5.9054	1.0451	0.1895	1.022	4.49	3.61	0	5	52	13.1	52.4	5.0	0.8919	0.9265	0.8919	0.9100
4	32.6	474.4	5.9785	1.0480	0.1881	1.020	4.40	3.49	0	5	52	13.1	52.4	5.0	0.8948	0.9286	0.8948	0.9125

1963: 1	32.5	477.2	6.0191	1.0505	0.1876	1.020	4.38	3.33	5.0	5	52	13.1	52.4	0.8962	0.9296	0.9137
2	33.1	481.8	6.0373	1.0533	0.1879	1.022	4.40	3.17	5.0	5	52	13.1	52.4	0.8964	0.9297	0.9139
3	34.7	489.9	6.0380	1.0551	0.1885	1.023	4.45	3.16	5.0	5	52	13.1	52.4	0.8952	0.9288	0.9128
4	35.9	497.4	6.0518	1.0585	0.1890	1.025	4.47	3.14	5.0	5	52	13.1	52.4	0.8947	0.9285	0.9124
1964: 1	36.7	503.9	6.3684	1.0609	0.1806	1.030	4.49	3.07	5.0	0	50	13.1	52.4	0.8941	0.9281	0.9119
2	37.7	511.5	6.3926	1.0637	0.1807	1.029	4.54	2.98	5.0	0	50	13.1	52.4	0.8932	0.9275	0.9111
3	39.5	517.6	6.4327	1.0676	0.1806	1.030	4.52	2.91	5.0	0	50	13.1	52.4	0.8941	0.9281	0.9119
4	40.0	520.0	6.4354	1.0734	0.1818	1.036	4.53	2.96	5.0	0	50	13.1	52.4	0.8936	0.9277	0.9115
1965: 1	41.5	532.2	6.4719	1.0766	0.1817	1.038	4.52	2.96	5.0	0	48	13.1	52.4	0.8934	0.9276	0.9113
2	41.7	538.9	6.5084	1.0829	0.1820	1.038	4.56	2.98	5.0	0	48	13.1	52.4	0.8922	0.9268	0.9103
3	44.2	548.9	6.5185	1.0845	0.1824	1.036	4.63	3.01	5.0	0	48	13.1	52.4	0.8902	0.9253	0.9086
4	45.2	561.6	6.4944	1.0883	0.1840	1.041	4.72	2.98	5.0	0	48	13.1	52.4	0.8879	0.9238	0.9067
1966: 1	46.4	569.4	6.4578	1.0974	0.1869	1.045	4.94	3.12	5.0	0	48	13.1	52.4	0.8813	0.9192	0.9011
2	47.7	571.4	6.4013	1.1095	0.1909	1.055	5.15	3.33	5.0	0	48	13.1	52.4	0.8747	0.9046	0.8956
3	49.8	576.2	6.1191	1.1167	0.2012	1.056	5.51	3.71	3.3	0	48	13.1	52.4	0.8634	0.9067	0.8861
4	50.7	582.8	5.6861	1.1243	0.2180	1.073	5.62	3.67	0	0	48	13.1	52.4	0.8607	0.9048	0.8838

a Source: U.S. Department of Commerce.

b Source: Derived from equation (3.42).

c Source: See discussions, pp. 82–88.

d Source: Survey of Current Business, various issues.

e Used as ratio in estimating parameters.

f See discussion on pp. 87–88.

g See discussion on p. 86.

h Source: U.S. Treasury Department.

i See discussion on p. 86.

j See discussion on p. 85.

k Source: Derived from equation (3.50).

l Source: Derived from equation (3.52). Available for tax purposes beginning in 1954.

m Average of straight-line and sum-of-the-years-digits methods weighted according to the estimated proportion of equipment depreciated by accelerated methods (equation 3.53).

CHAPTER IV

The Effect of Cash Flow on the Speed of Adjustment

ROBERT M. COEN *Stanford University*

FEDERAL TAX POLICIES AIMED at stimulating plant and equipment expenditures in the United States have taken various forms. Beginning in 1954, firms were permitted to accelerate depreciation through use of the declining-balance and sum-of-the-years-digits depreciation methods. In 1962 Congress passed legislation granting a 7 percent tax credit (3 percent for utilities) on purchases of many types of equipment, and the Internal Revenue Service published new guidelines for depreciation that generally liberalized depreciation rates. Finally, the Revenue Act of 1964 provided for substantial reductions in corporate income tax rates and for a liberalization of the investment tax credit through repeal of the Long amendment. Wide debate on the effectiveness of such tax incentives has, up until this time, produced surprisingly little direct empirical evidence on which a sound evaluation might be based.

The purpose of this study is to assess the impact of these tax incentives on plant and equipment expenditures in the manufacturing sector during the 1954–66 period. Since the methods to be followed are by no means obvious, much of this study must be devoted to the development of an analytical framework.

The Impact of Accelerated Depreciation

Of all the investment incentives the government has sought to apply through the tax system, accelerated depreciation has received the most intense analytical attention. An examination of the approaches taken in these studies may serve to illustrate the nature of the existing literature on tax incentives generally.[1]

Accelerated depreciation is thought to stimulate capital expenditures in two ways. First, by increasing after-tax returns in the early years of an asset's life and reducing those in the later years by an equal amount, it increases the after-tax rate of return on the asset.[2] This will be referred to as the "rate-of-return effect." The second stimulative effect of accelerated depreciation is felt through an increase in cash flow, or the "liquidity effect."

Accelerated Depreciation and Rates of Return

To illustrate the rate-of-return effect, suppose that a particular asset can currently be purchased for q dollars. The asset is expected to yield a stream of returns before taxes and depreciation denoted by R_t, $t = 1, \ldots, T$. On the assumption that the asset has no salvage value, the rate of return after taxes, r', during period t, is defined implicitly by

$$q = \sum_{t=1}^{T} (R_t - TC_t)(1+r')^{-t}, \tag{4.1}$$

where TC_t is direct taxes in period t. If a depreciation deduction D_t is permitted in calculating taxable returns during period t with tax rate u, so that $TC_t = u(R_t - D_t)$, then

$$q = (1-u)\sum_{t=1}^{T} R_t(1+r')^{-t} + u\sum_{t=1}^{T} D_t(1+r')^{-t}. \tag{4.2}$$

---

[1] For a large sample of the extensive literature on accelerated depreciation, see Richard A. Musgrave, *The Theory of Public Finance* (McGraw-Hill, 1959), pp. 337–38. The limited work on tax credits for investment consists primarily of analyses of their application to net investment. See E. Cary Brown, "Comments on Tax Credits as Investment Incentives," *National Tax Journal*, Vol. 15 (June 1962), pp. 198–204; Sam B. Chase, Jr., "Tax Credits for Investment Spending," *National Tax Journal*, Vol. 15 (March 1962), pp. 32–52; William H. White, "Illusions in the Marginal Investment Subsidy," *National Tax Journal*, Vol. 15 (March 1962), pp. 26–31; and Jack Wiseman, "Public Policy and the Investment Tax Credit," *National Tax Journal*, Vol. 16 (March 1963), pp. 36–40.

[2] Throughout this study, the problems associated with a tax structure that does not allow full loss offsets in the period in which the losses occur are ignored. It may be assumed that the investor has a large enough gross income in each period to take advantage of the allowable depreciation charges; otherwise, the possibility of negative tax liabilities would have to be admitted. The corporation income tax in the United States permits losses to be carried back three years and forward five years. This scheme may provide nearly full loss offsets, but the timing problem involved would complicate the analysis.

Total allowable depreciation over the asset's life would, according to U.S. practice, be equal to q. Accelerated depreciation changes the timing of the deductions in favor of the earlier years and consequently increases the after-tax rate of return.

The investor is assumed to compare this return with the return on an alternative use of his funds—for example, the after-tax return on long-term bonds r. By raising the former relative to the latter, accelerated depreciation aims to make investment in depreciable assets more attractive.

Various writers have quantified the rate-of-return effect by computing rates of return on a typical asset, using different assumptions regarding the useful life of the asset for tax purposes, the tax rate, and the depreciation method. The results of these calculations are suggestive, but they fall far short of demonstrating the effectiveness of accelerated depreciation in stimulating investment. The difficulty is the lack of any readily available estimate of the elasticity of investment with respect to the rate of return. Indeed, a major problem in econometric studies of investment is the measurement of policy-induced changes in the rate of return. Expected sales or profits, or their proxies, are frequently assumed to be the prime determinants of the expected rate of return, since they determine the returns in equation (4.1). The role of prices and of policy parameters has received very little attention.

The approach taken here is to capture the rate-of-return effect in an appropriately defined "user cost of capital" variable. In the case of the asset discussed above, the investor can be thought of as comparing the value of the after-tax returns, discounted at the after-tax market rate r, with the current price of the asset. He would invest in the asset if

$$\sum_{t=1}^{T} (R_t - TC_t)(1+r)^{-t} > q, \qquad (4.3)$$

which may also be written as

$$\sum_{t=1}^{T} R_t(1+r)^{-t} > \frac{1}{1-u}\left[q - u\sum_{t=1}^{T} D_t(1+r)^{-t}\right]. \qquad (4.4)$$

If there were no direct tax on the returns, that is, if $u = 0$, the investor simply compares the discounted returns with q, the price of the asset. The existence of the tax raises the cost of the asset by a factor $1/(1-u)$, if depreciation deductions are not allowed (and assuming that establishment of the tax leaves the discount rate r unchanged). With depreciation permitted, the price of the asset is reduced by the discounted value of the tax savings stemming from the depreciation deductions, and this net price is inflated by the factor $1/(1-u)$. Accelerated depreciation will reduce the cost of the assets by increasing the discounted value of these tax savings.

All the variables on the right-hand side of equation (4.4) are observable; thus the appropriate cost of the capital good can be found empirically. It is this cost that, along with the factors determining the gross revenues, should affect the investor's decision. An investment tax credit can easily be incorporated into the problem. If the investor is permitted to credit a proportion k of the price paid for the asset against his present tax liabilities, then he should compare the discounted future returns with

$$[1/(1-u)]\left[q(1-k)-u\sum_{t=1}^{T}D_t(1+r)^{-t}\right].$$

In the section beginning on page 137, this notion of the cost of capital goods is developed for the firm that continually invests in them. The firm's demand for capital is shown to depend on the level of demand for its output and on the relative prices of its factors of production—capital (the derived expression for user cost) and labor (the wage rate). Given the level of demand and the wage rate, a policy-induced reduction in user cost will lead the firm to substitute capital for labor, that is, it will increase the firm's desired stock of capital and desired capital-output ratio. The strength of this effect depends, of course, on the magnitude of the reduction in user cost and on the scope for factor substitution in the production process. The following section, beginning on page 153, presents estimates of the user cost of capital for manufacturing during the postwar period, giving particular attention to the reductions in user cost brought about by tax incentives. Estimates of the investment function presented in the section beginning on page 163 provide evidence on the substitutability of factors.

Accelerated Depreciation and Cash Flow

The second way in which accelerated depreciation might stimulate investment is by increasing each firm's cash flow (after-tax income plus depreciation charges for tax purposes), which is one measure of the amount of internal funds available for financing investment and which is thought by some to be an important determinant of investment expenditures. This is called the liquidity effect.

In the absence of a tax credit for investment, cash flow can be written as

$$F_t = (1-u)(R_t-D_t)+D_t, \tag{4.5}$$

where

u = the tax rate on business income

R_t = gross business income during period t (including depreciation, but net of all other deductions)

D_t = depreciation charges for tax purposes.

Suppose that beginning in period τ, firms are permitted to accelerate depreciation. Let D_t^B, $t = \tau, \tau+1, \ldots$, be a measure of depreciation for period t that is consistent with depreciation methods prevailing prior to period τ. Cash flow in the absence of the acceleration of depreciation would have been

$$F_t^B = (1-u)(R_t - D_t^B) + D_t^B, \qquad t = \tau, \tau+1, \ldots, \tag{4.6}$$

and the increase in cash flow resulting from accelerated depreciation is

$$F_t - F_t^B = u(D_t - D_t^B), \tag{4.7}$$

which is the tax savings in period t resulting from accelerated depreciation.

Several writers have established the relation between depreciation before and after acceleration for hypothetical cases based on various assumptions about the depreciation method, the useful life of assets for tax purposes, and the rate of growth of the firm's capital expenditures. The results may be summarized as follows: For a firm that invests the same amount each period, accelerated depreciation will exceed "normal" depreciation for a number of periods (generally for the useful life of assets assumed for tax purposes) and then will fall to the level of normal depreciation and remain there. For a firm whose capital expenditures are growing each period, accelerated depreciation will always exceed normal depreciation. Thus accelerated depreciation may be viewed as a stream of interest-free loans in the amounts $u(D_t - D_t^B)$, $t = \tau, \tau+1, \ldots$, which will never be repaid in whole or in part unless the firm reduces absolutely its gross capital expenditures. Indeed, if the rate of capital expenditures grows, the amount of these permanent interest-free loans will actually grow.

If the firm were permitted a tax credit on its gross capital expenditures, total tax savings resulting from the tax incentives would be

$$F_t - F_t^B = u(D_t - D_t^B) + CDT_t, \tag{4.8}$$

where CDT_t is the amount of the credit in period t. The section starting on page 153 presents estimates of the amounts of normal depreciation for aggregate manufacturing during the postwar period and derives measures of the tax savings that can be attributed to accelerated depreciation, the investment tax credit, and the 1964 and 1965 reductions in the corporate income tax rate.[3]

Cash flow and its components have frequently been included in econometric studies of the determinants of investment, but not always in a manner consistent with the theoretical arguments advanced in their favor. As a result, interpretation of the results is somewhat precarious. In particular, it is often difficult to distinguish the role of cash flow as a measure of the expected profitability of investment from its role as a measure of the availability of funds for investment. Yet it is the latter that is generally intended for measurement, and it is through it that the liquidity effect is thought to operate. The following section presents a theory of investment demand based on a capital stock adjustment process in which the speed of adjustment is a function of cash flow. This seems to be the appropriate way of introducing cash flow into the investment relation, and the estimated investment relations reported here (pages 163–74) lend support to this view.

In the concluding section, the estimated investment relations and the estimated changes in the user cost of capital and cash flow brought about by tax incentives are employed to determine the amount of manufacturing investment attributable to the incentives from 1954 through the third quarter of 1966. These figures must be used with caution. A particularly serious shortcoming is that this approach ignores the interdependence of many of the variables included in the analysis. For example, new orders in manufacturing are found to be an important determinant of plant and equipment expenditures in manufacturing. In estimating investment attributable to tax incentives, new orders are assumed to be exogenous, which is to say, unaffected by changes in tax policy. But to the extent that tax incentives stimulate investment demand in other sectors, new orders in manufacturing will be increased, and the expansion of manufacturing investment in response to these increased orders should clearly be laid to tax incentives. To allow for such interdependencies, a multi-equation model of the economy would have to be constructed—a task far beyond the scope of this study. It is hoped, however, that the results reported below will help to improve the specification of investment functions included in macroeconometric models, particularly with regard to the inclusion of tax policy parameters.

---

[3] If the tax rate is changing, it is not possible to distinguish between tax savings stemming from such changes and those stemming from accelerated depreciation. This problem is taken up in the section beginning on p. 153.

Tax Incentives and Investment Theory

Investment is a dynamic adjustment of firms to changes in their desired or optimum stocks of capital. This suggests that development of a theory of investment might proceed in two stages. In the first, the determinants of the optimum stock of capital would be postulated or derived. The results would provide certain propositions, in a comparative statics framework, concerning the impact of changes in policy or other parameters on the optimum stock of capital. In the second stage, the nature of the adjustment process would be investigated, with special consideration given to technological and economic constraints on the rate at which discrepancies between the optimum and actual stocks can or will be eliminated.

Perhaps because it greatly simplifies the analysis, this two-stage approach has been widely adopted in the literature on investment theory. Irving Fisher's theory,[4] or some other theory of capital, is employed to deduce the determinants of the optimum stock; then various arguments are presented to demonstrate that adjustment cannot in fact take place instantaneously. These arguments involve considerations such as uncertainty, the time required to arrange for financing of expenditures, and the lag between appropriations and actual outlays. It is generally assumed that the factors that delay adjustment are relatively stable over time, so that the adjustment process can be represented by a fixed lag distribution whether of simple or complex form.

Nevertheless, it seems preferable to develop the theory in a single stage and to justify the form of the lag distribution adopted by deriving it from the profit-maximizing behavior of firms. For if the lag distribution is to be determined empirically rather than derived as part of the theory, there is always a danger that the researcher will choose the form that vindicates his particular preconceptions about the variables important in determining the optimum stock. For example, one might feel that the level of sales determines the optimum stock of capital and search for a lag distribution that produces statistically significant regression coefficients for sales variables. Yet it can be conjectured, probably correctly, that some lag distribution can be found that will lead to significant results for practically any variable; and if the theory is incapable of at least narrowing the set of possible lag distributions, futile controversies may arise concerning the relative importance of different variables in determining capital expenditures.

---

[4] Irving Fisher, *The Theory of Interest* (Macmillan, 1930).

The single-stage approach has been pursued by Robert Eisner and Robert Strotz, in work unique in this respect.[5] They amended the usual statement of the neoclassical theory of capital by assuming that the price of capital goods depends on the rate of investment, and showed that, under certain conditions, a Koyck-type lag distribution would be followed by a firm that is attempting to maximize its current net worth.[6] They were able not only to derive the form of the lag distribution, but also to specify the economic variables that determine the speed of adjustment. For the problem considered, the speed of adjustment was shown to depend on the rate of interest. As long as the interest rate is constant, the speed of adjustment (and consequently the lag distribution) would be fixed; but in the more general case it would vary over time, leading to what might be called a "flexible capital stock adjustment model."

Most arguments for introducing cash flow or some measure of liquidity as a variable determining capital expenditures stress the importance of short-term financial conditions for the timing of expenditures rather than for the long-run optimum capital stock. These arguments are usually based on the assumption of an imperfect capital market in which firms can borrow only at a rate higher than that at which they can lend, or in which the borrowing rate they face increases with the ratio of their debt to earnings.[7] This is certainly not an unreasonable assumption; but instead of accepting its implications based on ad hoc arguments, it would be interesting to investigate them using the analytical approach of Eisner and Strotz. In this way, a sound theoretical foundation might be laid for including cash flow as a determinant of the adjustment speed and for specifying more accurately the variables and functional forms to be used in empirical investigations of the determinants of investment. Unfortunately, the difficulties encountered

[5] Robert Eisner and Robert H. Strotz, "Determinants of Business Investment," in Commission on Money and Credit, *Impacts of Monetary Policy*, Research Study Number Two (Prentice-Hall, 1963).

[6] See L. M. Koyck, *Distributed Lags and Investment Analysis* (Amsterdam: North-Holland, 1954).

[7] See, for example, James S. Duesenberry, *Business Cycles and Economic Growth* (McGraw-Hill, 1958), Chap. 5; Edwin Kuh, "Theory and Institutions in the Study of Investment Behavior," in American Economic Association, *Papers and Proceedings of the Seventy-fifth Annual Meeting, 1962* (*American Economic Review*, Vol. 53, May 1963), pp. 260–68; John R. Meyer and Edwin Kuh, *The Investment Decision: An Empirical Inquiry* (Harvard University Press, 1957); and John R. Meyer and Robert R. Glauber, *Investment Decisions, Economic Forecasting, and Public Policy* (Harvard University, Graduate School of Business Administration, Division of Research, 1964).

in carrying out such an analysis are formidable. For this reason, the two-stage approach is adopted here, but the notion of a flexible capital stock adjustment model will be used in exploring the role of cash flow in the investment function.

The Demand for Capital

The only statement of the neoclassical theory of capital in which explicit attention is given to tax policy parameters is that of Dale Jorgenson.[8] The problem he considers may be described as follows for the case of discrete time and no direct taxation. At the beginning of period one, a firm in a competitive industry is to choose an investment program for the entire future, I_t, $t = 1, 2, \ldots$, and to decide on labor inputs at each future date, L_t, $t = 1, 2, \ldots$. All transactions and applications of inputs are assumed to occur at the close of each period. The firm wishes to maximize its net worth W, which may be written as

$$W = \sum_{t=1}^{\infty} (pQ - wL_t - qI_t)(1+r)^{-t}, \tag{4.9}$$

where

Q_t = output at date t
p = price of output
w = wage rate
q = price of the capital good
r = rate of interest at which the firm may borrow or lend any amount at any date.

There are two constraints on the firm. The first is a production function relating Q_t to L_t and K_{t-1}, the capital stock on hand at the end of the preceding period:

$$Q_t = \Phi(L_t, K_{t-1}). \tag{4.10}$$

The second is a relation indicating how current and past investments contribute to the current capital stock. If it is assumed that the capital good decays at a constant rate δ, this relation is

$$K_t = I_t + (1-\delta)I_{t-1} + (1-\delta)^2 I_{t-2} + \ldots, \tag{4.11}$$

or

$$K_t = I_t + (1-\delta)K_{t-1}. \tag{4.11.1}$$

[8] Dale W. Jorgenson, "Capital Theory and Investment Behavior," in American Economic Association, *Papers and Proceedings of the Seventy-fifth Annual Meeting, 1962* (*American Economic Review*, Vol. 53, May 1963), pp. 247–59.

The parameter δ may be viewed as the true depreciation rate or as the proportion of the capital stock that must be replaced each period if it is to remain intact—in short, the replacement rate.[9] It should be noted that depreciation is assumed to occur only because of the passage of time and does not depend on the intensity at which capital goods are used.

The maximization of (4.9) subject to (4.10) and (4.11.1) yields the marginal productivity conditions

$$\frac{\partial Q_t}{\partial L_t} = \frac{w}{p},$$

(4.12)

$$\frac{\partial Q_t}{\partial K_{t-1}} = \frac{q(r+\delta)}{p},$$

(4.13)

for $t = 1, 2, \ldots$. The expression c is what Jorgenson refers to as the "user cost of capital"—the implicit rental price per period of a unit of capital. While his terminology will be used here, it does not correspond to that in previous literature. In particular, c is not user cost in the sense that Keynes used the term,[10] for Keynes's concept was based on the assumption that depreciation depends, at least in part, on the intensity of use of capital goods.[11]

Taxes

A direct tax on the firm's income is easily included in the analysis. If TC_t is direct taxes at date t, the firm's present net worth is

$$W = \sum_{t=1}^{\infty} (pQ_t - wL_t - qI_t - TC_t)(1+r)^{-t},$$

(4.14)

[9] Equation (4.11.1) may be valid for true depreciation schemes other than that underlying (4.11), since, for any constant stream of gross expenditures or for any stream growing at a constant rate, replacement requirements ultimately will be a constant proportion of the capital stock. Nevertheless, the true depreciation function implicit in (4.11) is the only one that implies (4.11.1) for *any* stream of gross expenditures at *any* point in time.

[10] John Maynard Keynes, *The General Theory of Employment, Interest and Money* (Harcourt, Brace, 1936).

[11] User cost c is the appropriate cost of capital goods for the usual static analysis of the firm. Static production theory seeks to determine the optimum capital and labor inputs for a firm wishing to maximize profits. But the cost of capital goods to be used in defining profits is not always made clear. With the solution of the capital theory problem above, that cost is clearly determined. Maximization of profits, defined as $pQ - wL - cK$, subject to $Q = Q(L, K)$, treating K as a variable, will yield the same solution as (4.12) and (4.13). Furthermore, c is the appropriate cost of capital to use in constructing the firm's long-run cost curves.

which is maximized subject to the constraints (4.10) and (4.11.1) and an additional constraint defining TC_t, namely,

$$TC_t = u(pQ_t - wL_t - D_t) - kqI_t, \tag{4.15}$$

where

  u = tax rate
  D_t = depreciation charges permitted for tax purposes at date t
  k = the proportion of investment expenditures permitted as a credit against tax liabilities.[12]

The deductibility of interest payments and nondeductibility of payments to equity capital raise many conceptual and analytical problems concerning the manner in which investment expenditures are financed and the appropriate measure of the cost of funds. If debt were the only means of finance, then the deductibility of interest payments could be incorporated simply by defining r in (4.14) as the after-tax market rate on bonds $(1-u)r_b$, where r_b is the market rate. If equity finance is also possible, then in a competitive capital market in which risk is absent the rate that the firm must pay to obtain equity capital r_e must be equal to $(1-u)r_b$. If this were the case, then defining r to equal $(1-u)r_b$ in (4.14) would again be the proper way to incorporate deductibility of interest payments. But if capital markets are not competitive or if investors view equities as more risky than bonds, which appears the more likely set of circumstances, then $r_e \neq (1-u)r_b$; that is to say, the firm's borrowing rate and tax payments in any period will depend on the type of financing it undertakes, and the mix of debt and equity finance chosen by the firm should itself depend upon the tax rate, among other things. Furthermore, the firm's lending rate would no longer necessarily be equal to its borrowing rate; even if it were to lend to another firm it would have to find one with the same capital structure as it has. Hence it is no longer clear how (4.14) and (4.15) should be written. For this reason, the deductibility of interest payments and the taxation of interest income are ignored in this analysis. Thus r in (4.14) is again simply the market rate of interest.[13]

Depreciation

Depreciation charges are determined by the prevailing depreciation formula for tax purposes. Depreciation policy stipulates the proportion of

[12] The tax treatment of capital gains and losses is omitted here on the assumption that the expected value of capital gains is zero.
[13] For further discussion of the appropriate discount rate, see pp. 158–59.

the depreciable base of assets that can be written off in each period after their acquisition. If the depreciable base is equal to the cost of the assets, then

$$D_t = \sum_{s=0}^{\infty} D(s)q I_{t-s}, \tag{4.16}$$

where $D(s)$ is the proportion of the depreciable base of assets acquired s periods ago allowed as a depreciation deduction at date t.[14] For example, the straight-line depreciation rule stipulates that

$$D(0) = D(1) = D(2) = \ldots = D(T-1) = \frac{1}{T},$$

where T is the useful life of assets for tax purposes, so that

$$D_t = \sum_{s=0}^{T-1} \frac{1}{T} q I_{t-s}.$$

If the depreciable base is equal to the cost of the assets less the amount of the tax credit claimed, then

$$D_t = \sum_{s=0}^{\infty} D(s)(1-k)q I_{t-s}. \tag{4.17}$$

The user cost measure obtained by maximizing (4.14) subject to (4.10), (4.11.1), and (4.15) depends upon whether (4.16) or (4.17) is substituted for D_t in (4.15). If the tax credit is not deducted from the depreciable base of acquisitions, then

$$c = q(r+\delta)(1-k-uz)/(1-u), \tag{4.18}$$

where z is the discounted value of the stream of depreciation charges generated by a dollar of current investment, that is,

$$z = \sum_{s=0}^{\infty} D(s)(1+r)^{-s}. \tag{4.19}$$

If the tax credit must be deducted from the depreciable base, then

$$c = q(r+\delta)(1-k)(1-uz)/(1-u). \tag{4.20}$$

---

[14] In the empirical work employing quarterly data, I have assumed that investment expenditures at date t do not begin to generate tax depreciation charges until date $t+1$, that is, $D(0) = 0$.

For a given rate of interest, accelerating depreciation will increase the discounted value of depreciation charges and will therefore reduce the user cost of capital. Furthermore, if there is no tax credit ($k = 0$), and if the firm is permitted to write off the entire cost of assets in the period in which they are acquired ($z = 1$), then direct taxation would not affect the user cost of capital and therefore would not change the optimum stock of capital. Under these circumstances the definition of taxable income corresponds exactly to net revenue, and the capital stock that maximizes net worth will also maximize net worth after taxes.[15]

The Acceleration Principle and the Adjustment Process

Although this analysis began with what appeared to be an investment problem, it has resulted in maximization conditions stated in terms of the stock of capital, the optimum stock K^* being implicitly defined by (4.12) and (4.13). Of course, the optimum path of investment expenditures could easily be derived by recursive use of (4.11.1). If the initial capital stock were zero, real investment at the end of period one should be K^*; and for each period thereafter, investment should be δK^*, if the capital stock is to be maintained at its optimum level. Trivial as this result may seem, it reflects the fact that one cannot get any more out of a piece of analysis than one builds into it. Given the initial assumptions, there is nothing to bar the firm from adjusting within one period to the optimum stock.

A gradual adjustment process could be introduced (rather than tacked on) in at least two ways. First, it might be assumed that the firm goes through an iterative process over time in attaining the optimum stock. Labor input and the level of production would be determined from (4.10)

---

[15] In his original derivation of the user cost measure in the case of a direct tax in "Capital Theory and Investment Behavior," Jorgenson assumed that depreciation for tax purposes is a constant proportion v of replacement, so that $D_t = vq\delta K_{t-1}$. The user cost measure thus derived would be correct only for the special case in which (a) the depreciation formula was of the declining-balance form with a tax depreciation rate equal to δ and (b) policy makers stipulate that the cost basis of acquisitions for depreciation purposes is vqI_t rather than qI_t. If policy makers alter the proportion of depreciation to replacement, they would not change the timing of depreciation charges, but rather the total amount of the write-off.

This shortcoming of Jorgenson's formulation and the user cost measures relevant to the U.S. experience were set forth in an unpublished paper, "Depreciation Policy and Professor Jorgenson's Measure of User Cost," which I circulated in the spring of 1965, and in a paper, "Accelerated Depreciation and Investment Decisions," which I delivered at the December 1965 North American Regional Conference of the Econometric Society in New York City.

and (4.12), given the initial capital stock K_0. Call the output so determined $\overline{Q}_1$. Then instead of investment in the first period I_1 being set equal to $K^* - (1-\delta)K_0$, it would be set equal to $\overline{K}_1 - (1-\delta)K_0$, where $\overline{K}_1$ is determined by finding the factor combination that would produce $\overline{Q}_1$ at a minimum total cost. The capital stock for the next period would then be $\overline{K}_1$, and the procedure would be repeated. The iteration will converge to K^*, given the usual assumptions regarding the shapes of the short- and long-run average cost curves. Second, an assumption that the price of the asset q is not constant but is a function of investment expenditures during the given period could be introduced. This is the modification considered by Eisner and Strotz;[16] as they showed, it establishes the Marshallian short run and long run as matters of degree rather than as arbitrarily and rigidly fixed.

The derived user cost measure is particularly useful here since it is the cost of capital goods that should enter the firm's long-run demand function for capital. Provided that the long-run average cost curve is U-shaped or simply rising, solving (4.12) and (4.13) will yield unique values for the optimum capital and labor inputs, K^* and L^*. The solutions are the long-run demand curves of the firm for capital and labor, and they can be written as

$$K^* = \Phi_{K^*}[w/p, c/p], \tag{4.21}$$

$$L^* = \Phi_{L^*}[w/p, c/p]. \tag{4.22}$$

That output does not enter the demand function for capital may disappoint "accelerationists," but it should not surprise them. Output appears in this problem as a decision variable, not as a parameter. The situation is quite similar to the absence of income in the consumption function derived in the classical theory of consumer behavior. Just as additional assumptions are required to get income into the consumption function, so are they required to get output into the demand function for capital.[17]

[16] Eisner and Strotz, "Determinants of Business Investment."

[17] Jorgenson presents what appears to be a misleading argument for including output in (4.21). He states that if the production function is of the Cobb-Douglas form, say

$$Q_t = AL_t^{1-\alpha} K_{t-1}^{\alpha},$$

then (4.13) can be solved explicitly for desired capital stock K^*:

$$K^* = \frac{\alpha p}{c} Q^*.$$

This is true definitionally; it has nothing to do with causation, because Q^* is not exogenously given to the firm but is determined by it. Output and capital stock are jointly deter-

Rationalizations of the acceleration principle range from the assumption of a fixed technological relationship between output and capital stock to consideration of the importance of current and past output as proxies for the expected rate of return on current investment. Such arguments do not fit in well with neoclassical theory; but they are plausible, and continued success in empirical tests of properly specified acceleration models provides strong evidence to support the principle. Yet its practicability is not a very persuasive reason for the insertion of output into the demand function; nor are the ad hoc arguments for the modification any more satisfactory, particularly when they are inconsistent with, or only loosely related to, the theory initially developed.

A crucial and unrealistic assumption made in deriving the demand function is that orders are produced and sales completed by the end of each period. If production and sales were so neatly synchronized, there would be no reason for firms intentionally to hold inventories of finished goods. But in the more plausible case of nonsynchronization, firms can be expected to hold inventories, if only to smooth the impact on production of fluctuating sales. Furthermore, inventories held for this purpose would probably be approximately proportional to the level of sales. Given the existence of inventories, sales (rather than output) could enter the firm's demand function for capital.

The theory developed above has focused on the determinants of *desired* or *planned* output, labor input, and capital stock, but there is no reason to assume that the plans of all firms will be consistent with the attainment of market equilibrium at output price p. Suppose, for example, that all

---

mined on the basis of wage and interest rates, prices of assets and of output, and the rate of decay. However, Jorgenson's remarks are cryptic on this point, and it is possible that he intended to state a proposition, based on the iterative process described above, that would lead to the demand for capital being a function of current output *during the period of adjustment*. But again it is impossible to interpret this proposition as a statement of the acceleration principle, since it is simply the entrepreneur's own groping, not exogenous demand shifts, that introduces current output as a determinant of the demand for capital.

Furthermore, the Cobb-Douglas form imposes a unitary elasticity of substitution between capital and labor. If Jorgenson had instead assumed a constant-elasticity-of-substitution production function with constant returns to scale, he would have obtained

$$K^* = A^\sigma (p/c)^\sigma Q^*,$$

where σ is the elasticity of substitution and A is a constant. If $\sigma = 0$, relative prices, even when altered by policy, will not affect the desired capital stock. Surely one should determine the value of the elasticity of substitution from the data, rather than arbitrarily assigning it a value of unity.

firms in the market or industry are identical and that each plans to sell an amount Q^* during the current period, so that total supply is the number of firms multiplied by Q^*. If buyers wish to purchase more than this quantity at price p, consistency of buyers' and sellers' plans is usually thought to be established by a change in price. But in a world with inventories, prices could remain fixed, trading could take place, and consistency of desired sales and planned output could be brought about by an undesired decumulation of inventories. If realized sales were to exceed planned sales for a number of periods, firms would undoubtedly come to view the level of realized sales as permanent and would rationally maximize their net worth by finding the labor input and capital stock at which it could be produced at minimum cost. In this way, realized sales—exogenously given—would indeed appear in the demand function for capital along with user cost.

Implicit in this argument is a presumption that prices are relatively sticky, so that shorter-run adjustments in markets take place via unintended changes in inventories. This is not to say that prices will necessarily be inflexible in the long run; for if the level of market demand is high enough to permit existing firms to make large profits, new firms may be expected to enter the industry and cut prices. Even so, the lag between the rise in market demand and the entrance of new firms suggests that capital expenditures by new firms are in fact caused by the high level of sales in the industry. The complexity of such long-run adjustments is very great, and these remarks are meant to be only suggestive. But there does seem to be ample justification for including realized sales as a determinant of the demand for capital even within the confines of neoclassical capital theory.

The argument for including realized sales in the demand function implies that prices and output are given and that the firm is faced with a problem of cost minimization rather than profit maximization. The relevant prices of the two inputs are, of course, the wage rate for labor and the appropriate user cost measure for capital. First-order conditions for cost minimization imply that the marginal rate of substitution of the two factors should be equated to the ratio of their prices. Thus the demand function for capital can be written

$$K^* = \Phi_{K^*}[S_R, c/w], \qquad (4.23)$$

where S_R is the realized level of sales in real terms or an average of realized sales of several previous periods and c is user cost (which is, of course, a function of tax policies).

Investment Demand

A theory of investment must specify how the demand for capital (a stock) is translated into investment demand (a flow). Investment demand is made up of two components—net investment and replacement. Net investment results from changes in the desired stock of capital, while replacement is here assumed always to be a fraction δ of the capital stock on hand at the beginning of the period. A change in the desired stock of capital may generate net expenditures over a number of periods, reflecting the various adjustment lags mentioned above. In general, net investment during period t is

$$I_{N_t} = \sum_{i=0}^{n} \beta_i (K_{t-i}^* - K_{t-1-i}^*), \qquad (4.24)$$

where $n+1$ is the number of periods over which a change in the desired stock generates net expenditures with a distributed lag pattern given by the set of β_i coefficients. Stability requires that

$$\sum_{i=0}^{n} \beta_i = 1. \qquad (4.25)$$

Gross investment during period t is then

$$I_t = \sum_{i=0}^{n} \beta_i (K_{t-i}^* - K_{t-1-i}^*) + \delta K_{t-1}. \qquad (4.26)$$

Ideally, the β's would be determined by fitting equation (4.26) to a set of data, given some specification of the determinants of desired stock.[18] With time series data, however, this procedure is often impossible, because of multicollinearity of changes in the variables determining K^* and because the series generally available are short relative to the number of β's one would typically wish to estimate. Two alternative approaches have been used. First, one might specify precise numerical values for the β's on some a priori grounds. After comparing the results obtained for different specified values, one could select the set that yields the best fit or that best confirms the hypotheses regarding the determinants of K^*. Second, one might specify the form of the relation among the β's and use this specification to reduce the number of lagged variables needed to estimate the parameters of the lag distribution.

[18] Robert Eisner has done this with cross-sectional data in "A Distributed Lag Investment Function," *Econometrica*, Vol. 28 (January 1960), pp. 1–29.

For several reasons, I have chosen to follow the second approach and to specify initially that the β's form an infinite decaying geometric series (a Koyck distribution). Thus

$$\beta_i = b(1-b)^i, \qquad i = 0, 1, \ldots, \tag{4.27}$$

where b is a constant, $0 < b \leq 1$; and

$$I_t = \sum_{i=0}^{\infty} b(1-b)^i (K_{t-i}^* - K_{t-1-i}^*) + \delta K_{t-1}. \tag{4.28}$$

This specification is the one suggested by the work of Eisner and Strotz noted earlier. Other forms of the lag distribution often impose a behavioral relation that leads to apparently irrational actions. To illustrate, consider a situation in which capital goods do not deteriorate. Assume that a particular firm has not been investing for a number of periods, because its actual capital stock of 100 machines has been equal to its desired stock. In period t, however, its desired stock jumps to 200; and in period $t+1$, its desired stock falls to 150, where it remains for an indefinite number of periods. Suppose, for example, that the postulated lag distribution is

$$I_t = \tfrac{1}{2}(K_t^* - K_{t-1}^*) + \tfrac{1}{2}(K_{t-1}^* - K_{t-2}^*). \tag{4.29}$$

Then $I_t = 50$, $I_{t+1} = 25$, and $I_{t+2} = -25$. At the end of period t, the firm actually had accumulated a stock of 150 machines—its desired stock in the ensuing periods. Yet, because of the nature of this adjustment process, the firm goes on investing and disinvesting for the next two periods.

The Koyck distribution avoids such anomalous predictions. Examination of equation (4.28) reveals that

$$I_t = \sum_{i=0}^{\infty} b(1-b)^i K_{t-i}^* - \sum_{i=0}^{\infty} b(1-b)^i K_{t-1-i}^* + \delta K_{t-1} \tag{4.30}$$

$$= bK_t^* + (1-b)\sum_{i=0}^{\infty} b(1-b)^i K_{t-1-i}^* - \sum_{i=0}^{\infty} b(1-b)^i K_{t-1-i}^* + \delta K_{t-1}$$

$$I_t = b\Big[K_t^* - \sum_{i=0}^{\infty} b(1-b)^i K_{t-1-i}^*\Big] + \delta K_{t-1}.$$

By definition, K_t is equal to the sum of all past net investments, that is,

$$K_t = \sum_{\tau=0}^{\infty} \sum_{i=0}^{\infty} b(1-b)^i (K_{t-\tau-i}^* - K_{t-\tau-1-i}^*) \tag{4.31}$$

$$= b(K_t^* - K_{t-1}^*) + b(1-b)(K_{t-1}^* - K_{t-2}^*) + b(1-b)^2(K_{t-2}^* - K_{t-3}^*) + \cdots$$

$$+ b(K^*_{t-1} - K^*_{t-2}) + b(1-b)(K^*_{t-2} - K^*_{t-3}) + \ldots$$
$$+ b(K^*_{t-2} - K^*_{t-3}) + \ldots$$

and so forth,

$$= bK^*_t + b(1-b)K^*_{t-1} + b(1-b)^2 K^*_{t-2} + \ldots$$

$$K_t = \sum_{i=0}^{\infty} b(1-b)^i K^*_{t-i}.$$

Thus (4.30) can be written

$$I_t = b(K^*_t - K_{t-1}) + \delta K_{t-1}. \tag{4.32}$$

Use of the Koyck lag is equivalent to assuming that net investment is always a fraction b (called the "speed of adjustment") of the gap between the desired capital stock and the actual capital stock. When these two stocks are equal, net investment is zero, which seems to be in accord with rational behavior.

The Role of Cash Flow

A further advantage of initially assuming a Koyck lag distribution is that the implied capital stock adjustment model (4.32) can be modified to allow for a variable adjustment speed, that is, an adjustment speed that depends on economic variables. Such a modification would seem to be in the spirit of most arguments concerning the role of cash flow in investment decisions.

Cash flow, or some measure of internal funds available for investment, is generally viewed as a constraint on the volume of investment expenditures rather than as a determinant of the optimum capital stock. It is argued that firms prefer to finance expenditures from internal sources and rely on external sources (borrowing and equity issues) only when absolutely necessary. Presumably, absolute necessity arises when the anticipated return on an investment would fall greatly if it were postponed until sufficient internal funds were available.

Proponents of this view often call attention to the fact that much investment is internally financed. But, in itself, this does not reveal a preference for internal financing. Firms should be indifferent to the mode of finance. The opportunity cost of using internal funds to finance investment is the lending rate, which in a perfect market is equal to the borrowing rate. Thus observed behavior is not inconsistent with the theory presented so far.

Many arguments have been suggested to support the proposition that firms prefer internal sources. At their heart is a divergence between the borrowing and lending rates faced by the firm, at least in the short run. Firms may face a higher borrowing than lending rate—an imperfection in the capital market that may arise where, for some reason, there is specialization among institutions in specific types of debt instruments. It is hard, however, to imagine such a situation persisting for very long. Ultimately, firms should be able to lend to one another, and a discrepancy between the borrowing and lending rates seems logically impossible. Perhaps a more plausible argument is that while the lending rate is fixed, the borrowing rate may be an increasing function of the ratio of interest payments to net income or of the ratio of total debt to total assets. The reasoning here is that lenders will become more cautious as the firm appears to become increasingly burdened with debt. A related argument stresses the importance of the firm's current profitability in determining the terms on which it can borrow, although the current ratio and interest coverage can be satisfactory even if profitability is low.

Emphasis on finding a rationalization for preference for internal funds appears misplaced. Perhaps what must be explained is why firms tend to retain such a high proportion of their earnings. Some may argue that this is simply a reflection of the preference for internal financing, but a more appealing explanation is that because of the divergence between ordinary income tax rates and tax rates on capital gains, shareholders prefer to receive their income in the form of capital gains rather than dividends. Thus the importance of retained funds as a source of finance may reflect not so much the preference of management for internal financing as the preference of shareholders for capital gains income.[19]

Tenuous as the arguments in favor of cash flow may be, its role in investment decisions should at least be tested. One must be careful, however, to include the internal funds variable in a manner that is consistent with the considerations just noted. In particular, the role of cash flow would seem most important in determining the speed at which discrepancies between the desired and optimum stocks of capital are eliminated. What is suggested here is that the speed of adjustment b in (4.32) be taken not as a constant but as a function of cash flow, which is assumed to measure the availability of internal funds. Thus the model might be written

$$I_t = b_t(K_t^* - K_{t-1}) + \delta K_{t-1}, \tag{4.33}$$

[19] For some evidence in support of this view, see John A. Brittain, *Corporate Dividend Policy* (Brookings Institution, 1966).

where

$$b_t = \phi_b(F_t), \qquad (4.34)$$

F_t being the level of cash flow during period t. Alternatively, the model may be written

$$I_t = b_t[K_t^* - (1-\delta)K_{t-1}], \qquad (4.35)$$

reflecting the hypothesis that the firm considers the adequacy of internal funds to meet both expansion and replacement expenditures. If the adjustment speed in period t is always less than unity, (4.35) has the undesirable implication that the stationary value of capital stock is less than the optimum.

Two recent empirical studies have attempted to isolate the role of internal funds in this manner. In an analysis of cross-sectional data from McGraw-Hill surveys of capital expenditures, Edward Greenberg tested a model similar to (4.35) and specified b_{it}—the adjustment speed of firm i at time t—as an exponential function of after-tax profits lagged one year and two years, Moody's index of common stock prices lagged one year, and Moody's index of the average price of new capital lagged one year.[20] The major shortcoming of this specification is that it does not take account of the ratio of internal funds to the funds required to accomplish what might be called the investment chore—the expansion from the current to the desired stock of capital. Suppose that in one situation profits are $1 million and the investment chore is $1 million, while in another profits are again $1 million, but the investment chore is $10 million. The model implies that the adjustment coefficient is the same in both instances, yet it appears that a larger fraction of the investment chore would be completed in the first case than in the second.

This shortcoming is not present in the model tested by Harold Hochman.[21] Employing aggregate annual time series data for the postwar period, he estimated a relation similar to (4.33),

$$I_t = \left[b_0 + b_1 \frac{F_{t-1} - \delta K_{t-1}}{K_t^* - K_{t-1}}\right](K_t^* - K_{t-1}) + \delta K_{t-1}. \qquad (4.36)$$

Here the amount of internal funds available for expansion $F_{t-1} - \delta K_{t-1}$, relative to desired expansion $K_t^* - K_{t-1}$, determines the speed of adjustment.

[20] Edward Greenberg, "A Stock-Adjustment Investment Model," *Econometrica*, Vol. 32 (July 1964), pp. 339–57.

[21] Harold M. Hochman, "Some Aggregative Implications of Depreciation Acceleration," *Yale Economic Essays*, Vol. 6 (Spring 1966), pp. 217–74.

Hochman's specification has the further advantage that it leads to an investment relation whose parameters are easily estimated—

$$I_t = b_0(K_t^* - K_{t-1}) + b_1(F_{t-1} - \delta K_{t-1}) + \delta K_{t-1}. \qquad (4.37)$$

Given a linear relation specifying the determinants of desired stock, least squares or maximum likelihood estimates of the parameters of (4.37) can be readily obtained. It should be noted, however, that b may behave in a strange way when $K_t^* - K_{t-1}$ becomes very small; and the relation makes little sense if $K_t^* - K_{t-1}$ is negative.

Perhaps a more reasonable specification would be

$$I_t = \left[b_0 + b_1 \frac{F_{t-1}}{K_t^* - (1-\delta)K_{t-1}} \right] [K_t^* - (1-\delta)K_{t-1}]. \qquad (4.38)$$

Here the firm is assumed to adjust more rapidly the higher the ratio of cash flow to desired expansion plus replacement. The term $K_t^* - (1-\delta)K_{t-1}$ is not likely to be small and certainly would not be negative in the postwar U.S. economy.

One criticism that might be made of both Greenberg's and Hochman's treatments of the adjustment process is that no constraints are imposed on the adjustment speed. When dealing with models involving a constant speed of adjustment, it is reasonable to assume that the adjustment coefficient is greater than zero but no greater than unity, for otherwise the model would imply a high degree of instability. (Whether observed behavior suggests stability of adjustment processes is not easily determined, and it is not altogether clear that unstable models should be rejected on such grounds.) However, the adjustment speed in a flexible adjustment model may temporarily equal zero or exceed unity without implying long-run instability of the adjustment process. Thus, if constraints are to be imposed, they must be defended on grounds other than stability. It might be argued that an adjustment speed even temporarily greater than unity would be inconsistent with rational behavior. But this may not be the case, at least not in the problem considered here. If a firm realizes cash flow during the current period in excess of current investment requirements, and if management feels compelled to distribute any unused funds as dividends, additional investment may be undertaken in anticipation that, in the future, investment requirements will exceed cash flow. In other words, rather than distribute dividends in one period and be forced to use external sources or even to curtail investment in the next, management may over-invest in the current period. Of course, if the lending rate is greater than the return on this additional investment, the firm will lend out the excess funds for the current period, and the adjustment speed would not exceed unity.

As a further consideration, it should be noted that an unconstrained adjustment rate permits the use of vastly simpler estimation methods. An example of a constrained flexible adjustment model is

$$I_t = [1 - e^{-v_1 - v_2(F_t - \delta K_{t-1})/(K^*_t - K_{t-1})}](K^*_t - K_{t-1}) + \delta K_{t-1}. \quad (4.39)$$

The adjustment speed has a lower bound of $1 - e^{-v_1}$ (with $v_1 \geq 0$) and an upper bound of unity. The estimation difficulties are apparent; no transformation will achieve linearity in the parameters. If the expression for the adjustment speed were to be expanded in a Maclaurin series treating $(F_t - \delta K_{t-1})/(K^*_t - K_{t-1})$ as the variable and retaining only the first two terms of the expansion, the resulting linear approximation of (4.39) would have exactly the same form as Hochman's model.

Hochman's specification has several obvious advantages and is adopted in the empirical analysis reported below. To summarize, the following three forms of the investment function will be tested:

$$I_t = b(K^*_t - K_{t-1}) + \delta K_{t-1}, \quad (4.32)$$

or

$$I_t = \left[b_0 + b_1 \frac{F_{t-1} - \delta K_{t-1}}{K^*_t - K_{t-1}} \right] (K^*_t - K_{t-1}) + \delta K_{t-1}, \quad (4.36)$$

and

$$I_t = \left[b_0 + b_1 \frac{F_{t-1}}{K^*_t - (1-\delta)K_{t-1}} \right] [K^*_t - (1-\delta)K_{t-1}], \quad (4.38)$$

where

$$K^* = \Phi_{K^*}[S_R, c/w].$$

Impact of Tax Incentives on Cash Flow and User Cost

This section presents estimates of the impact of tax incentives on cash flow and the user cost of capital in manufacturing during the postwar period.

Cash Flow

Previously it was shown that tax savings during period t stemming from accelerated depreciation and an investment tax credit can be written as

$$F_t - F^B_t = u(D_t - D^B_t) + CDT_t, \quad (4.8)$$

where

F = cash flow

F^B = cash flow that would have been realized had there been no accelerated depreciation or tax credit

u = the tax rate

D = actual depreciation charges for tax purposes

D^B = depreciation charges calculated according to the depreciation formula prevailing prior to the acceleration of depreciation

CDT = the tax credit

Equation (4.8) can be used to compute tax savings for the 1954–63 period; but in 1964 and 1965 the tax rate on corporate income was reduced below the 1954–63 level, and a measure of tax savings that includes those stemming from the rate reductions would be useful. If u^B is defined as the tax rate that would have prevailed had there been no rate reduction (that is, the rate from 1954 to 1963), then

$$F_t^B = (1-u^B)(R_t - D_t^B) + D_t^B, \tag{4.40}$$

$$F_t = (1-u)(R_t - D_t) + D_t, \tag{4.40.1}$$

where R is income gross of depreciation. Therefore,

$$F_t - F_t^B = (u^B - u)(R_t - D_t) + u^B(D_t - D_t^B) + CDT_t. \tag{4.41}$$

It is tempting to call $(u^B - u)(R_t - D_t)$ the tax savings resulting from a tax rate change and $u^B(D_t - D_t^B)$ the savings resulting from accelerated depreciation. But this would be incorrect. If the tax rate had been changed but accelerated depreciation had not been granted, the savings would be $(u^B - u)(R_t - D_t^B)$. One cannot add these savings to $u^B(D_t - D_t^B)$ to obtain savings due to both the tax rate change and accelerated depreciation, because there is an interaction effect between the two changes, that is,

$$
\underbrace{(u^B - u)(R_t - D_t) + u^B(D_t - D_t^B)}_{\substack{\text{Savings due to tax rate} \\ \text{change and accelerated} \\ \text{depreciation}}} = \underbrace{(u^B - u)(R_t - D_t^B)}_{\substack{\text{Savings due} \\ \text{to tax rate} \\ \text{change only}}} +
$$

$$
\underbrace{u^B(D_t - D_t^B)}_{\substack{\text{Savings due to} \\ \text{accelerated de-} \\ \text{preciation only}}} - \underbrace{(u^B - u)(D_t - D_t^B)}_{\text{Interaction term}}. \tag{4.42}
$$

As an approximation, the interaction term will be distributed in proportion to the separate effects in the identification of tax savings reported below. For example, the tax savings attributed to the change in the tax rate will be

$$(u^B - u)(R_t - D_t^B) \left[1 - \frac{(u^B - u)(D_t - D_t^B)}{(u^B - u)(R_t - D_t^B) + u^B(D_t - D_t^B)} \right]. \qquad (4.43)$$

Distributing the interaction in this way can be defended. Suppose that tax savings resulting from accelerated depreciation only—$u^B(D - D^B)$—were to be expressed in terms of an equivalent change in the tax rate, namely, $(u^B - u) = u^B(D - D^B)/(R - D^B)$. Then a tax rate change could be directly compared with a change in depreciation accounting, and it would seem reasonable to distribute the interaction term in proportion to the tax rate change and the tax-rate-change equivalent of accelerated depreciation. The procedure shown in (4.43) amounts to doing just this.

Another problem introduced by tax rate changes is the selection of a base against which the changes are to be measured. For example, should the 1966 rate be compared with the 1965 rate, in which case there would be no change? Or should it be compared with the 1953 rate, in which case there would be a decrease of four percentage points? The latter comparison is in keeping with the measurement of tax policy effects adopted throughout this study; that is, the question concerns the effects on manufacturing investment if no change in tax policy had occurred after 1953. If estimates are to be made well beyond 1966, then it would probably be advisable to shift the basis of comparison to the tax structure prevailing in, say, 1965.

To obtain estimates of D^B for aggregate manufacturing during the postwar period, a straight-line depreciation formula is applied to annual capital expenditures for new plant and equipment by manufacturing firms. The expenditure series, useful lives for tax purposes, and depreciation formula are described in Appendix 4-A.

The impact of tax incentives on corporate tax liabilities for 1954–66 is summarized in Table 4-1. In computing tax savings, the general statutory rate on corporate income was used as an estimate of u and u^B. Part A of Table 4-1 shows the separate effect of each policy change on the assumption that no other changes in policy occurred. For example, the first column indicates the reductions in tax liabilities attributable to accelerated depreciation assuming that the tax rate had remained at 52 percent throughout the period. The tax-rate-change equivalent of each tax incentive and the total for all incentives are presented in the last four columns. A tax-rate-change equivalent is found by dividing consistently measured before-tax

TABLE 4-1. Estimates of Tax Savings Resulting from Tax Incentives, Corporate Manufacturing, 1954–66

Year	Accelerated depreciation[a]	Tax credit[b]	Tax cut[c]	Interaction[d]	Total	Accelerated depreciation[e]	Tax credit[f]	Tax cut[g]	Total[h]
	Tax savings (millions of dollars)					*Equivalent tax rate reduction (percentage points)*			
A. Separate and interaction effects									
1954	$559				$559	2.8			2.8
1955	816				816	2.9			2.9
1956	797				797	3.0			3.0
1957	781				781	3.1			3.1
1958	699				699	3.5			3.5
1959	592				592	2.2			2.2
1960	462				462	2.0			2.0
1961	382				382	1.7			1.7
1962	927	$421			1,348	3.4	1.6		5.0
1963	840	573			1,413	2.9	1.9		4.8
1964	955	680	$663	—$37	2,261	2.9	2.0	2.0	
1965	1,194	819	1,593	—92	3,514	3.0	2.1	4.0	
1966[i]	1,011	731	1,315	—78	2,979	3.1	2.2	4.0	
B. Interaction effects distributed in proportion to separate effects									
1964	933	680	648		2,261	2.8	2.0	2.0	6.8
1965	1,155	819	1,540		3,514	2.9	2.1	3.9	8.9
1966[i]	977	731	1,271		2,979	3.0	2.2	3.9	9.1

Note: $u^B = 0.52$.
a $u^B(D–D^B)$.
b CDT.
c $(u^B–u)(R–D^B)$.
d $-(u^B–u)(D–D^B)$.
e $u^B(D–D^B)/(R–D^B)$.
f $CDT/(R–D^B)$.
g $u^B–u$.
h Total rate reductions include interaction effects in 1964–66 and therefore are given only in Part B.
i First three quarters.

income (see Table 4-2) into the calculated tax savings. To illustrate the interpretation of these figures, accelerated depreciation reduced tax liabilities by $699 million in 1958; firms would have enjoyed the same reduction of tax liabilities without accelerated depreciation if they had been given a reduction of 3.5 percentage points in the tax rate. Part B of Table 4-1 is

TABLE 4-2. Reported and Consistent Before-Tax Income, All Corporate Manufacturing, 1954–66

(Millions of dollars)

Year	Reported before-tax income $(R-D)$	Consistent before-tax income $(R-D^B)$
1954	18,703	19,778
1955	26,310	27,879
1956	25,164	26,697
1957	23,848	25,350
1958	18,481	19,825
1959	25,713	26,851
1960	22,743	23,632
1961	22,061	22,796
1962	25,161[a]	26,944
1963	27,846[a]	29,462
1964	31,362[a]	33,199
1965	37,568[a]	39,865
1966[b]	30,965[a]	32,910

Source: July issues of *Survey of Current Business*, 1954–61, Table 56; for 1962–66, Table 6.13.

[a] Estimates of before-tax income consistent with the definition on which 1954–61 data are based. Beginning in 1962, profits before taxes in the national income accounts include (a) oil well drilling costs in excess of depreciation on oil wells, (b) oil well bonus payments written off, (c) income of mutual financial intermediaries, and (d) bad debt adjustment, and exclude (e) costs of trading and issuing corporate securities. Item (c) does not affect the data for manufacturing. The remaining items raised profits before taxes for all industries about 5 percent above what they would have been in 1962–63. Hence the estimates given here for manufacturing are 95 percent of the reported figures.

[b] First three quarters. See App. 4-A.

derived from Part A by distributing the interaction effects in the manner described above. The combined figure shown in the fourth column is the total reduction of tax liabilities resulting from the three tax incentives. When this total is converted into an equivalent tax rate change, it may be seen that in 1965, for example, the entire bundle of tax incentives was equivalent to a reduction of 8.9 percentage points in the tax rate. Accelerated depreciation and the tax credit accounted for about 5.0 percentage points of that reduction, indicating the extent to which these policies have served to erode the corporate income tax.

Quarterly estimates of cash flow and of cash flow corrected for tax incentives were derived from these annual estimates by methods described in Appendix 4-A.

User Cost

Quarterly estimates of the user cost of capital for manufacturing were calculated according to the formulas derived in pages 139–43. In the absence of a tax credit, the basic relation is

$$c_{j_t} = q_t(r_t + \delta)(1 - u_t z_{j_t})/(1 - u_t), \qquad (4.18.1)$$

where

c_{j_t} = user cost (rental price) using the jth depreciation method

q_t = price of capital goods

r_t = interest rate

δ = replacement rate

u_t = tax rate

z_{j_t} = discounted value of future depreciation charges stemming from a dollar of current investment depreciated according to the jth depreciation method.

The implicit price deflator for nonresidential fixed investment employed in the gross national product accounts[22] was used as an estimate of q. The series was rebased to 1954. Jorgenson's method of estimating the replacement rate was adopted here.[23] He assumed that replacement during period t is a fixed proportion of net capital stock at the beginning of period t. Using estimates of real net capital stocks at the beginning of 1948 and 1960 from the OBE Capital Goods Study, he found the replacement rate that, when applied to real quarterly investment expenditures (seasonally adjusted) and the 1948 capital stock estimate, would yield the 1960 capital stock estimate. The value of the replacement rate obtained was 0.0271 per quarter, which implies that a unit of capital loses about 85 percent of its real value in eighteen years. The general (statutory) corporate income tax rate was used as an estimate of u.

Choosing an appropriate measure of the interest rate raises many difficult problems. The issues involved in defining and measuring the cost of funds to firms have been most thoroughly discussed by Merton Miller and Franco Modigliani.[24] They have shown that, with a proportional tax on business income that permits interest payments to be deducted, the cost of funds can be considered an average of the costs of debt and equity, weighted by the proportions of the two in the firm's desired capital structure. The cost of equity is the market's capitalization rate for streams of unlevered

[22] *Survey of Current Business*, Vol. 45 (August 1965), pp. 52–53.

[23] Jorgenson, "Capital Theory and Investment Behavior."

[24] Merton H. Miller and Franco Modigliani, "Some Estimates of the Cost of Capital to the Electric Utility Industry, 1954–57," *American Economic Review*, Vol. 56 (June 1966), pp. 333–91.

equity earnings of firms in a given risk class and the cost of debt is the product of 1 minus the tax rate and the cost of equity. Determination of the capitalization rate from data on a firm's recent earnings and on the market value of its debt and equity would be relatively easy if the market did not take potential growth into account in evaluating securities. The importance of growth in market valuations enormously complicates estimation of the capitalization rate. Miller and Modigliani have estimated the capitalization rate for the electric utility industry for 1954, 1956, and 1957 (a relatively easy case because growth has been rather steady and predictable). The implied estimates of the cost of funds (using average proportions of debt and equity in the capital structure of firms in the industry) are, respectively, 3.6 percent, 4.5 percent, and 4.6 percent in those years.

The authors compare these estimates, which are the best available, with two commonly used measures of the cost of funds—the yield on Aaa bonds and a weighted average of the bond yield and the yields on equities. They find that the Aaa bond yield is far superior to the weighted average yield in predicting both the level of, and the magnitude of changes in, the cost of funds. Whether this is true in the manufacturing sector is unknown, since research in this important area is just beginning. Nevertheless, I have decided to adopt Moody's industrial bond yield as an estimate of r. The original monthly series was averaged for each quarter, and the averages were divided by four to obtain estimates of quarterly interest rates. To check the sensitivity of the results of this study to the specification of the interest rate, all computations were also run using two arbitrary alternative estimates of the rate—double Moody's industrial bond yield and a constant 10 percent per year. Appendix B presents investment relations and estimates of investment attributable to tax incentives for these alternative specifications. In general, the results are not very sensitive to the choice of the rate.

Estimates of the discounted value of depreciation charges were computed for the following five depreciation methods:

1. Straight-line, assumed tax life of seventy-two quarters (eighteen years);

2. Double-declining-balance, assumed tax life of seventy-two quarters, with a switch to straight-line in the thirty-seventh quarter;

3. Sum-of-the-years-digits, assumed tax life of seventy-two quarters;

4. Double-declining-balance, assumed tax life of sixty quarters (fifteen years), with a switch to straight-line in the thirty-first quarter;

5. Sum-of-the-years-digits, assumed tax life of sixty quarters.

The first three variants relate to pre-1962 guideline lives, while the last two reflect the reduction in lives brought about by the new depreciation guidelines. Both of the declining-balance variants allow for a switch to the straight-line method midway through the asset's life, the point at which the discounted value of declining-balance depreciation charges is maximized.

TABLE 4-3. Discounted Value of Depreciation Charges Stemming from One Dollar of Current Investment, by Depreciation Method and Selected Tax Lives, 1947-66

(Dollars)

| | Tax life of 18 years | | | Tax life of 15 years | | |
| | | | | | | Interest |
Year	Straight line	Declining balance	Sum-of- the years- digits	Declining balance	Sum-of-the- years- digits	rate (percent)
1947	0.792					2.67
1948	0.779					2.87
1949	0.787					2.74
1950	0.792					2.67
1951	0.778					2.89
1952	0.770					3.00
1953	0.752					3.30
1954	0.765	0.807	0.835			3.09
1955	0.759	0.802	0.830			3.19
1956	0.740	0.786	0.816			3.50
1957	0.704	0.755	0.789			4.12
1958	0.712	0.762	0.794			3.98
1959	0.681	0.736	0.771			4.53
1960	0.678	0.733	0.769			4.59
1961	0.681	0.736	0.771			4.54
1962[a]	0.683	0.738	0.773			4.50
1962[b]	0.686	0.740	0.775	0.775	0.805	4.44
1963	0.687	0.741	0.776	0.776	0.806	4.42
1964	0.682	0.737	0.772	0.772	0.803	4.52
1965	0.677	0.733	0.768	0.768	0.799	4.61
1966[c]	0.647	0.707	0.745	0.745	0.778	5.20

Source: Equation (4.19), except last column, for which the source is Moody's Investors Service, *Moody's Industrial Manual* (1967).

[a] First two quarters.

[b] Last two quarters.

[c] First three quarters.

Since the estimates are on a quarterly basis, there is no reasonable way of allowing for the convention of taking half a year's depreciation in the year of acquisition, but this should make little difference in the results.

Annual averages of the quarterly values for each of the five variants, computed according to (4.19), are presented in Table 4-3, along with the average interest rate (Moody's industrial bond yield) for the year.[25] The sum-of-the-years-digits variants are seen always to yield higher discounted values than the declining-balance variants; hence, the sum-of-the-years-digits method is the most advantageous from the firm's viewpoint. Also, the increase in the value of depreciation resulting from acceleration varies considerably with changes in the interest rate. For example, the discounted value produced by the sum-of-the-years-digits method exceeded the straight-line discounted value by about 9 percent in 1954 when the interest rate was about 3 percent; however, the rise in the interest rate to about 4.6 percent in 1960, decreasing the value of depreciation, increased the excess produced by sum-of-the-years-digits over straight-line to approximately 13.4 percent. This simply reflects the fact that changes in the rate of interest bring about relatively smaller changes in the discounted value of accelerated depreciation than in the discounted value of straight-line depreciation. Thus the impact of interest rate changes on investment is reduced by accelerated depreciation, since the user cost of capital is less sensitive to interest rate changes when an accelerated depreciation method is used. It is also interesting to note that rising interest rates quickly rob firms of the benefits conferred by accelerated depreciation. For example, the declining-balance figures indicate that by 1957 firms would have been better off if accelerated depreciation had not been granted but interest rates had been maintained at their 1954 levels.

User Cost Estimates

Annual totals of three measures of user cost are presented in Table 4-4. The consistent straight-line variant gives an estimate of what user cost would have been had no tax incentives been enacted during the period—that is to say, it is based on the straight-line depreciation formula; the tax life is constant at eighteen years and the tax rate at 52 percent; there is no allowance for the tax credit. The two remaining variants—the actual user cost measures—incorporate all tax incentives enacted during the period: to be precise, (a) accelerated depreciation, beginning with the first quarter

[25] It is merely a coincidence that the discounted value for an eighteen-year life and sum-of-the-years-digits depreciation is the same as that for a fifteen-year life and declining-balance depreciation.

TABLE 4-4. Consistent Straight-Line and Actual User Costs, and Equivalent Tax Rate Reductions, 1947-66

| | User cost (discounted dollars per $100 of investment, 1954 prices) | | | Equivalent tax rate reduction (percentage points) | |
| | | Actual | | | |
Year	Consistent straight line	Declining balance	Sum-of-the years-digits	Declining balance	Sum-of-the-years-digits
1947	11.60	11.60	11.60		
1948	12.98	12.98	12.98		
1949	13.17	13.17	13.17		
1950	13.62	13.62	13.62		
1951	16.01	16.01	16.01		
1952	16.83	16.83	16.83		
1953	17.76	17.76	17.76		
1954	17.47	16.84	16.42	4.9	8.8
1955	18.08	17.42	16.98	4.9	8.7
1956	20.04	19.26	18.75	4.9	8.6
1957	22.81	21.85	21.23	4.7	8.4
1958	22.94	21.99	21.38	4.8	8.3
1959	24.93	23.83	23.12	4.7	8.3
1960	25.24	24.12	23.40	4.7	8.3
1961	25.23	24.11	23.40	4.7	8.3
1962[a]	25.28	24.16	23.45	4.8	8.3
1962[b]	25.16	22.67	22.06	12.2	16.2
1963	25.22	22.54	21.94	13.4	17.5
1964	25.80	22.14	21.55	19.4	24.1
1965	26.40	22.35	21.79	21.4	25.9
1966[c]	28.64	24.12	23.48	20.2	24.5

[a] Average of first two quarters expressed at annual rates.
[b] Average of last two quarters expressed at annual rates.
[c] Average of first three quarters expressed at annual rates.

of 1954; (b) the reduction in useful lives, beginning with the third quarter of 1962; (c) the tax credit, beginning with the third quarter of 1962, with the provision, embodied in the Long amendment, that the amount of the credit be deducted from the depreciable basis of the acquisitions; (d) the tax rate reduction of 1964 and the repeal of the Long amendment to the tax credit, thus permitting the credit to be taken without reducing the depreciable basis of the acquisitions, beginning with the first quarter of 1964; and (e) the tax rate reduction of 1965 (as specified in the Revenue Act of 1964), beginning with the first quarter of 1965. These two variants differ in that one is based on the double-declining-balance depreciation method, and the other on the sum-of-the-years-digits method. The fraction of the value of acquisitions permitted as a credit (k in the notation of pages 139–43) was taken to be 0.029 for 1962, which was the ratio of the credit in corporate manufacturing in 1962 to manufacturing investment in 1962, and 0.037 for 1963–66, which was the ratio of the credit in 1963 to investment in 1963 (the last year for which information on the credit was available).

The last two columns of Table 4-4 present estimates of tax rate reductions that would have yielded the reductions in user cost that actually occurred. They are found by solving, for $\tilde{u}$,

$$q(r+\delta)(1-\tilde{u}z^{\mathrm{B}})/(1-\tilde{u}) = c, \tag{4.44}$$

where c is actual user cost and z^{B} is the discounted value of straight-line depreciation for a tax life of eighteen years (column 1 of Table 4-3). The equivalent tax rate reduction is $0.52-\tilde{u}$. The results are striking. In 1965, for example, with the sum-of-the-years-digits variant, a drop of 25.9 percentage points in the tax rate (from 52 to 26.1 percent) would have been required to bring about a reduction in user cost as large as that produced by the entire bundle of tax incentives! It is also interesting to examine the 1962–66 period more closely to assess the relative importance of tax incentives in reducing user cost. Precise calculations would be tedious and difficult because of the many interaction effects. Rough calculations show that the new guidelines accounted for about 63 percent of the reductions in 1962 and 1963, with the remaining 37 percent attributable to the tax credit. As a result of the 1964 tax rate reduction, the increase in the tax rate reductions should have been about 2 percentage points in 1964, but the actual increases were of the order of 6 to 7 percentage points, which indicates the substantial impact of the 1964 change in the tax credit provision.

The Investment Function

Three alternative specifications of the investment function were suggested earlier. They are:

$$I_t = b(K_t^* - K_{t-1}) + \delta K_{t-1}, \tag{4.32}$$

$$I_t = \left[b_0 + b_1 \frac{F_{t-1} - \delta K_{t-1}}{K_t^* - K_{t-1}} \right] (K_t^* - K_{t-1}) + \delta K_{t-1}, \tag{4.36}$$

and

$$I_t = \left[b_0 + b_1 \frac{F_{t-1}}{K_t^* - (1-\delta)K_{t-1}}\right][K_t^* - (1-\delta)K_{t-1}], \qquad (4.38)$$

where

$K^* = $ the desired capital stock
$K = $ the actual capital stock
$F = $ cash flow
$\delta = $ replacement rate.

The actual capital stock variable can be eliminated from each of these relations by noting that capital stock is by definition equal to the sum of past net investments, that is,

$$K_t = \sum_{i=0}^{\infty}(1-\delta)^i I_{t-i}. \qquad (4.45)$$

For example, (4.32) can be written as

$$I_t = bK_t^* + (\delta - b)\sum_{i=0}^{\infty}(1-\delta)^i I_{t-1-i}. \qquad (4.46)$$

If $(1-\delta)I_{t-1}$ is subtracted from both sides of (4.46), then

$$I_t - (1-\delta)I_{t-1} = bK_t^* - b(1-\delta)K_{t-1}^* + (\delta - b)I_{t-1}, \qquad (4.47)$$

$$I_t = b(K_t^* - K_{t-1}^*) + b\delta K_{t-1}^* + (1-b)I_{t-1}. \qquad (4.48)$$

This result indicates that a distributed lag model explaining *gross* investment must include not only changes in the variables determining the desired capital stock but also the absolute levels of those variables.

It should also be noted that the parameters of (4.48) will be overidentified if the desired stock is a function of more than one variable. The overidentification problem can be avoided if the replacement rate is known, since (4.48) can then be written as[26]

$$I_t = b[K_t^* - (1-\delta)K_{t-1}^*] + (1-b)I_{t-1}. \qquad (4.49)$$

This transformation of (4.32) is the one that is used here, with δ assumed

---

[26] This can be seen more easily if (4.49) is rewritten as

$$I_t - I_{t-1} = b[K_t^* - (1-\delta)K_{t-1}^* - I_{t-1}].$$

to be equal to 0.0271. The corresponding transformations of (4.36) and (4.38) are[27]

$$I_t = b_0[K_t^* - (1-\delta)K_{t-1}^*] + (1 - b_1\delta - b_0)I_{t-1} \qquad (4.50)$$
$$+ b_1[F_{t-1} - (1-\delta)F_{t-2}],$$

and

$$I_t = b_0[K_t^* - (1-\delta)K_{t-1}^*] + (1 - b_1)(1-\delta)I_{t-1} \qquad (4.51)$$
$$+ b_1[F_{t-1} - (1-\delta)F_{t-2}].$$

Expectation Lags

In deducing the determinants of a firm's optimum capital stock, it was assumed that the firm knew with certainty the values of future prices of inputs and outputs. As an alternative interpretation, the firm might expect current prices to persist into the indefinite future and act accordingly. In reality, the future is seldom certain and expectations are not likely to be formed in such a simple way. These considerations must be taken into account in specifying the determinants of the desired stock when the model is applied to actual data.

According to the theory developed in the second section of this chapter, the desired stock is determined by two variables—sales, which capture acceleration influences, and the user cost of capital divided by the wage rate. The current values of these variables as viewed by firms are likely to contain both transitory and permanent components. It is assumed that the firm bases its decisions on the permanent components only, and that the permanent component of each variable can be approximated by a weighted average of current and past values of the variable. Three plausible, though hardly exhaustive, choices of weights were tested. If n (always chosen as an even number) is the number of quarters of data to be averaged, then the weights can be described as follows:

    1. The rectangular, or uniform, distribution. Each quarter receives equal weight, namely, $1/n$.

    2. The inverted-V distribution. The weights are proportional to $1, 2, 3, \ldots, n/2, n/2, n/2$ minus $1, \ldots, 3, 2, 1$. The proportionality factor that makes the weights sum to unity is $4/(n^2 + 2n)$.

[27] If nonautocorrelated disturbances were added to (4.32), (4.36), and (4.38), the transformed relations presented here would contain autocorrelated disturbances. I have assumed that the disturbances to be added to (4.49), (4.50), and (4.51) are not autocorrelated, which implies that (4.32), (4.36), and (4.38) contain autocorrelated disturbances.

3. The arithmetic distribution. The weights are proportional to $n, n-1, n-2, \ldots, 1$. The proportionality factor that makes the weights sum to unity is $2/n(1+n)$.

Various values of n were selected and tested for each of the three sets of weights, and the results were assessed on the basis of the signs obtained for each variable, the significance of the variables, and the overall ability of the estimated relations to explain actual expenditures.

The Relations To Be Estimated

Before the two preceding sections are pieced together, some special consideration must be given to the acceleration variable that is to enter the investment relations. It has been argued here that sales would be a more appropriate acceleration variable than output, capturing more accurately the current state of demand in the output market and hence providing a better indication of capital requirements. If the delay between the receipt of orders for the firm's output and final delivery (sales) were short relative to the period of analysis, sales would certainly be the relevant variable. But this study employs quarterly data for aggregate manufacturing, and it would be unwise to ignore this delay. Current sales are likely merely to reflect past new orders, and the current state of demand may be better indicated by current new orders. For this reason, the acceleration variable finally adopted is new orders rather than sales. Results obtained in investment studies by Reynold Sachs and Albert Hart and by Otto Eckstein suggest that orders do play an important role in determining capital expenditures.[28]

New orders during period t will be denoted as O_t and the ratio of user cost to the wage rate by $(c/w)_t$. The K^* function (see equation (4.23) above) is assumed to be linear:

$$K_t^* = d_0 + \sum_{i=0}^{n-1} \gamma_{t-i}[d_1 X_{t-i} + d_2(c/w)_{t-i}], \qquad (4.52)$$

where the γ's are the weights given by the expectations lag distribution.

[28] Reynold Sachs and Albert G. Hart, "Anticipations and Investment Behavior: An Econometric Study of Quarterly Time Series for Large Firms in Durable-Goods Manufacturing," in Robert Ferber (ed.), *Determinants of Investment Behavior*, A Conference of the Universities-National Bureau Committee for Economic Research (Columbia University Press for the National Bureau of Economic Research, 1967); and Otto Eckstein, "Manufacturing Investment and Business Expectations: Extensions of de Leeuw's Results," *Econometrica*, Vol. 33 (April 1965), pp. 420–24.

Thus,

$$K_t^* - (1-\delta)K_{t-1}^* = \delta d_0 + \sum_{i=0}^{n-1} \gamma_{t-i}\{d_1[O_{t-i}-(1-\delta)O_{t-1-i}]$$

$$+ d_2[(c/w)_{t-i}-(1-\delta)(c/w)_{t-1-i}]\}. \tag{4.53}$$

If

$$\mu(S)O_t = \sum_{i=0}^{n-1} \gamma_{t-i}[O_{t-i}-(1-\delta)O_{t-1-i}]$$

and

$$\mu(S)(c/w)_t = \sum_{i=0}^{n-1} \gamma_{t-i}[(c/w)_{t-i}-(1-\delta)(c/w)_{t-1-i}],$$

then

$$K_t^* - (1-\delta)K_{t-1}^* = \delta d_0 + d_1\mu(S)O_t + d_2\mu(S)(c/w)_t. \tag{4.54}$$

If (4.54) is substituted in (4.49), (4.50), and (4.51) the basic investment relations are

$$I_t = b\delta d_0 + bd_1\mu(S)O_t + bd_2\mu(S)(c/w)_t + (1-b)I_{t-1}, \tag{4.55}$$

$$I_t = b_0\delta d_0 + b_0 d_1\mu(S)O_t + b_0 d_2\mu(S)(c/w)_t + (1-b_1\delta-b_0)I_{t-1}$$

$$+ b_1[F_{t-1}-(1-\delta)F_{t-2}], \tag{4.56}$$

$$I_t = b_0\delta d_0 + b_0 d_1\mu(S)O_t + b_0 d_2\mu(S)(c/w)_t + (1-b_0)(1-\delta)I_{t-1}$$

$$+ b_1[F_{t-1}-(1-\delta)F_{t-2}]. \tag{4.57}$$

Equation Estimates

Complete descriptions of sources of data estimates and methods are presented in Appendix 4-A. Where appropriate, all data were seasonally adjusted and expressed at quarterly rates. Investment, new orders, and cash flow are measured in billions of 1954 dollars. The replacement rate was assigned a value of 0.0271. All relations were fitted by the direct least squares method.

Preliminary investigations revealed several things. First, the rectangular and arithmetic expectations lag distributions consistently gave the wrong sign for the coefficient of the user cost variable. Second, the inverted-V distribution gave the wrong sign on the user cost variable for values of n less than eight quarters. Third, a twelve-quarter inverted-V expectations lag on the orders variable seemed to work best. A shorter lag gave a slightly higher $\bar{R}^2$ (coefficient of multiple determination corrected for lost degrees of freedom), but it also gave a negative constant term, which led to absurd results for the constant term in the function describing the desired stock.

In view of these findings, estimates of the relations involving the inverted-V distribution for eight, ten, and twelve quarters on user cost and for twelve quarters on new orders are the only ones reported. For notational convenience, the change in user cost, divided by the wage rate, with an eight-quarter inverted-V expectations lag is denoted as $\mu(8)(c/w)$; the other variables are similarly designated.

The estimates are summarized in Tables 4-5 and 4-6. The first three relations in each table contain the declining-balance variant of user cost, and the last three relations contain the sum-of-the-years-digits variant. Both variants were tested, since the variable is a somewhat artificial construct to begin with and it did not seem reasonable to rule out one variant a priori, even though the declining-balance method is the more widely used.

TABLE 4-5. Investment Regressions: Constant Adjustment Speed Model, by Depreciation Method and Length of Lag Distribution

$$I_t - I_{t-1} = a_0 + a_1\mu(12)O_t + a_2\mu(S)(c/w)_t + a_3 I_{t-1}$$

Param-eter or statistic	Declining-balance user cost			Sum-of-the-years-digits user cost			Mean of variable
	8 quarters	10 quarters	12 quarters	8 quarters	10 quarters	12 quarters	
a_0	0.1305	0.1898	0.2529	0.1271	0.1817	0.2398	0.0515[a]
	(1.659)	(2.367)	(2.889)	(1.633)	(2.304)	(2.807)	
a_1	0.1254	0.1140	0.1014	0.1282	0.1174	0.1048	2.843
	(6.103)	(5.662)	(4.901)	(6.250)	(5.882)	(5.134)	
a_2	—1.702	—2.520	—3.122	—1.695	—2.476	—3.036	0.0481[b]
	(—2.538)	(—3.457)	(—3.752)	(—2.565)	(—3.468)	(—3.740)	0.0465[b]
a_3	—0.1155	—0.1116	—0.1108	—0.1180	—0.1141	—0.1126	3.066
	(—3.604)	(—3.615)	(—3.640)	(—3.681)	(—3.699)	(—3.700)	
$\bar{R}^2$							
$\quad I_t - I_{t-1}$	0.401	0.445	0.460	0.402	0.446	0.460	
$\quad I_t$	0.972	0.974	0.975	0.972	0.974	0.975	
S_e	0.1171	0.1127	0.1111	0.1170	0.1126	0.1112	
DW	1.250	1.334	1.342	1.253	1.336	1.340	

Note: Fitted to 67 observations, first quarter 1950 through third quarter 1966. Numbers in parentheses are t-statistics.

$\qquad\qquad$ $t > 2.58$. Significant at the 0.01 probability level.
$\qquad\qquad$ $t > 1.96$. Significant at the 0.05 probability level.
[a] Mean of the dependent variable.
[b] Means of $\mu(12)(c/w)$ for declining-balance and sum-of-the-years-digits user cost, respectively. Means for shorter lags differ by only two points in the last decimal place.

TABLE 4-6. Investment Regressions: Variable Adjustment Speed Model, by Depreciation Method and Length of Lag Distribution

$$I_t - I_{t-1} = a_0 + a_1\mu(12)O_t + a_2\mu(S)(c/w)_t + a_3 I_{t-1} + a_4[F_{t-1} - (1-\delta)F_{t-2}]$$

Param-eter or statistic	Declining-balance user cost			Sum-of-the-years-digits user cost			Mean of variable
	8 quarters	10 quarters	12 quarters	8 quarters	10 quarters	12 quarters	
a_0	0.0166	0.0683	0.1125	0.0191	0.0673	0.1087	0.0515[a]
	(0.226)	(0.871)	(1.295)	(0.263)	(0.880)	(1.297)	
a_1	0.1346	0.1286	0.1211	0.1349	0.1298	0.1225	2.843
	(7.413)	(6.956)	(6.258)	(7.465)	(7.129)	(6.470)	
a_2	—0.2533	—1.020	—1.517	—0.3033	—1.039	—1.514	0.0481[b]
	(—0.376)	(—1.348)	(—1.770)	(—0.460)	(—1.413)	(—1.830)	0.0465[b]
a_3	—0.1225	—0.1204	—0.1196	—0.1229	—0.1214	—0.1205	3.066
	(—4.346)	(—4.324)	(—4.336)	(—4.362)	(—4.371)	(—4.381)	
a_4	0.2108	0.1877	0.1802	0.2091	0.1871	0.1804	0.1829
	(4.447)	(3.976)	(3.901)	(4.439)	(3.994)	(3.946)	
$\bar{R}^2$							
$I_t - I_{t-1}$	0.539	0.551	0.560	0.539	0.552	0.561	
I_t	0.978	0.979	0.980	0.979	0.979	0.980	
S_e	0.1028	0.1014	0.1004	0.1027	0.1013	0.1002	
DW	1.620	1.599	1.599	1.616	1.602	1.603	

Note: Fitted to 67 observations, first quarter 1950 through third quarter 1966. Numbers in parentheses are t-statistics.

$t > 2.58$. Significant at the 0.01 probability level.
$t > 1.65$. Significant at the 0.10 probability level.

[a] Mean of the dependent variable.
[b] Means of $\mu(12)(c/w)$ for declining-balance and sum-of-the-years-digits user cost, respectively. Means for shorter lags differ by only two points in the last decimal place.

Two $\bar{R}^2$'s are presented for each equation. The first indicates the ability of the relation to explain changes in investment, that is, it is the $\bar{R}^2$ obtained when the dependent variable is $I_t - I_{t-1}$. The second indicates the ability of the relation to explain the level of investment, that is, it is the $\bar{R}^2$ obtained when the dependent variable is I_t. The regression coefficients are the same in either case, except for the coefficient of I_{t-1}, which would be 1 plus its value in the table when I_t is the dependent variable.

Investment shows a very high first-order autocorrelation, and the $\bar{R}^2$ obtained by regressing I_t on I_{t-1} and anything else is bound to be quite high.

The first measure is a better indicator of the ability of the relation to explain investment because it does not include the explained variance due to first-order autocorrelation. Inspection of the tables reveals that each of the equations explains about 98 percent of the variance of investment and that there is little to choose among them on this basis. However, the $\bar{R}^2$'s measured in terms of $I_t - I_{t-1}$ vary considerably and are quite useful in evaluating the relations.

The estimated relations for the constant adjustment speed model (4.55) are shown in Table 4-5. The user cost (or factor-price ratio) variable performs well in each case. The longer expectations lags on c/w yield higher values of $\bar{R}^2$, and this seems contrary to what might be expected. One would think that the expectations lag applying to user cost would be shorter than that for new orders, because there is probably a larger amount of transitory variance in the latter. However, it is unrealistic to assume that a sharp distinction can be drawn between adjustment lags and expectations lags. The better fit with the longer expectations lag on user cost may well be the result of a misspecification of the adjustment lag distribution.[29] Furthermore, beginning in 1954 the user cost variable incorporates the full impact of accelerated depreciation when, in fact, firms were quite slow to adopt the new write-off methods.[30] Thus, the long lag may simply reflect delay by management in recognizing the reduction in user cost brought about by accelerated depreciation. As businessmen become more aware of the advantages of rapid write-offs, one would expect to find an improvement in the performance of the shorter lags.

The new orders variable is consistently significant, but its coefficient is reduced slightly as the lag on user cost is lengthened. The coefficient of I_{t-1} is an estimate of the negative of the adjustment speed b. The estimates of the adjustment speed are all about the same and indicate that 11 percent of the gap between desired and actual stocks is eliminated each quarter. This seems rather low, particularly since substantial expectations lags have already been imposed on the variables determining optimum stock. Actually, there is a serious collinearity problem (the only one in these data) between

[29] From the viewpoint of economic policy, it is important to distinguish between the two types of lags. If government convinced businessmen that all necessary steps would be taken to assure economic stability, the expectations lag might be markedly changed, while the adjustment lag would be unaltered.

[30] On this point, see the evidence in Norman B. Ture, *Accelerated Depreciation in the United States, 1954–60* (Columbia University Press for the National Bureau of Economic Research, 1967). His study came to my attention after this work was completed.

the change in orders with a twelve-quarter inverted-V lag and lagged investment, so that the distribution of weight between these two variables may be greatly affected by just a few observations. For example, when these relations were first estimated with observations for the period from the first quarter of 1950 through the fourth quarter of 1963, the adjustment speed was estimated to be about 0.25 and the coefficient of the orders variable was somewhat larger. The presence of collinearity makes it difficult in this instance to sort out the adjustment speed and the importance of new orders.

Finally, it should be noted that the two variants of user cost give very similar results.

Table 4-6 presents estimates of the transformed variable adjustment speed models (4.56) and (4.57). Both models lead to the same regression equation, the difference lying in the structural interpretation of the coefficient of I_{t-1}. Inclusion of the change in cash flow substantially raises the $\bar{R}^2$ in every case, and the variable itself performs very well.[31] But the improvement obtained is at the expense of the user cost variable, the coefficient of which is reduced by more than 50 percent in most cases.

Structural Parameters

In addition to examining the signs and significance of the coefficients and the closeness of fit, one can evaluate the relations by inspecting the structural parameters estimated from them. Tables 4-7, 4-8, and 4-9 present the estimated structural parameters and give the functional relations between the structural parameters and the parameters of the transformed relations. An effort has been made to convert the slope-coefficients of the demand for capital into elasticities. The means of the variables O and c/w in the tables are sample means of "permanent" new orders and "permanent" user cost divided by the wage rate, that is, they are means of weighted averages of the variables, the weights being given by the appropriate expectations lag distribution. With these means, the average level of the desired stock over the period can be estimated; these estimates are also shown in the tables. The elasticities of optimum stock are then evaluated at the mean values of the variables. (The two variable adjustment speed models must, by necessity, yield the same elasticity estimates.)

With constant returns to scale, one would expect the elasticity of the demand for capital with respect to new orders to be unity. The values range

[31] There is no problem of collinearity between the change in cash flow, as defined here, and any other variable in the analysis.

TABLE 4-7. Structural Parameters of the Constant Adjustment Speed Model, by Depreciation Method and Length of Lag Distribution

$$I_t = b(K_t^* - K_{t-1}) + \delta K_{t-1}$$
$$K_t^* = d_0 + d_1 O_t + d_2(c/w)_t$$

Parameter or statistic	Declining-balance user cost			Sum-of-the-years-digits user cost		
	8 quarters	10 quarters	12 quarters	8 quarters	10 quarters	12 quarters
$b = -a_3$	0.1155	0.1116	0.1108	0.1180	0.1141	0.1126
$d_0 = a_0/(\delta b)$	41.69	62.76	84.22	39.75	58.76	78.59
$d_1 = a_1/b$	1.086	1.022	0.915	1.086	1.029	0.931
$d_2 = a_2/b$	—14.74	—22.58	—28.18	—14.36	—21.70	—26.96
Mean O	77.71	77.71	77.71	77.71	77.71	77.71
Mean c/w	2.130	2.075	2.021	2.092	2.038	1.985
Mean K^*	94.69	95.33	98.37	94.10	94.50	97.42
Elasticity K^*: O	0.891	0.833	0.723	0.897	0.846	0.743
Elasticity K^*: c/w	—0.332	—0.491	—0.579	—0.319	—0.468	—0.549

TABLE 4-8. Structural Parameters of the Variable Adjustment Speed Net Investment Funds Model, by Depreciation Method and Length of Lag Distribution

$$I_t = \left[b_0 + b_1 \frac{F_{t-1} - \delta K_{t-1}}{K_t^* - K_{t-1}} \right] (K_t^* - K_{t-1}) + \delta K_{t-1}$$
$$K_t^* = d_0 + d_1 O_t + d_2(c/w)_t$$

Parameter or statistic	Declining-balance user cost			Sum-of-the-years-digits user cost		
	8 quarters	10 quarters	12 quarters	8 quarters	10 quarters	12 quarters
$b_1 = -a_3 - \delta a_4$	0.1168	0.1153	0.1147	0.1172	0.1163	0.1156
$b_1 = a_4$	0.2108	0.1877	0.1802	0.2091	0.1871	0.1804
$d_0 = a_0/(\delta b_0)$	5.24	21.86	36.19	6.01	21.35	34.70
$d_1 = a_1/b_0$	1.152	1.115	1.056	1.151	1.116	1.060
$d_2 = a_2/b_0$	—2.17	—8.85	—13.23	—2.59	—8.93	—13.10
Mean O	77.71	77.71	77.71	77.71	77.71	77.71
Mean c/w	2.130	2.075	2.021	2.092	2.038	1.985
Mean K^*	90.14	90.14	91.51	90.04	89.88	91.07
Elasticity K^* : O	0.993	0.961	0.897	0.993	0.965	0.904
Elasticity K^* : c/w	—0.051	—0.204	—0.292	—0.060	—0.202	—0.286

TABLE 4-9. Structural Parameters of the Variable Adjustment Speed Gross Investment Funds Model, by Depreciation Method and Length of Lag Distribution

$$I_t = \left[b_0 + b_1 \frac{F_{t-1}}{K_t^* - (1-\delta)K_{t-1}} \right] [K_t^* - (1-\delta)K_{t-1}]$$

$$K_t^* = d_0 + d_1 O_t + d_2(c/w)_t$$

Parameter or statistic	Declining-balance user cost			Sum-of-the-years-digits user cost		
	8 quarters	10 quarters	12 quarters	8 quarters	10 quarters	12 quarters
$b_0 = (a_3+\delta)/(\delta-1)$	0.0981	0.0959	0.0951	0.0985	0.0969	0.0960
$b_1 = a_4$	0.2108	0.1877	0.1802	0.2091	0.1871	0.1804
$d_0 = a_0/(\delta b_0)$	6.24	26.28	43.65	7.16	25.63	41.78
$d_1 = a_1/b_0$	1.372	1.341	1.273	1.370	1.340	1.276
$d_2 = a_2/b_0$	—2.58	—10.64	—15.95	—3.08	—10.72	—15.77
Mean O	77.71	77.71	77.71	77.71	77.71	77.71
Mean c/w	2.130	2.075	2.021	2.092	2.038	1.985
Mean K^*	107.36	108.41	110.34	107.18	107.91	109.63
Elasticity $K^* : O$	0.993	0.961	0.897	0.993	0.965	0.904
Elasticity $K^* : c/w$	—0.051	—0.204	—0.292	—0.060	—0.202	—0.286

from 0.72 to 0.99, with the higher elasticities obtained for the variable adjustment speed models. (The estimates at the low end of the range would indicate marked increasing returns to scale.) The estimated elasticities of the demand for capital with respect to relative factor prices vary over a fairly wide range—from -0.05 to -0.58. The higher elasticities (in terms of absolute value) occur in the case of the constant adjustment speed model.

It has already been noted that the constant adjustment speed model yields an estimated adjustment rate of about 11 percent per quarter. Tables 4-8 and 4-9 give estimated values of b_0 and b_1 in the variable adjustment speed models. For example, according to the structural parameters of the relation in Table 4-8, if cash flow available for expansion is quite small relative to the gap between desired and actual stocks of capital, then only about 12 percent of the gap will be closed during the quarter; but if cash flow available for expansion is about equal to the gap, then 30 to 33 percent of the gap will be closed. The corresponding figures for the alternative interpretation of the model (Table 4-9) are 10 percent and 28 to 31 percent.

On an overall basis, the variable adjustment speed models seem superior to the constant adjustment speed model. They provide better fits to these data; they give more reasonable estimates of the adjustment rate; and, in my opinion, they give more reasonable estimates of the elasticity of the demand for capital with respect to new orders.

Effects of Tax Incentives

Impact on Desired Capital Stock

According to the model developed in this study, a reduction in the user cost of capital will produce a one-shot increase in the desired stock of capital. Net investment expenditures will be increased for a number of periods, until the new desired stock of capital is attained; and replacement investment will be permanently increased, its new stationary value being $\delta \Delta K^*$ larger than its previous stationary value, where ΔK^* is the increase in the desired stock. Thus one way to measure the impact of tax incentives is to estimate the increases they brought about in the desired stock of capital. [32]

Table 4-10 presents estimates of increases in desired capital stock based on the estimated demand functions for capital shown in Tables 4-7, 4-8, and 4-9. Part A of the table gives the results for the declining-balance variant of user cost, Part B the results for the sum-of-the-years-digits variant. Rather than calculate estimates for each of the demand functions, I have selected from within each class of models the demand function that is most favorable to the user cost variable. In each case, this means using the demand function derived from the investment relation containing a twelve-quarter inverted-V lag on user cost divided by the wage rate. The induced change in desired stock K^* is calculated according to

$$\Delta K^* = d_2 \overline{[(c/w)_t - (c^B/w)_t]}, \tag{4.58}$$

[32] Other models could be developed in which a reduction in user cost would permanently increase the volume of net investment expenditures if demand for output is growing. For example, one might specify that the desired capital-output ratio is determined only by relative factor prices (user cost divided by the wage rate), rather than by relative factor prices and the level of orders, as in this study. A fall in relative factor prices would then increase the desired capital-output ratio; and if orders are growing, net investment must be permanently increased, because production of each additional unit of output will require a greater addition to capital stock than before.

TABLE 4-10. Reduction in Factor-Price Ratio and Increase in the Demand for Capital Stock Resulting from Tax Policy Changes, Estimated by Selected Demand Functions for Selected Periods, 1954–66[a]

| | | | Increase in desired capital stock (millions of 1954 dollars) | |
| | | | Variable adjustment speed | |
Variant and period	Average reduction in factor-price ratio c^B/w	Constant adjustment speed model[b]	Net investment funds model[c]	Gross investment funds model[d]
A. Declining-balance user cost variant				
1954 : 1–1962 : 2	0.08856	$2,496	$1,172	$1,413
1962 : 3–1963 : 4	0.11966	3,372	1,583	1,909
1964 : 1–1964 : 4	0.06955	1,960	920	1,109
1965 : 1–1966 : 3	0.02762	778	365	440
1954 : 1–1966 : 3	0.30539	8,606	4,040	4,871
B. Sum-of-the-years-digits user cost variant				
1954 : 1–1962 : 2	0.14578	3,930	1,910	2,299
1962 : 3–1963 : 4	0.11001	2,966	1,441	1,735
1964 : 1–1964 : 4	0.06676	1,800	874	1,053
1965 : 1–1966 : 3	0.02546	686	334	401
1954 : 1–1966 : 3	0.34801	9,382	4,559	5,488

[a] Policy changes were as follows:
    1954 : 1 – 1962 : 2—Accelerated depreciation.
    1962 : 3 – 1963 : 4—Depreciation guidelines and tax credit with Long amendment.
    1964 : 1 – 1964 : 4—Repeal of Long amendment, and corporate tax rate reduction.
    1965 : 1 – 1966 : 3—Corporate tax rate reduction.
[b] Table 4-7.
[c] Table 4-8.
[d] Table 4-9.

where

d_2 = the long-run response coefficient found in Table 4-7, 4-8, or 4-9
c/w = actual user cost divided by the wage rate
c^B/w = the ratio of factor prices that would have prevailed had there been no change in tax policy.

The bar over the difference indicates that it is an average over a number of periods of the reductions in the factor-price ratio brought about by tax

TABLE 4-12. Investment in Manufacturing Attributable to Tax Incentives, Variable Adjustment Speed Model, by Depreciation Method, 1954–66

(Millions of 1954 dollars)

| Year | Declining-balance user cost | | Sum-of-the-years-digits user cost | | Actual investment |
	10 quarters	12 quarters	10 quarters	12 quarters	
1954	70	72	102	105	11,065
1955	239	271	361	409	11,113
1956	245	340	379	533	13,690
1957	204	296	319	465	13,870
1958	185	268	293	425	9,790
1959	146	228	238	365	9,972
1960	129	198	215	321	11,928
1961	111	179	186	291	11,253
1962	208	262	268	352	11,954
1963	365	422	405	483	12,673
1964	554	704	578	734	14,848
1965	647	882	671	903	17,663
1966[a]	494	689	512	704	15,476
Total, 1954:1–1962:2	1,413	1,965	2,208	3,076	98,518
Total, 1962:3–1966:3	2,184	2,846	2,318	3,015	66,777

[a] First three quarters.

the-years-digits variant of user cost give considerably higher estimates of $I_t - I_t^B$ for the 1954–62 period than those containing the declining-balance variant. The timing of expenditures is about the same in each case, with peaks occurring in 1955 or 1956 and in 1965. At the 1965 peak, investment attributable to tax incentives was about 9 percent of actual gross investment, according to the more liberal estimates.

Conclusions

The variation of the estimates in Tables 4-11 and 4-12 prohibits a decisive judgment on the effectiveness of tax incentives unless one is willing to pass judgment on the relative merits of (a) the constant and variable adjustment speed models and (b) the two variants of user cost. With regard to the models, the variable adjustment speed models were found to be definitely superior in terms of goodness of fit to the sample data; furthermore, they gave more reasonable estimates of the adjustment speed and of the elasticity of the demand for capital with respect to new orders. On these grounds, it would appear that the variable adjustment speed models are to be preferred to the constant adjustment speed models.

With regard to the user cost variables, both are undoubtedly subject to important measurement errors. In particular, because of the slow adoption of accelerated depreciation, they both must overstate the reductions in user cost actually perceived by businessmen in the periods immediately following major policy changes. But evidence on the relative popularity of the two methods suggests that the sum-of-the-years-digits variant probably gives larger overestimates than the declining-balance variant, since the latter is more widely used. In light of these considerations, it would seem that the estimates based on the declining-balance variant ought to be preferred to those based on the sum-of-the-years-digits variant.

If these arguments are accepted, the first two columns of Table 4-12 give the most accurate estimates of the impact of tax incentives. These are the lowest estimates obtained and suggest that the performance of tax incentives has been quite disappointing. Policies that produced an estimated $5.1 billion (constant 1954 dollars) in tax savings in manufacturing from 1954 through mid-1962 increased manufacturing capital expenditures by only $2.0 billion during the same period; and policies that produced an estimated $8.6 billion in tax savings from mid-1962 through the third quarter of 1966 increased expenditures by only $2.8 billion. Perhaps a more sensible yardstick is net additions to capital stock, since under stationary conditions tax savings from accelerated depreciation would ultimately fall to zero (D would approach, but would never fall below, D^B), while gross investment would continue to be enlarged by the amount of replacement generated by the increase in the desired capital stock. It may be seen from Table 4-10 that policies that through the third quarter of 1966 had produced $13.7 billion in tax savings would ultimately generate only a $4.0 billion net growth in capital stock.

I_{39}^{OBE} = the OBE-SEC figure for 1939

I_t^C = Chawner's estimate for year t.

The OBE-SEC figure for 1939 was extrapolated forward for the period 1940–44 using a series estimated by Wilson, who employed the same methods as Chawner.[35] The extrapolated values were calculated as

$$\hat{I}_t^{OBE} = (I_{39}^{OBE}/I_{39}^W)I_t^W, \qquad t = 40, \ldots, 44, \qquad (4.61)$$

where I_t^W is Wilson's estimate for year t: I_{39}^W equals I_{39}^C.

The OBE-SEC series, extrapolated OBE-SEC series, and underlying series are summarized in Table 4-A-1. While the extrapolated values probably should not be taken too literally, they are considered sufficiently accurate for present purposes.

Useful Lives of Plant and Equipment

Tenuous as the capital expenditures series is, plant and equipment lives actually used for tax purposes are even more difficult to establish. An immediate source of information would appear to be the Treasury Department's *Bulletin F*, which suggested useful lives for tax purposes for a detailed breakdown of capital goods.[36] However, as Hickman notes, "*Bulletin F* ... reflects the average experience of the 1930's with its low standards of obsolescence. Although used until quite recently as a guideline for fixing expected lives when the taxpayer's own records were inadequate to establish probable service lives, *Bulletin F* has never been binding, and it is clear that many companies have been able to demonstrate to the satisfaction of Treasury officials that their own retirement experience calls for shorter lives." [37]

Estimates of useful lives can be inferred from corporate income tax returns published annually in summary form by the Treasury Department in *Statistics of Income*. Depreciation charges for tax purposes are available from the income statement data, and gross depreciable assets are available from the balance sheet data. If all assets are depreciated according to a straight-line formula, then the ratio of gross depreciable assets to depreciation charges should approximate the composite service life of plant and

[35] D. Stevens Wilson, "Planned Capital Outlays and Financing," *Survey of Current Business*, Vol. 25 (July 1945), pp. 15–23.

[36] U.S. Treasury Department, Bureau of Internal Revenue, *Income Tax Depreciation and Obsolescence: Estimated Useful Lives and Depreciation Rates*, Bulletin F (revised January 1942), referred to as *Bulletin F*.

[37] Hickman, *Investment Demand and U.S. Economic Growth*, p. 241.

equipment. Huntley computed this ratio for two-digit manufacturing industries for the prewar and early postwar periods and found a steady decline in estimated useful lives in most industries for the postwar years.[38] His findings suggest that capital goods acquired during the postwar years had shorter tax lives than those acquired in earlier years, which could be due either to a general shortening of both plant and equipment lives or to a shift in the composition of capital expenditures toward shorter-lived equipment and away from longer-lived plant.

To account for this reduction in useful lives, prewar and wartime acquisitions are depreciated here at a slower rate than postwar acquisitions. Hickman has computed postwar lives from income tax records for 1954 and 1955, which are probably the last years for which data are both largely free from distortions caused by accelerated depreciation and characteristic of the lives of postwar acquisitions.[39] The useful lives estimated by Hickman are adopted for acquisitions after 1945, and Huntley's estimates are adopted for acquisitions through 1945. Both sets of estimates for a two-digit breakdown of manufacturing are presented by Hickman and are reproduced here in Table 4-A-2. To obtain an estimate of the composite useful life for all manufacturing, a weighted harmonic mean of the two-digit lives is computed, the weights being gross capital assets (excluding land) for each two-digit industry as reported in *Statistics of Income.* For the lives for 1945 and earlier years, gross capital assets at the end of 1940 are used as weights; for the post-1945 lives, gross capital assets at the end of 1954 are used as weights. If K_i is gross capital assets of manufacturing industry i, T_i is the useful life of assets in industry i, and T is the composite (weighted harmonic mean) useful life for all manufacturing, then

$$T = \frac{\Sigma K_i}{\Sigma (K_i/T_i)}. \tag{4.62}$$

Table 4-A-3 presents the gross capital assets data employed as weights.

The new guideline lives for equipment from the Treasury Department's *Depreciation Guidelines and Rules* are also presented in Table 4-A-2.[40] The breakdown of manufacturing found there does not correspond precisely

[38] Patrick Huntley, "State Distribution of Manufacturers' Plant and Equipment in Place, 1954–1956" (Ph.D. thesis, University of North Carolina, 1961).

[39] Hickman, *Investment Demand and U.S. Economic Growth*, pp. 238–45.

[40] U.S. Treasury Department, Internal Revenue Service, *Depreciation Guidelines and Rules*, Publication No. 456 (July 1962).

useful lives inferred from income tax records should certainly approximate tax lives more closely than actual service lives.

There is one serious shortcoming of the *Statistics of Income* data that could produce a significant bias in the inferred tax lives. The balance sheet item, gross depreciable assets, does not correspond to the true measure of gross depreciable assets required to compute tax lives. To quote *Statistics of Income*:

> The amount of depreciable assets is, in some cases, greater than the value of the assets on which depreciation is claimed. The latter figure cannot be readily tabulated from the corporate return form. Depreciable assets reported on the balance sheet of the return generally include assets on which accelerated amortization is claimed, and fully depreciated assets, as well as the assets for which depreciation is claimed.[42]

Both of these measurement errors will lead to overestimates of tax lives, even if the sum of amortization and depreciation (rather than just depreciation) is divided into measured gross depreciable assets. Part of the observed decline in tax lives could, in fact, be due to an increasing tendency of firms to retire fully depreciated assets from the gross stock more rapidly.

One objective test can be constructed to determine the credibility of the estimated tax lives. Apart from disturbances resulting from accelerated amortization of emergency facilities during the Second World War and the Korean war, an estimated consistent straight-line depreciation series for the postwar period based on these estimated lives should very closely approximate observed depreciation through about 1954. As will be seen, comparison of the series suggests that the estimated tax lives at least pass this test. Ideally, the disturbance due to accelerated amortization should be eliminated by removing from the capital expenditures series those expenditures subject to amortization, but data on such expenditures could not be obtained, and it is extremely risky to try to infer the expenditures series from annual data on amortization.

Depreciation Formula

The simplest approach to writing a general expression for straight-line depreciation when a change in the tax life is introduced at some point is to define two capital expenditures series as follows. Let I_t be actual capital

---

[42] U.S. Treasury Department, Internal Revenue Service, *Statistics of Income—1958–59, Corporation Income Tax Returns* (1961), p. 5.

expenditures during year t, $t = 1921$–66. Capital expenditures through 1945 are to be depreciated according to the estimated useful life of acquisitions through 1945 T. Define a capital expenditures series I_t^T such that

$$I_t^T = I_t \text{ for } t = 1945 \text{ or earlier}$$

$$I_t^T = 0 \text{ for } t \text{ after 1945}. \tag{4.63}$$

Similarly, let the estimated useful life of postwar acquisitions be T' and define a capital expenditures series $I^{T'}$ such that

$$I_t^{T'} = 0 \text{ for } t = 1945 \text{ or earlier}$$

$$I_t^{T'} = I_t \text{ for } t \text{ after 1945}. \tag{4.64}$$

Then, with the adoption of the convention of taking half a year's depreciation in the year of acquisition, estimated consistent straight-line depreciation for year t is

$$D_t^B = \left(\frac{1}{2T}\right) I_t^T + (1/T) \sum_{i=1}^{T-1} I_{t-i}^T + \left(\frac{1}{2T}\right) I_{t-T}^T$$

$$+ \left(\frac{1}{2T'}\right) I_t^{T'} + (1/T') \sum_{i=1}^{T'-1} I_{t-i}^{T'} + \left(\frac{1}{2T'}\right) I_{t-T'}^{T'}. \tag{4.65}$$

Values of D_t^B were calculated using the OBE-SEC expenditure series given in Table 4-A-1 and setting T and T' equal to 25 and 18 respectively. The results appear in the first column of Table 4-A-4. The second column presents values of D_t^B for all corporate manufacturing which are based on the assumption that the ratio of consistent straight-line depreciation of corporations to consistent straight-line depreciation of all manufacturing firms is the same as the corresponding ratio found in the reported depreciation series shown in the third and fourth columns.

In a comparison of D_t^B and D_t, it should be carefully noted that D_t includes accelerated amortization of emergency facilities. Excluding amortization would make sense if amortized acquisitions could be eliminated from the expenditure series used to calculate D_t^B, but it was not possible to do this. Hence the difference between D_t and D_t^B reflects not only the impact of accelerated depreciation granted in 1954 and the new guideline lives of 1962, but also the impact of accelerated amortization. Since D_t^B includes normal depreciation of Second World War acquisitions that were in fact amortized, it should slightly exceed D_t during the early postwar

Current Business. The 1945–55 data are found in the issue for June 1956, pages 6 and 7. The 1956–66 data are found in subsequent March, June, September, and December issues.

Quarterly expenditures were deflated by the GNP implicit price deflator for nonresidential fixed investment found in the *Survey of Current Business,* August 1965, pages 52 and 53, and subsequent issues. The deflator was rebased from 1958 to 1954, so that the deflated series is in billions of 1954 dollars.

Straight-Line Depreciation Charges

To obtain quarterly estimates of straight-line depreciation charges, the following interpolation method was used. D_t^B designates estimated straight-line depreciation for year t, and D_{it}^B estimated straight-line depreciation for quarter i of year t, expressed at an annual rate. Then

$$D_{1t}^B = [\tfrac{3}{4}D_t^B + \tfrac{1}{4}D_{t-1}^B]A_t$$
$$D_{2t}^B = D_t^B A_t \qquad\qquad (4.68)$$
$$D_{3t}^B = [\tfrac{3}{4}D_t^B + \tfrac{1}{4}D_{t+1}^B]A_t$$
$$D_{4t}^B = [\tfrac{1}{2}D_t^B + \tfrac{1}{2}D_{t+1}^B]A_t,$$

where

$$A_t = \frac{D_t^B}{\tfrac{1}{4}D_{t-1}^B + 3D_t^B + \tfrac{3}{4}D_{t+1}^B}. \qquad (4.69)$$

Multiplication by the factor A_t was necessary to assure that

$$\sum_{i=1}^{4} D_{it}^B = D_t^B.$$

The quarterly estimates were converted to quarterly rates.

Actual Depreciation Charges

Quarterly depreciation charges for 1947–61 and 1963–64 were obtained from annual charges according to the same interpolation formula used in the case of straight-line depreciation.

Special methods had to be adopted for 1962, because application of the new guideline lives caused an abrupt jump in the level of actual depreciation charges. Quarterly estimates at annual rates for 1962 were calculated as

$$D_{1,62} = [\tfrac{5}{4}D_{62} - \tfrac{1}{4}D_{63}]A_{62}$$
$$D_{2,62} = D_{62}A_{62} \tag{4.70}$$
$$D_{3,62} = [\tfrac{3}{4}D_{62} + \tfrac{1}{4}D_{63}]A_{62}$$
$$D_{4,62} = [\tfrac{1}{2}D_{62} + \tfrac{1}{2}D_{63}]A_{62},$$

where D_{62} and D_{63} are actual depreciation charges for 1962 and 1963, and

$$A_{62} = \frac{D_{62}}{\tfrac{7}{2}D_{62} + \tfrac{1}{2}D_{63}}. \tag{4.71}$$

This procedure is not completely satisfactory, particularly because it assumes that the new guidelines took effect at the beginning of 1962, whereas they were not published until mid-1962. Firms filing annual tax returns after the release of the guideline lives were permitted to use the new lives in computing their tax liabilities for the year, so the new guidelines were retroactive to some extent. However, it might make more sense in explaining investment behavior to attribute the impact of the guidelines in 1962 entirely to the third and fourth quarters of the year.

Special methods also had to be adopted for 1965 and 1966, because actual depreciation charges for 1966 were not yet available at the time the calculations were made. Quarterly estimates at annual rates for 1965 and for the first three quarters of 1966 were calculated as

$$D_{1,65} = [\tfrac{3}{4}D_{65} + \tfrac{1}{4}D_{64}]A_{65}$$
$$D_{2,65} = D_{65}A_{65}$$
$$D_{3,65} = [\tfrac{5}{4}D_{65} - \tfrac{1}{4}D_{64}]A_{65}$$
$$D_{4,65} = [\tfrac{3}{2}D_{65} - \tfrac{1}{2}D_{64}]A_{65} \tag{4.72}$$
$$D_{1,66} = [\tfrac{7}{4}D_{65} - \tfrac{3}{4}D_{64}]A_{65}$$
$$D_{2,66} = (2D_{65} - D_{64})A_{65}$$
$$D_{3,66} = [\tfrac{9}{4}D_{65} - \tfrac{5}{4}D_{64}]A_{65},$$

where

$$A_{65} = \frac{D_{65}}{\tfrac{9}{2}D_{65} - \tfrac{1}{2}D_{64}}. \tag{4.73}$$

The quarterly estimates of actual depreciation charges were converted to quarterly rates.

Cash Flow Corrected for Tax Incentives

Quarterly estimates of cash flow in the absence of tax incentives were obtained in exactly the same way as annual estimates, as described on pages 153–57, using the quarterly estimates of straight-line and actual depreciation charges and the quarterly estimates of the tax credit.

Corrected quarterly cash flow was also converted to 1954 dollars using the GNP implicit price deflator for nonresidential fixed investment.

New Orders

Manufacturers' monthly new orders in current dollars, seasonally adjusted and expressed at monthly rates, were taken from *Manufacturers' Shipments, Inventories, and Orders: 1947–1963, Revised* (U.S. Department of Commerce, Bureau of the Census, 1963) and from subsequent issues of the *Survey of Current Business*. This series was deflated month by month using the wholesale price index for commodities other than farm products and foods converted to a 1954 base. This price index is also found in the *Survey*. The deflated monthly data were then summed for each quarter. The final series is in billions of 1954 dollars and is expressed at quarterly rates.

Wage Rate

The underlying data used to compute the wage rate in manufacturing were supplied by the Brookings econometric model project. The underlying data are total compensation of employees (quarterly, seasonally adjusted, at annual rates) and total man-hours of production and nonproduction workers (quarterly, seasonally adjusted, at annual rates). The wage rate is simply total compensation per man-hour. Compensation is measured in billions of dollars, and man-hours in billions of man-hours, so the wage rate is measured in dollars per man-hour.

These data extended only through the fourth quarter of 1963, so special methods had to be adopted for 1964–66. An alternative series that was available was average hourly earnings of production workers, reported by the Bureau of Labor Statistics and published in the *Survey of Current Business*. The Brookings wage rate w was regressed on the BLS wage rate w_{BLS_t}, giving, for the first quarter of 1959 through the fourth quarter of 1963, the relation

$$w_t = -0.7892 + (1.6110)w_{\mathrm{BLS}_t}. \qquad \bar{R}^2 = 0.992 \qquad (4.78)$$

This relation was used to project the Brookings series through the third quarter of 1966.

Sensitivity of the Results to Specification of the Interest Rate

IT HAS BEEN POINTED OUT that an accurate measure of the cost of funds to firms is difficult to obtain. Moody's measure of the yield on industrial bonds was used throughout this study, although there are objections to it as a measure of the cost of funds.[45] While estimating an accurate measure of the cost of funds is beyond the scope of this study, it is possible to check the sensitivity of the results to the specification of r, the interest rate. Two alternatives to Moody's industrial bond yield were selected—twice Moody's industrial bond yield and a constant 10 percent per annum. All equations and estimates were run with the alternatives. The latter are not necessarily meant to be more realistic, although the bond yield would seem to be a rather low discount rate in view of rates of return in manufacturing that may be three to five times as high.

Compared with the case in which r is Moody's industrial bond yield, the coefficients on the user cost variable are lower and slightly more significant when r is twice Moody's bond yield and considerably lower and less significant when r is 10 percent per annum (see Table 4-B-1). The coefficients of other variables and the degree of explained variance is hardly affected in either case.

[45] Moody's Investors Service, *Moody's Industrial Manual* (1967).

This principle was later modified to include both output (or its rate of change) and capital stock. After many studies and much debate, nearly all investigators have settled on output, profits, cash flow (retained earnings plus depreciation), the interest rate, the rental price of capital, capital stock, capacity utilization, other factor costs, and indicators of technical change as the relevant set of variables for investment functions. These may be modified to allow for rates of change or distributional effects among firms or industries.

While most investigators refer to the same list of variables and usually select some subset for their own studies, the ways the variables are combined differ considerably. The least restrictive assumption is that investment is a linear or log-linear function of several of these independent variables. It is possible to derive highly specific functions on the basis of assumed rational behavior, competitive markets, and parametric specifications of the production process. Some scope for choice exists in formulating these versions of the investment function, in terms of rates of change or levels of explanatory variables; otherwise the form of the function is strictly constrained.

Whether, after adoption of a general approach, investment is specified as a linear function of the explanatory variables or as some constrained function based on rational behavior, the lag relationship cannot be fixed a priori. There must be delay in investment planning to allow for decision making, ordering, completion of lengthy projects, and adaptation of actual behavior to the unfolding of uncertain events over the time span of an investment. Theory or other a priori information does not say very much about the structure of the lag pattern. Formerly, relationships were estimated between investment and explanatory variables, dated at specific *prior* times. Now, individual values of explanatory variables are more often replaced by lag distributions such as the geometric, general rational function, or Almon type based on Lagrangian interpolation formulas. We feel that the final choice of lag structure will be empirically determined, and have been guided by the general consideration that investment planning takes time and that shipments of goods resulting from decisions are spread in a unimodal-humped pattern over a span of two to three years. (If short- and long-lived items are lumped together, the distribution need not be unimodal. Cancellation and order revisions can also produce a bimodal distribution.[1])

---

[1] For calculations involving standard industrial classification two-digit industries that consider this aspect, see Michael K. Evans, "A Study of Industry Investment Decisions," *Review of Economics and Statistics*, Vol. 49 (May 1967), pp. 151–64.

Up to this point, investment has been treated as though it is a homogeneous macroeconomic variable. While we will not take up microeconomic investment at this stage, we will consider some types of disaggregation. We shall discuss at least some broad industry categories of investment, and we hope eventually to separate plant and equipment investment.

Not only is there uncertainty as to the exact specification of investment functions, leaving wide scope for alternative research strategies, but there are alternative approaches to estimation. If investment is a pure lag relationship, some variant of least squares regression can usually be employed for parameter estimation. It may involve nonlinearities, especially for the proper estimation of lag distributions. Since the time shape of investment decision making is so important, attention is paid to this aspect of estimation theory. Autoregressive transformations may prove useful in eliminating or reducing serial correlation of errors in the investment functions.

Given these considerations, this investigation employs investment functions that are specified to have lag distributions, a stock adjustment form of the flexible accelerator, cash flow variables, a capacity utilization variable, and an interest or capital rental cost variable. Alternative approaches to estimation have been used and functions estimated for some separate categories of investment. It should be clear, however, that despite general agreement on most explanatory variables, the specification and estimation of investment functions are not yet settled. There is much room for research, and the last word on empirical investment functions plainly has not been written.

Alternative Investment Functions

To evaluate our contribution on the impact of investment incentives, it is useful to appraise the work of authors whose results differ from ours. Investment functions account for a major part of the differences in results.

While slightly less stringent assumptions than those of Hall and Jorgenson would yield the same answers, we interpret their vision of the world in the following way:[2]

Perfect competition exists, implying complete knowledge, perfect capital markets, and prices freely determined by market supply and demand.

Profit is maximized over the long run.

Perfect rationality is applied.

[2] Robert E. Hall and Dale W. Jorgenson, "Tax Policy and Investment Behavior," *American Economic Review*, Vol. 57 (June 1967), pp. 391–414.

profitable; that is, the cost of capital is greater than the rate of return, or, in the terminology Jorgenson uses, the expected discounted net worth of the firm would decline if the project were undertaken.[7] If a firm, with its more complete knowledge, assessed its prospects or the risks of a project differently from a lender, or if a firm had a different risk aversion function, then a project would be considered profitable and undertaken *provided* funds could be raised internally. Profits after taxes and depreciation are a source of such capital. On these grounds, a theory of investment ought to include cash flow. The method of introducing it for these purposes is not entirely clear, but that used by Coen in Chapter 4 above is certainly sensible.[8]

Several other aspects of cash flow should be considered. Internal financing is cheaper than external financing because of the tax treatment of capital gains. By reinvesting earnings, a company can grow and its price per share can rise. Even if the total value of the company is exactly the same, owners gain a tax rate reduction through the conversion of earnings into capital gains rather than dividends. (Capital gains are taxed at a maximum of one-half the rate of dividends, which are taxed as ordinary income.) To the owners, therefore, internal financing is cheap and the amount of cash flow or its ratio to total investment is relevant to investment decisions. This has both a long-run and a cyclical effect on marginal investments.

A related argument on cash flow recognizes that management, often separate from ownership in large corporations, can be expected to run a company in part to satisfy its own income objectives. Because of the tax structure, a major portion of management's remuneration is taken in the form of stock options. Management's consequent interest in the greatest possible rise in the price per share is served by reinvestment of dividends, but not, perhaps, by raising funds externally.[9] Cash flow is important to

[7] Dale W. Jorgenson, "The Theory of Investment Behavior," in Robert Ferber (ed.), *Determinants of Investment Behavior*, Conference of the Universities-National Bureau Committee for Economic Research (Columbia University Press for the National Bureau of Economic Research, 1967).

[8] It would also make sense to investigate dividend policy and investment behavior jointly. For an excellent discussion, see Phoebus J. Dhrymes and Mordecai Kurz, "Investment, Dividend, and External Finance Behavior of Firms," in Ferber (ed.), *Determinants of Investment Behavior*.

[9] We ignore the increase in the discounted net worth of the firm since it occurs regardless of whether internal or external funds are used. Also the statement is true even if the price-earnings ratio is reduced to reflect potential dilution from the options.

management because external financing has many risks associated with innovation and growth, without having any compensating benefits.

The final significance of cash flow lies in its effect on the timing of investment even when it has none on the equilibrium level of capital stock. This is easiest to see for investments not directly related to the production process. When profits are falling, dividends are maintained partly to sustain the stock price. This means a declining cash flow. At this point firms can cut back on certain types of investment not used directly for production or delivery of goods. While such things as office furniture and office buildings are needed for companies to operate, anything above the minimal amount, quality, and frequency of replacement is subject to considerable discretion.

The discussion turns now to complete knowledge and foresight, or their opposites, risk and uncertainty. It has often been pointed out that a production process with higher minimum average cost than another will be selected if it is cheaper over broader ranges of output and if the firm can expect wide cyclical variations in demand. Since the average cost curve depends partially upon the wage rate and production level, and since the choice will hinge on the extent of risk and the firm's aversion to it, uncertainty clearly complicates matters. While major attempts to deal with uncertainty are not made here,[10] the related problems of distinguishing between permanent and transitory changes in the determinants of investments are considered.

In order to avoid the problems involved in analyzing a series of changes known to be temporary, investment studies usually adopt some form of smoothing to obtain "permanent" output or prices.[11] It is unfortunate, given this approach, that the significantly different impacts of transitory changes have hardly ever been analyzed.[12] The issue assumes even greater importance when policy changes plainly labeled as temporary are being evaluated.

Like cash flow, transitory changes in output or prices can alter the timing of investment without affecting long-run equilibrium capital stock. If output

[10] Presumably the problem is more important for Bischoff, who assumes only ex ante substitution, than for Hall and Jorgenson or Coen, who assume ex ante and ex post substitutability. However, plant is more general purpose than equipment (ex post), so there could still be incompatibilities between the two functions in Hall and Jorgenson.

[11] Robert Eisner, "A Permanent Income Theory for Investment: Some Empirical Explorations," *American Economic Review*, Vol. 57 (June 1967), pp. 363–90.

[12] The Hall and Jorgenson mathematical derivation of net worth is correct since the interrelationships over time of the various arguments are included. The empirical implementation and, indeed, the critical discussion of the implications of changing output or prices are the points at which the problems arise.

function. Too much sophistication can lead to a too great departure from the real world.

On the matter of factor substitution, in an ex ante sense, firms can choose any capital-labor combination, but once the combination is in place, this flexibility is limited. Bischoff has investigated the consequences for such a putty-clay model with relative prices as a function of the rate of use; we believe that he has introduced relative prices in a more appropriate fashion than Hall and Jorgenson.

The implications of a user cost depreciation function are very important for neoclassical investment theory. Taubman and Wilkinson have shown that the selling price of capital, the interest rate, and the user cost function all have different impacts on investment and on the desired level of capital stock, measured in physical number of machines.[16] This result depends upon the ability of the firm to substitute a greater number of hours, or a more intensive rate of speed of use of capital, for more physical units of capital.[17] An investment function should recognize the distinction between hours of use and physical units available, but up to this time little empirical work has done so. However, data developed by Murray Foss, which suggest a marked change in hours of use since the 1920s, could be introduced into the production or investment functions.[18]

As to the production function, Bischoff's idea of using the constant elasticity of substitution (CES) function and determining the elasticity of substitution appears to be preferable to the Hall and Jorgenson practice of using the Cobb-Douglas function, because the CES function admits the Cobb-Douglas formulation results as a special case and thus can reflect the wider possibility that relative price and output have different effects. While CES is a fairly general function, it is not incontrovertibly the most appropriate one, especially when output is a multiproduct aggregate such as gross national product (GNP). Under the assumption of a particular form of the production function, relative prices would help to determine capital-labor ratios. Even if the form of the function is unknown, relative prices (adjusted for taxes) could be added separately, as in Hickman.[19] In the context of

[16] Taubman and Wilkinson, "User Cost, Capital Utilization and Investment Theory."

[17] Speed is an important element. Assembly lines can be run faster or slower (with different size labor forces). The marginal product of speed may be variable since the faster the operation, the less accurate the machine.

[18] Murray F. Foss, "The Utilization of Capital Equipment: Postwar Compared with Prewar," *Survey of Current Business*, Vol. 43 (June 1963), pp. 8–16.

[19] Bert G. Hickman, *Investment Demand and U.S. Economic Growth* (Brookings Institution, 1965).

production functions, the whole question of measurement of capital stock comes to the fore. The problems of technical change (vintage models) and capital services rather than units must be dealt with.

The problem of nonhomogeneous capital arises in another context. Fixed capital can be in either plant or equipment. If these items have separate influences on output, they should enter the production function as different variables.[20] In a generalized Cobb-Douglas function, the omission of the split in capital would make no difference to the Hall and Jorgenson estimates, because of the assumption of a unitary elasticity of substitution among all inputs, including plant and equipment. For the CES function, the problem is to estimate the elasticity of substitution.

Presumably the distinction between plant and equipment is important because the ratio between them has altered sharply in this century—indeed, over the postwar period.[21] In any event, plant and equipment are complements in the short run. For complementary goods, a weighted average of prices, rather than any one price, should be employed. Since the impact of accelerated depreciation on the rental price of plant and equipment was different from that of the investment tax credit, some weighted average should have been employed to study their effects. In other words, although the investment tax credit does not apply to structures, stimulation of equipment investment generates an increase in expenditures for plant. To judge correctly the impact on demand for capital, the value of the credit for the combined package of plant and equipment should be used.

Estimation of Lag Distributions

The timing of investment decisions is of critical importance in the final specifications of the proper investment function. A general pattern has emerged from past studies, showing that a lag process is involved and that the shape of the distribution is humped. However, similar agreement has not been reached on the method of estimating the lag distribution and the parametric specifications of the lag structures must remain somewhat arbitrary.

The approaches used in specifying the lag distribution may be grouped under two headings, according to present practices: (1) the rational function

[20] Robert M. Solow has done this in a study of technological progress, "On a Family of Lag Distributions," *Econometrica*, Vol. 28 (April 1960), pp. 393–406.

[21] U.S. Department of Commerce, Office of Business Economics, *The National Income and Product Accounts of the United States, 1929–1965: Statistical Tables* (1966), pp. 80–85.

distribution of the type made familiar in econometrics through the work of Jorgenson;[22] (2) the interpolation formulas made familiar through the work of Almon.[23]

The rational function lag distribution, which includes as special cases the Koyck distribution [24] and the Pascal distribution,[25] can be written:

$$I_t = \frac{\gamma(S)}{\omega(S)} K_t^* + v_t, \tag{5.2}$$

where I_t is defined as the time series of investment and K_t^* as the time series of the desired capital stock (which Jorgenson makes proportional to output multiplied by the ratio of output price to capital rental price). Random error is represented by v_t.

The rational function $\gamma(S)/\omega(S)$ is a ratio of two polynomials in the lag displacement operator ($Sx_t = x_{t-1}$). The numerator polynomial is written as

$$\gamma(S) = \gamma_0 + \gamma_1 S + \gamma_2 S^2 + \gamma_3 S^3 + \dots, \tag{5.3}$$

and the denominator polynomial as

$$\omega(S) = 1 + \omega_1 S + \omega_2 S^2 + \omega_3 S^3 + \dots. \tag{5.4}$$

The objective of statistical inference is to estimate the coefficients γ_i and ω_i that determine the distributed lag response of I_t to K_t^*. Before estimation can be carried out, however, the degree of polynomials must be specified. In working with quarterly data, Hall and Jorgenson use

$$\gamma_0, \gamma_1, \gamma_2, \gamma_6, \dots = 0$$

$$\gamma_3, \gamma_4, \gamma_5 = \text{unknown, nonzero parameters}$$

$$\omega_1, \omega_2 = \text{unknown, nonzero parameters}$$

$$\omega_3, \dots = 0.$$

This is a very particular parametric specification. It assumes a delayed response for two full quarters and an extension for three more. Many other combinations may be plausible, and until a complete empirical search has been carried out, the appropriate investment function for any industry or product aggregate will remain in doubt.

[22] Dale W. Jorgenson, "Rational Distributed Lag Functions," *Econometrica*, Vol. 34 (January 1966), pp. 135–49.

[23] Shirley Almon, "The Distributed Lag between Capital Appropriations and Expenditures," *Econometrica*, Vol. 33 (January 1965), pp. 178–96.

[24] L. M. Koyck, *Distributed Lags and Investment Analysis* (Amsterdam: North-Holland, 1954).

[25] Solow, "On a Family of Lag Distributions."

It will be assumed, however, that the arbitrariness of parametric specification has been decided upon. A simple estimation approach is then to write

$$\omega(S)I_t = \gamma(S)K_t^* + \omega(S)v_t$$
$$I_t = -\omega_1 I_{t-1} - \omega_2 I_{t-2} + \gamma_3 K_{t-3}^* + \gamma_4 K_{t-4}^* + \gamma_5 K_{t-5}^* + \varepsilon_t. \tag{5.5}$$

Using the same approach as Jorgenson, we assumed that ε_t is a series of mutually independent random variables and made the least squares regression of I_t on I_{t-1}, I_{t-2}, K_{t-3}^*, K_{t-4}^*, K_{t-5}^*. If it is assumed that ε_t is a serially independent series of random errors, then v_t is serially dependent. The implicit assumption here is that the dependence of v_t is precisely such that $\omega(S)v_t$ is independent. Empirically we find that direct estimates of v_t from an analogous method do reveal serial dependence and that direct estimates of ε_t appear to reveal serial independence. Tests of the latter finding are clouded by the presence of lagged dependent variables in the least squares regression.

We propose an alternative estimation procedure, forming the criterion function

$$G = \sum_{t=1}^{m_2} \left[I_t \frac{\gamma(S)}{\omega(S)} K_t^* \right]^2 \tag{5.6}$$

and minimizing with regard to $\gamma(S)$ and $\omega(S)$ for m_2 observations. The relevant estimation equations are

$$\frac{\partial G}{\partial \gamma_i} = -2 \sum_{t=1}^{m_2} \left[I_t - \frac{\gamma(S)}{\omega(S)} K_t^* \right] \frac{S^i K_t^*}{\omega(S)} = 0 \qquad i = 0, 1, 2, \ldots; \tag{5.7}$$

$$\frac{\partial G}{\partial \omega_j} = 2 \sum_{t=1}^{m_2} \left[I_t - \frac{\gamma(S)}{\omega(S)} K_t^* \right] \frac{S^j \gamma(S) K_t^*}{[\omega(S)]^2} = 0 \qquad j = 1, 2, \ldots. \tag{5.8}$$

The i and j subscripts, in this case, assume values that depend on the parametric specifications of the polynomials. Steiglitz and McBride, in engineering applications, have proposed an iterative algorithm for solving these estimation equations.[26] If

$$I_t' = I_t / \omega(S) \tag{5.9}$$

$$K_t^{*'} = K_t^* / \omega(S) \tag{5.10}$$

$$K_t^{*''} = \frac{\gamma(S)}{\omega(S)} K_t^{*'}, \tag{5.11}$$

[26] K. Steiglitz and L. E. McBride, "A Technique for the Identification of Linear Systems," *IEEE Transactions on Automatic Control*, Vol. AC-10 (October 1965).

then the estimation equations may be written as

$$\sum_{t=1}^{m_2} [\omega(S)I'_t - \gamma(S)K^{*'}_t] K^{*'}_{t-i} = 0 \tag{5.12}$$

and

$$\sum_{t=1}^{m_2} [\omega(S)I'_t - \gamma(S)K^{*'}_t] K^{*''}_{t-j} = 0. \tag{5.13}$$

These equations are linear in the unknown parameters, provided the transformed variables can be estimated. Consistent estimators of $\gamma(S)$ and $\omega(S)$ are first obtained by, say, some application of instrumental variable methods,[27] and are called $\gamma^0(S)$ and $\omega^0(S)$. Initial estimates of I'_t, $K^{*'}_t$, and $K^{*''}_t$ are then formed. The estimation equations for $\gamma^1(S)$ and $\omega^1(S)$ are then solved and the procedure carried out as before until the parameter estimates converge to a given order of accuracy.

Since $I_t/\omega(S)$ and the other terms involve the calculation of infinite sums, these are approximated by summing only from the first sample observation. In a sampling experiment in which this method was combined with others, it was found that truncation of these infinite sums had little effect on the performance of this method in the special case of the Koyck distribution.[28] Steiglitz and McBride have also applied it successfully in experimental calculations that go beyond simple Koyck distributions.[29]

If, after application of this method, it is found that the residual variation is serially correlated, autoregressive transformations of the original series may be made, for example, to

$$\tilde{I}_t = I_t - \rho_1^0 I_{t-1} - \rho_2^0 I_{t-2} - \cdots \tag{5.14}$$

$$\tilde{K}^*_t = K^*_t - \rho_1^0 K^*_{t-1} - \rho_2^0 K^*_{t-2} - \cdots, \tag{5.15}$$

and the same iteration procedure applied to the $\tilde{I}_t$ and $\tilde{K}^*_t$ variables, iterating also, as indicated by the superscripts on ρ, on the autoregressive structure of error. This would seem to be better than simply assuming that $\omega(S)v_t$ is serially independent. In fact, in other work Jorgenson ends up with an

[27] Nissan Liviatan, "Consistent Estimation of Distributed Lags," *International Economic Review*, Vol. 4 (January 1963), pp. 44–52.

[28] See J. L. Morrison, "Small Sample Properties of Selected Distributed Lag Estimators," *International Economic Review*, Vol. 11 (February 1970), pp. 13–23.

[29] Steiglitz and McBride, "A Technique for the Identification of Linear Systems," p. 462.

equation that regresses I_t on I_{t-1} and I_{t-2}.[30] This is equivalent to the second-order autoregressive correction described above, and the evidence presented below indicates that that is what is required. Although we end up with the same parametric form as Jorgenson, we prefer our method of parameter estimation for determining the structure of the lag distribution because it avoids correlation between the error term and the independent variables.

Because we have not yet completed the estimation of investment functions using the Steiglitz-McBride iterative procedure, we have made use of Almon's weights.[31] Her method is simply a polynomial interpolation formula over a set of values $x_1, \ldots, x_n$. It is capable of describing the humped distribution thought to be typical of the investment decision process. It is less general than the rational lag function and typically does not have a bell shape; nevertheless, from an empirical point of view it should approximate the lag distribution as well as most other functions.

Consequently, our investment function takes the form

$$I_t = a \sum_{i=0}^{n} \mu_i K_{t-i}^* + \varepsilon_t. \tag{5.16}$$

If early values of μ_i—say, μ_0, μ_1, μ_2—are set equal to zero, the lag effect does not begin immediately; n determines the end point of the distribution.

---

[30] Dale W. Jorgenson, "Capital Theory and Investment Behavior," in American Economic Association, *Papers and Proceedings of the Seventy-fifth Annual Meeting, 1962* (*American Economic Review*, Vol. 53, May 1963), pp. 247–59.

[31] If K_{t-j}^* is replaced by I_{t-j}' in the second of the two normal equations, the set of equations to be solved is somewhat simpler. They are then symmetrical and retain their consistency properties. We have in fact made this calculation with data from the Brookings econometric model project for manufacturing durables. Our result is

$$I_{N_{MD,t}} = \frac{0.00243S^3 - 0.00069S^4 - 0.00145S^5}{1 - 1.97S + 0.98S^2} X_{MD_t}.$$

In this case, I_{MD} = net investment in billions of 1958 dollars, and X_{MD} = change in gross national product originating in durable manufacturing, deflated by an index of user cost.

If we regress net investment on its values in $t-1$ and $t-2$, and output in $t-3$, $t-4$, and $t-5$, the result is

$$I_{N_{MD,t}} = \frac{0.00075S^3 + 0.00076S^4 + 0.00028S^5}{1 - 1.56S + 0.60S^2} X_{MD_t}.$$

In the first case, the Durbin-Watson statistic is 0.15, and in the second it is 2.05. The first set of estimates will have to be autoregressively transformed and recomputed before they are completely acceptable. We put these estimates forward at this point, however, to show how much the coefficients can be affected by the method of estimation.

In contrast with the rational function lag distribution, this type is of a finite length. Mrs. Almon determined her values of the distribution by considering the lag between appropriations and investment. Rather than recalculating her type of interpolation formulas for the data on investment and output, we have used her weights, which are

$$\mu_2 = 0.074 \quad \mu_6 = 0.171$$
$$\mu_3 = 0.132 \quad \mu_7 = 0.138$$
$$\mu_4 = 0.170 \quad \mu_8 = 0.091$$
$$\mu_5 = 0.183 \quad \mu_9 = 0.041.$$

The first two weights, μ_0 and μ_1, were set equal to zero to reflect the lag between investment decisions and appropriations as well as between appropriations and actual investment.

Initial Investment Equations

The Wharton Econometric Forecasting Unit (Wharton-EFU) model, which is the basis for estimating the economy-wide effects of the investment incentives, contains equations that make use of the Almon weights given above.[32] For manufacturing, the equation for investment in plant and equipment is

$$I_{\text{BUS}_M} = -17.45 + 24.59 JCAP_{M-1} + 0.1308 \sum_{i=0}^{7} \mu_i X_{M-i-2}$$
$$(10.69) \qquad\qquad (9.41)$$

$$+ 0.1644 \sum_{i=0}^{7} \mu_i (RE_M + CCA_M)_{-i-2} - 1.158 \sum_{i=0}^{7} \mu_i RM_{\text{MBCIND}-i-2}$$
$$(2.70) \qquad\qquad\qquad\qquad (3.97)$$

$$- 0.0248 \sum_{i=0}^{7} \mu_i K_{M-i-2}.$$
$$(3.82)$$

$$\bar{R}^2 = 0.895 \qquad S_e = 0.68 \qquad DW = 0.58 \qquad\qquad (5.17)$$

In this estimated relationship, we have formed Almon-type weighted averages of manufacturing output X_M, cash flow $(RE_M + CCA_M)$, the long-term bond yield RM_{MBCIND}, and the stock of capital in manufacturing K_M. The short-term lag variable $JCAP_M$ indicates that the rate of capacity utilization may induce short-run changes (cancellation or expansion of

---

[32] See Michael K. Evans and Lawrence R. Klein, programmed by George R. Schink, *The Wharton Econometric Forecasting Model* (University of Pennsylvania, Wharton School of Finance and Commerce, Department of Economics, Economics Research Unit, 1967).

plans) in investment outlays at the final stage between long-run investment planning and actual investment.

This equation fits the data well (*t*-ratios are shown in parentheses below the coefficients). The overall multiple correlation is high (0.895), but there is a high degree of serial correlation present in the residuals between actual and estimated manufacturing investment. This is shown by the low Durbin-Watson ratio (0.58). Thus it cannot be assumed that the residuals are a series of mutually independent random errors.

This same equation has been updated by adding observations for 1965–66 and by utilizing revised data for the later years of the sample previously used. The newly estimated equation showed the same high serial correlation of residuals; so all the variables were subjected to a second-order autoregressive transformation, for example,

$$\rho\{x\} = x - \rho_1 x_{-1} - \rho_2 x_{-2}, \tag{5.18}$$

and the following relationship estimated, using best fitting values of ρ_1, ρ_2, and all the other coefficients:

$$\rho\{I_{\text{BUS}_M}\} = \underset{(3.84)}{0.6050 + 8.0099\rho\{JCAP_{M-1}\}} + \underset{(4.56)}{0.1620\rho\{\sum_{i=0}^{7} \mu_i X_{M-i-2}\}}$$

$$+ \underset{(1.94)}{0.2990\rho\{\sum_{i=0}^{7} \mu_i (RE_M + CCA_M)_{-i-2}\}} - \underset{(3.05)}{2.6129\rho\{\sum_{i=0}^{7} \mu_i RM_{\text{MBCIND}-i-2}\}}$$

$$- 0.0285\rho\{\sum_{i=0}^{7} \mu_i K_{M-i-2}\}.$$

$$\text{Estimated } \rho_1 = 1.11 \qquad \text{Estimated } \rho_2 = -0.308$$

$$\bar{R}^2 = 0.908 \qquad S_e = 0.453 \qquad DW = 1.84 \tag{5.19}$$

Apart from revealing how individual coefficients have changed as a result of changing both the sample and the method of estimation, the equation now gives rise to serially uncorrelated residuals. It may also be observed that the lag structure more closely resembles that of many of Jorgenson's formulations. The output variable affects current investment with a lag of two quarters or more. Also, investment one or two quarters ago affects current investment. There are basic differences in equation specification between this formula and Jorgenson's, but the lag structure is closer to his when our estimates are adjusted for the presence of serial correlation of residuals.

We prefer to come to this final result on the lag structure through autoregressive correction of residuals in a distributed lag equation instead of assuming that $\omega(S)v_t$ is an uncorrelated random variable and minimizing $\sum[\omega(S)v_t]^2$, but we are not yet prepared to comment on the empirical significance of this difference in statistical approach.

Data Sources and Estimates

In addition to theoretical economic and econometric issues, two types of practical problems arise in this analysis. These involve (1) the nature of the investment data to be used, and (2) the estimation of the rental price of capital.

Investment Data

Investment data are available from several sources, in various forms of disaggregation and for different time periods. The national income accounts contain quarterly data in current and constant dollars for sales to nongovernmental purchasers of nonresidential fixed investment, with separate subtotals for structures and producers' durable equipment. The OBE-SEC quarterly survey of business plans for plant and equipment expenditures is based on company data on both anticipated and actual investment. These data are subdivided into various sectors, such as manufacturing, mining, and utilities, and are available for a number of standard industrial classification two-digit manufacturing industries, but no separation is made between plant and equipment.[33] They show less investment than the national income accounts because they are based on a slightly different definition of investment and because they exclude capital outlays of farms and of nonprofit institutions, brokers' commissions, and dealers' margins on sales of used equipment, which are included in the national income account. Still another source of information is the Annual Survey of Manufactures, in which the U.S. Bureau of the Census has, since 1949, collected investment data for four-digit establishments, including separate totals for structures and equipment, which in turn is broken down into investment in new and used equipment. The national income accounts also provide annual information, in current and constant dollars, on types of investment, such as office buildings and railroad equipment, as well as complementary data

[33] Since 1961, information on the percentage of newly initiated and carryover projects has been collected. No study has been made with these data, though one would seem useful, given the problem of determining lags from orders to shipments.

on the magnitude of capital stocks. The latter estimates are prepared assuming alternative depreciation rates and retirement patterns, but they are available only for manufacturing, farming, and the total private economy. Finally, orders received by durable goods manufacturers are published by the Bureau of the Census.

Each of these sets of data has both virtues and faults which must be considered in selecting the series to be used. We believe, too, that the investment data employed explain a great deal of the difference in results among the authors represented here.[34]

The national income accounts, the series most familiar to econometricians, are the source of Bischoff's data for producers' durable equipment. One difficulty with this series is that no breakdown by purchasing industry is readily available. Such a breakdown is important for evaluating the impact of the investment tax credit because of the legislation's varying provisions for different industries and because some, such as utilities, are more concerned with minimizing costs than with maximizing profits. A breakdown would also be useful to exclude investment of nonprofit institutions, which is determined not at all by profit maximization and only to a limited extent by cost minimization, and, in the short run, is influenced by fund raising and government grants and loans. The measurement of investment in producers' durable equipment when shipped, rather than when ordered, creates a further deficiency, because the credit applies to orders and the lag between orders and shipments differs among various products and, consequently, is influenced in the aggregate by the product mix.[35]

Jorgenson and Hall are among those making use of the OBE-SEC data.[36] The major disadvantage of the series is the absence of a breakdown between structures and equipment. Furthermore, the present detail, while extremely useful, might be even more so were investment not assigned to industries on the basis of the main activity of companies. For one example, all investment undertaken by the Ford Motor Company is in the automotive area despite the fact that Ford now embraces Philco, a nonautomotive firm. The problem exists not only for two-digit industry classification but

[34] Paul Taubman, "Personal Saving: A Time Series Analysis of Three Measures of the Same Conceptual Series," *Review of Economics and Statistics*, Vol. 50 (February 1968), pp. 125–29.

[35] See pp. 207–12 for some results on the lag from orders to shipment.

[36] The Wharton model uses this series for investment by manufacturing and regulated industry. It also has a residual nonfarm investment total, so that the aggregate agrees with the total in the national income accounts.

also for sector designation: U.S. Steel falls into the manufacturing sector, although some of its investment is in mining subsidiaries.[37]

To gauge the magnitude of the discrepancy between the company and establishment data requires a comparable series on an establishment basis. For manufacturing, the Bureau of the Census provides annual investment data on an establishment basis. We have correlated data for each Census establishment-based industry with the corresponding SEC company-based industry. The results are given in a simple correlation table which shows all possible correlations between industries on the two bases. For total manufacturing, the correlation is 0.97, and for two-digit industries, the correlations range from about 0.50 to 0.96, with only a few as high as 0.90. In some cases, higher correlations exist between an SEC industry (j) and a different Census industry (k) than if the industry designations were reversed. For example, the correlation between investment of SEC manufacturing and that of Census mining could be greater than that for SEC mining and Census manufacturing (that is, the correlation of SEC_j-$Census_k$ is greater than SEC_k-$Census_j$). Also, asymmetry exists in that SEC_j and $Census_k$ might be highly correlated while SEC_j and $Census_j$ have weak association. Since the Census data are classified on an establishment basis, this indicates that much of the kth establishment-industry is incorporated within the jth company-industry in the SEC data. The results indicate that the SEC data conform poorly to an establishment basis at the two-digit or total manufacturing levels. The SEC data can be used, but the investment and derived capital stock numbers deviate from the true measurements and will generally yield biased results for activities or impacts classified or judged on an establishment basis.

If annual data were all that was required, the Census information with its subtotals for structures and equipment and its more complete industry details would be preferred over the SEC data. To determine the lag structure between investment and determinants, however, quarterly data are more appropriate. To obtain them, several industries from the SEC series were chosen on the basis of simple correlations, and information about them was used to posit a relationship of the following form between the annual SEC and Census data:

$$Census_j = a_j + b_j\, SEC_j + \sum_{k=1}^{N} c_{jk}\, SEC_k. \qquad (5.20)$$

[37] The magnitude of the problem of presenting the data on an industry basis is discussed below.

On the basis of these regressions, quarterly Census series for each industry were derived by using the existing quarterly values (seasonally adjusted) for each SEC series.[38] These new quarterly series were then divided into plant and equipment expenditures by plotting the ratio of equipment to total investment in the industry, centered at mid-year, and then reading off the quarterly ratios from a smooth linear function connecting the yearly points.

As an alternative, investment outlays could be studied by type of good rather than with the industry data just described. The advantage of the industry approach is that information on relative output, prices, interest rates, profits, and taxes is readily available. The advantage of the approach by type of good is that the lag structure from event to decision to order to shipment will be much more homogeneous, stable, and meaningful. More-over, leased investments are correctly classified, as they are not on an industry basis. It is known that the mix of investment goods varies greatly from year to year in a manner almost surely not attributable to changes in the mix of purchasing.[39] The lag structure should be studied by type of investment good, and this means that a variety of output and price measures is needed since some goods are bought by all industries and some by only a few. The data, including prices of the types of investment and capital stock, are readily available. We plan to explore this body of data also.

Finally, it should be emphasized that in all the sources noted, investment is recorded not when orders are placed but when shipments occur. The demand for investment goods is reflected in orders, while the lag to ship-ments reflects supply phenomena.

The old idea that this lag stretches out as capacity utilization rises in the supply industry has been tested empirically.[40] We have also estimated some regressions to determine this lag and find that it varies among products. Although there is little direct evidence of expansion and contraction of the

[38] There may be some danger that, within a year, the residuals from the annual equation will have the same sign so that the annual average of the quarterly figures will not equal the true annual figures. If so, the level can be adjusted, while the movement is kept the same.

[39] See U.S. Office of Business Economics, *National Income and Product Accounts*, pp. 80–85.

[40] Michal Kalecki, "A Macrodynamic Theory of Business Cycles," *Econometrica*, Vol. 3 (July 1935), pp. 327–44; Joel Popkin, "A Study of the Determinants of Both Plant and Equipment Spending", (U.S. Department of Commerce; processed); and P. A. Tinsley, "An Application of Variable Weight Distributed Lags," *Journal of the American Statistical Association*, Vol. 62 (December 1967), pp. 1277–89.

lags, much indirect evidence exists. For this reason, it makes sense—especially when the industry approach is used—to look at orders, the pure demand variable. Unfortunately, there are some difficulties with these data and correspondingly with Coen's analysis. The available data on orders contain double counting not found in the investment data in the gross national product accounts. This arises because durables orders placed with other concerns (that is, subcontracts) are added to the original order. If the percentage of subcontracting remained constant, the same elasticities would still be obtainable. This percentage depends upon the degree of vertical and horizontal industrial integration. Mergers can change the totals of orders for durables and cause trends in the regressions. Furthermore, some industries have no orders data, while data on others, such as machine tools, include foreign orders.

Rental Price of Capital and Tax Law Provisions

In the studies by Hall and Jorgenson, Bischoff, and Coen, the selling price of capital is translated into a rental price of capital adjusted for certain features of the tax law. In principle, we agree with them that these tax adjustments should be made. However, their methods raise some questions. For one thing, they have not taken all tax provisions into account; for another, the values assigned to the elements that are included are not correct.

The rental cost has been adjusted for changes in accelerated depreciation in 1954 and 1962; for the investment tax credit of 1962 and the 1964 amendment to it; and for changes in the corporate tax rate (exclusive of changes in the excess profits tax) whenever they occurred. The tax law, however, contains other important features which have been neglected. For example, none of the authors has considered accelerated amortization under the program of certificates of necessity, which were issued in substantial amounts in the mid-1950s.[41] Furthermore, in the early 1950s, final settlement of tax bills was not required for three years. After a succession of long-range adjustments and short-term fiscal actions, tax payments became equal to liabilities in 1968. Three-year deferral of tax payments constitutes a loan just as much as accelerated depreciation does; and this loan source no longer exists. If the rental price approach to capital costs is to be followed,

---

[41] For example, the private power interests in the Hell's Canyon dam project had a certificate. Presumably a dam and associated hydroelectric stations have a life of thirty years or more. Writing off two-thirds of the cost in five years substantially increases the rate of return.

some allowance should be made for this factor. Finally, the lower tax rate on the capital gains portion of income is ignored, and the nominal or average effective tax rate is employed in the rental cost calculations.

Besides these omissions, these authors use the effective (normal plus surtax) federal corporate income tax rate as the marginal tax rate in calculating the rental cost variable. While this is a convenient procedure, it glosses over several significant qualifications:

Not all investors and taxpaying businesses are corporations. Individuals and partnerships also invest and pay taxes, and nonprofit institutions, which pay no taxes, also invest.

Some companies, especially small firms that are growing and investing rapidly, have no taxable income. Profits of others fall below the level at which they would be subject to the surtax.

Depletion allowances permit oil and mining companies to be taxed at lower effective rates.

State and local governments impose income and gross revenue taxes, and the latter assess property taxes on plant and equipment.

Taxes were collected on excess profits during the Korean war period.

Some of these deficiencies may not be important. If manufacturing investment alone is studied, the use of the corporate tax rate by itself is defensible. For the economy as a whole, however, unincorporated businesses and nonprofit institutions are significant, accounting for about one-fourth of fixed investment and more than one-third of private business product in 1966. State corporate taxes represent 9 percent of federal corporate taxes. The impact of the other considerations varies according to industry and to stage of the business cycle. Average values could be calculated, but their usefulness might be compromised by aggregation biases; for example, small companies, subject to a relatively low tax rate, may be growing and investingr apidly.

The investment tax credit poses an even more difficult problem. It was governed by a complicated law and is not simply a flat percentage of investment either in total or for equipment only. According to Treasury data for various industries in 1963:[42]

a. The cost of prcperty used as an initial base in computing the investment credit was $27.7 billion. But all investment does not qualify

[42] U.S. Treasury Department, Internal Revenue Service, *Statistics of Income—1964, Corporation Income Tax Returns* (1969), p. 299.

in calculating the tax-credit base, and some qualifies only with a partial weight.

b. Qualified investment totaled $24.3 billion. The difference arises because equipment with a useful life of less than four years receives a weight of zero; that with a life of four to six years, a weight of one-third; that with a life of six to eight years, a weight of two-thirds; and that with a life of eight years and over, a weight of one.

c. The tentative credit was $1.4 billion. This is the credit that could be claimed if there were no restrictions on amounts claimed. A major restriction is that the credit cannot exceed $25,000 plus 50 percent of the tax over $25,000 (raised in 1967 from 25 percent). The unused credit can be carried forward and back. In addition, the tentative credit for manufacturing firms is figured as 7 percent of qualified investment while that for most utilities is 3 percent.

d. The investment credit claimed amounted to $1.1 billion.

e. The investment credit carried forward from 1962 totaled $0.3 billion (the difference between (c) and (d) in 1962).

f. The unused credit amounted to $0.6 billion (the sum of (c) and (e) less (d)).

Before the reduction in rental price of capital goods can be found, a decision must be made about the treatment of items (c) through (f). The tentative credit, employed by Hall and Jorgenson and others, seems inappropriate because not all of it was available in the first year. The discounted value of the allowable credit should be equated with

$$\sum_{t=1}^{5} \frac{\text{credit from year 1 claimed in year } t}{(1+r)^t}.$$

Not knowing how quickly the unused credit would be utilized, we employed only the $1.1 billion investment credit claimed, which is made up of the usable portions of the tentative credit and of the investment credit carried forward from 1962, and which amounts to 80 percent of the tentative credit. (The 1967 change in the amount claimable in a given year from 25 percent to 50 percent, and the permission to carry forward for seven rather than five years, will change the discounted value of the credit and the size of the investment credit claimed.)

The final step is to express the investment credit claimed, or the discounted measure, as a percentage of total investment in 1963 for each industry in the national income accounts. Investment, as defined in the national income accounts, differs from qualified investment, on which companies base their calculations of the credit, in three ways: (1) Structures are not included in qualified investment; (2) for purposes of calculating qualified investment, equipment of various lives receives various weights, as noted in point (b) above; and (3) some used equipment is included in qualified investment but, other than margins and commissions, is excluded from investment in the national income accounts.

The major question about dividing by national income account investment revolves around the inclusion of structures in the denominator. The answer is twofold. First, at a practical level, our regressions, which are to be used in calculating rate of return, combine structures and equipment. Second, since many structures are built to house new equipment, there is a joint product involved and the capital goods should be considered together. To the extent that this consideration is not as broadly applicable to office buildings, the effect of the credit will be understated. Hall and Jorgenson and others have applied 7 percent to producers' durable equipment in the national income accounts without making any adjustments for discounting, difference in coverage, or the fact that the rate applicable to utilities is 3 percent rather than 7 percent.

Evaluating the Suspension of Accelerated Depreciation and the Investment Tax Credit

For an understanding of how the effects of the investment tax credit and the suspension of accelerated depreciation were calculated and how our results compare with those of the other authors, a detailed description and justification of the steps taken are required.

Tax Credits and Rates of Return

First, the investment tax credit was conceptualized as a rate of return. If there is a stream of return over the lifetime of an asset and a selling price of a capital good, the following equation can be solved for r, the internal rate of return, or marginal efficiency of capital:

$$q = \sum_{t=0}^{T} \frac{F_t/I}{(1+r)^t}, \tag{5.21}$$

where q is the price of capital and F_t/I is gross profits (after income taxes but before depreciation) per dollar of investment. This calculation is made over the expected life of the asset T. It is not assumed that this asset will necessarily be replaced, but there is an implicit assumption that earnings on depreciation reserves will accumulate at the internal rate of return r.[43]

Assuming gross profits F are the same for all periods, equation (5.21) can be solved for the ratio of the price of capital to gross returns:

$$\frac{q}{F/I} = \frac{(1+r)^{T+1}-1}{(1+r)^T r} = \frac{1+r-[1/(1+r)^T]}{r} . \quad (5.21.1)$$

For short periods of time, the term $[1/(1+r)^T]$ is not negligible.

If a credit of k as a proportion of q is allowed and is assumed to be returned at once, it can be said that the given stream F/I has a price of $(1-k)q$.[44] Thus, given k, the new internal rate of return after the tax credit r^a can be found from the formula

$$\frac{(1-k)q}{F/I} = \frac{(1+r^a)^{T+1}-1}{(1+r^a)^T r^a} . \quad (5.22)$$

The ratio of (5.22) to (5.21.1) gives

$$(1-k) = \left[\frac{(1+r^a)^{T+1}-1}{(1+r^a)^T r^a}\right] \bigg/ \left[\frac{(1+r)^{T+1}-1}{(1+r)^T r}\right] . \quad (5.23)$$

Given the short lives of equipment, the relationship between r^a, r, and k is nonlinear and fairly sensitive to values of T.

Our calculations are carried out for (1) manufacturing, (2) regulated industries, and (3) residual industries, excluding farms and nonprofit institutions. The assumed values for r and T are given for each industry group in Table 5-1. It should be noted that regulated industries have a lower rate of return and longer-lived assets than do the other industries. These assumptions were made because the rate of return for regulated industries is kept fairly constant at the stated level and because *Bulletin F* lives for equipment are longer there than in manufacturing or the residual sector.[45]

For the calculations reported in Table 5-1, the size of the tax credit was realistically derived by using information on the mix and difference in credit between plant and equipment, potential credits, credits claimed, carryovers

---

[43] See Ezra Solomon (ed.), *The Management of Corporate Capital* (Free Press, 1959).

[44] This is easy enough to change, since it is assumed that r is known, that is, $(k)/(1+r)$ is constant.

[45] Regulated industry includes television, which is not restricted to such a low rate, but many utilities are limited to a 6 percent return. See U.S. Treasury Department, Bureau of Internal Revenue, *Income Tax Depreciation and Obsolescence: Estimated Useful Lives and Depreciation Rates*, Bulletin F (revised January 1942).

TABLE 5-1. Calculation of Post-Credit Rates of Return

Industry group	Assumed values			Calculated values	
	Pre-credit rate of return (r)	Amont of cred-it (k)	Asset lifetime T (years)	Post-credit rate of return (r^a)	Increase in pre-credit rate of return
Manufacturing	10 %	3.7 %	10	11.03 %	10.3 %
Regulated	7	2.6	20	7.39	5.6
Residual (except farm and non-profit institutions)	10	0.9	10	10.24	2.4

Source: Based on data on the investment tax credit in U.S. Treasury Department, Internal Revenue Service, *Statistics of Income—1963, Corporation Income Tax Returns* (1968).

of credits, and so forth. Our solution, which is far from ideal, divides the actual credit claimed in 1963 by the corresponding investment total —from the OBE-SEC series on investment for manufacturing and for regulated industry; and for the residual sector from the national income account nonresidential fixed investment less investment by manufacturing and regulated industries, farm, and nonprofit institutions.[46]

In manufacturing, the 3.7 percent credit means a 10.3 percent reduction in rental which is two-and-two-thirds times as large as the credit. For investments by utilities, which have longer lives, the credit of 2.6 percent increases the rate of return by only 5.6 percent, and so on. This information on rate of return allows us to gauge the impact of suspension of the credit, that is, of reducing the rate of return from r^a to r.[47]

[46] Unincorporated businesses can also use the credit, and have done so to the extent of about $300 million. U.S. Treasury Department, Internal Revenue Service, *Statistics of Income—1963, U.S. Business Tax Returns* (1967). We used the figures for corporate income since much of the data on unincorporated business refer to farms, which are exogenous, and because the exemption of up to $20,000 of eligible property allowed in the 1966 suspension would exempt most unincorporated businesses from it.

[47] On the grounds that the exemptions would not affect marginal investments, we have ignored the total exemption of investment in air and water pollution control facilities, and other exemptions, such as of equipment, machinery, and other property subject to the allowance if more than 50 percent of the cost of an equipped building or plant facility were already constructed or contracted for, or if more than 50 percent of the cost of the parts were already acquired or contracted for. These exemptions have, however, been taken into account in calculating cash flow.

Tax Credits and Investment Equations

The investment equations used in this study are of the following basic form for each of the three industry groups:

$$I = a_0 + a_1 \text{ (real output)}_j + a_2 \text{ (long-term interest rate)}$$
$$+ a_3 (K)_{t-1} + a_4 \text{ (cash flow variables)} + a_5 \text{ (capacity utilization)}_{t-1}.$$
$$(5.24)$$

(The actual coefficients are presented on page 229.)

Every variable except capacity utilization is a weighted average of past values, where the weights are distributed over eight past quarters, and are those estimated elsewhere by Shirley Almon in a study of capital appropriations.[48]

Since a neoclassical model has been much discussed, a few words about the rationale of these equations are in order. A more detailed account is published in descriptions of the Wharton model.[49]

Investment functions by purchasing industry were estimated for the manufacturing, regulated, and residual nonfarm sectors. The residual nonfarm sector requires special treatment because it is subject to capital rationing when money becomes tight. Much of the investment activity in this sector is commercial construction. The other two industries are estimated separately because of the previously discussed differences in behavior and treatment under tax laws. As a result of these differences, the coefficients in equation (5.24) may vary among industries. Since the manufacturing and regulated variants of output, cash flow, and capital behave differently —both cyclically and secularly—and since the coefficients vary, aggregation biases would arise if the industries were not separated. Within the context of the Wharton model, finer splits were not undertaken.

All the variables except cash flow are weighted averages and have the same weights, reflecting the lag from appropriations (orders) to shipment. The equations are of the usual stock adjustment form:

$$IO_t = b(K_t^* - K_{t-1}), \qquad (5.25)$$

[48] Almon, "Distributed Lag between Capital Appropriations and Expenditures."
[49] Evans and Klein, *The Wharton Econometric Forecasting Model*; and Evans, "A Study of Industry Investment Decisions."

where

IO_t = investment orders in period t

K_t^* = desired capital stock at end of period t

K_{t-1} = actual capital stock at end of period $t-1$.

Shipments at time t are a weighted average of orders in the past:

$$I_t = \sum_{i=0}^{n} \mu_i IO_{t-i}. \tag{5.26}$$

Shipments, therefore, will be an n-period weighted average of all variables in K_t^* and K_{t-1}. K^* depends on output and interest rates. Output is a proxy for expected future profits, which should be compared with alternative rates of return, represented by long-term interest rates. In future work we hope to introduce the tax law changes as separate variables since they alter future profits for the same output. The cash flow variable is included for reasons already given (pages 201–03). The capacity utilization variable is included (without lag) to measure unexpected changes in sales relative to capital as the fixed investment stages draw to a close. As argued previously, these changes induce order revisions or cancellations.

We assume that the interest rate in our equation stands for the negative of the expected rate of return. If they had no uncertainty, firms would invest only as long as the expected rate of return exceeds the interest rate. An increase in the interest rate cuts investment, since fewer projects have a rate of return in excess of the required rate. With uncertainty, the required return on investment will be greater than the long-term interest rate because people are risk-averters and insist upon risk premiums. We assume that these premiums are constant and added to the long-term rate.

Risk itself can be characterized by such things as variance and skewness of the distribution of returns.[50] Basically, we argue that the investment tax credit affects only the expected value of the rate of return, but leaves riskiness per se untouched. In the terminology of frequency distributions, the investment tax credit shifts the whole distribution in such a way that only the mean changes. With this line of argument accepted, the reduction in the rate of return on manufacturing from 11.03 percent to 10.0 percent brought about by the suspension of the tax credit (see Table 5-1) implies an equivalent absolute increase in the long-term interest rate of 1.03 points, that is, the rate moves from 5 percent to 6.03 percent. If it is assumed that

[50] Several moments of the distribution of returns, in addition to the first, the mean, may be necessary to describe risk.

the effect of the long-term rate changed by the same *percentage* as the change in the rate of return, the computed effect would be smaller, roughly 60 percent of the total effect of the incentive policies.

For a *permanent* elimination of the credit and depreciation provisions, the difference in post- and pre-incentives rates of return for each industry in Table 5-1 is added to the interest rate variable in the corresponding industry investment function.[51] Since cash flow variables also appear in these investment equations, it is appropriate to adjust the corporate tax functions for the credit by changing the constant term and to adjust the depreciation function for accelerated depreciation.[52] We did, in fact, make a computer run on this basis.

For a *temporary* suspension, corresponding to the 1966 law, a different approach is called for, since the same investment made when the credit is restored costs less.[53] This requires comparison of the discounted values of the income streams of investing during or after the suspension. Assume that there are two projects, A and B with cash flows of F_A and F_B respectively. Then the discounted values are given by

$$\text{Value of } A = \sum_{t=0}^{n} \frac{F_{A_t}}{(1+r)^t}, \tag{5.27}$$

$$\text{Value of } B = \sum_{t=0}^{n} \frac{F_{B_t}}{(1+r)^t}. \tag{5.28}$$

Project B is selected in preference to A if

$$\text{Value } B - \text{Value } A = \sum_{t=0}^{n} \frac{(F_{B_t} - F_{A_t})}{(1+r)^t} > 0. \tag{5.29}$$

Assume the streams from investment B to be the same as those from A, but delayed until January 1, 1968, which is period $t+1$. The credit kqI will be added to the cash flow of project B in period $t+1$, as will the interest earned by delaying the investment one year. But aside from this, assume that all future revenues are equal for A and B, that is,

$$F_{B_{t+j}} = F_{A_{t+j}} \qquad j = 1 \ldots T. \tag{5.30}$$

[51] For residual nonfarm investment, the equation in the model used the difference between the short- and long-term rates to reflect money tightness and the residual borrowing ability of the sector. We estimated another equation to get the appropriate interest rate.

[52] For the credit suspension, we used a $1.7 billion total for the five quarters to take account of the exemptions listed in note 47.

[53] For literature on this topic, see Solomon, *Management of Corporate Capital.*

In this case the value of B will be greater than the value of A only if

$$F_{B_t} - F_{A_t} + \frac{kqI}{1+r} > 0.$$

In general, $F_{B_t} - F_{A_t}$ would be expected to be negative since, apart from the interest to be earned from holding investment back for one year, it reflects either loss of sales (of the goods that the deferred addition to capacity would have produced) or extra production costs associated with using outmoded or inefficient capital instead of the current investment. Information on the loss of potential sales is difficult to get, though obviously such losses can occur only in a boom period, when capacity is highly utilized.

To evaluate extra production costs, it is necessary to know the timing of demands and the degree of diminishing returns with increasing output. It is also necessary to know how much more efficient today's investment is than previous investment, which is to say, how much technological progress is embodied in new investment. These questions are particularly difficult from an econometric standpoint, and while it may be possible to answer them eventually, we cannot do so at the present.

On purely ad hoc grounds, as the end of the suspension period approaches, the loss of revenues would become smaller and the value of the credit greater, so that the returns to waiting would be increased. Therefore, we multiplied the numbers to be added to the interest rate, the difference in the rate of return as explained above, by the following arbitrary factors:

1966:	4	1.00
1967:	1	1.00
	2	1.25
	3	1.50
	4	1.75
1968:	1	1.50

The first quarter of 1968 is included because some investment orders that ordinarily would have been placed in 1967 would not be produced or counted as investment until 1968. The temporary nature of the credit suspension would have caused a drying up of orders, especially in late 1967, but many manufacturers would have counted on a flow of orders in January 1968, and they would have produced standard items or components for inventories (especially if tacit agreements on intended orders were made).

To get the output feedback effects, therefore, it was necessary to adjust inventories upward at the end of 1967 and downward in 1968.

With all the above information and the lag structure of the investment functions, the impact on investment from the suspension of the credit and accelerated depreciation can be obtained for each quarter. We have done this for the permanent and temporary aspects, allowing first only for the impact on rate of return and then for the impact on cash flow and for feedbacks from the entire econometric model in both cases.

But before these results are discussed, two minor adjustments must be made. First, our investment functions use a weighted average of past output and interest rates to allow for lags—initially between recognition of changes in desired capital stocks and orders, and then between orders and production, shipment, and installation. In this case, the recognition lag should not be long, so we have shortened the lag structure by one quarter; that is, instead of occurring at $t+2$, the first response will occur at $t+1$.

Secondly, we have estimated $800 million for depreciation lost as a result of the suspension of accelerated depreciation. We allocated this among our three industry groups on the basis of the ratio of depreciation in each to total depreciation.

Complete System Solutions

The suspension of the tax credit and accelerated depreciation is best studied in the context of a complete model and its solution, since the variables affecting investment, depreciation, and profits are not independent of movements throughout the economy as a whole.

This phase of the study was carried out by using the Wharton model. While other models could serve this purpose, and some possibly would provide more investment detail, none is solved as repeatedly and with as current data as this model. Short of the more detailed and comprehensive study of investment behavior that is to be made in the next phase of this study, we have attempted to interpret as carefully as possible the effects of the legislation on investment and depreciation in terms of the equations of the Wharton model. We have also generated alternative simulation calculations forward from the fourth quarter of 1966, the point at which the tax credit and accelerated depreciation provisions were suspended. We first examine the full consequences of that suspension as though it were to be in force for the entire year 1967. We next try to assess the significance of an early reinstatement, in March 1967.

Shifts of Equation Coefficients

There are three points at which the legislative changes have a direct impact in the Wharton model: in investment equations, in the corporate tax function, and in the book-value depreciation equations. The relevant investment equations, as noted earlier, are estimated separately for manufacturing, regulated industry, and a residual nonfarm sector (commercial construction in large measure). These equations, with t-ratios shown parenthetically, are: [54]

$$I_{BUS_M} = -17.45 + \underset{(10.69)}{24.59 JCAP_{M-1}} + \underset{(9.41)}{0.1308} \sum_{i=0}^{7} \mu_i X_{M-i-2}$$

$$+ \underset{(2.70)}{0.1644} \sum_{i=0}^{7} \mu_i (RE_M + CCA_M)_{-i-2} - \underset{(3.97)}{1.158} \sum_{i=0}^{7} \mu_i RM_{MBCIND-i-2}$$

$$- \underset{(3.82)}{0.0248} \sum_{i=0}^{7} \mu_i K_{M-i-2}$$

$$\bar{R}^2 = 0.895 \qquad S_e = 0.68 \qquad DW = 0.58 \qquad\qquad (5.31)$$

$$I_{BUS_R} = 1.49 + \underset{(1.75)}{0.014} \tfrac{1}{2}(S_{F-1} + S_{F-2}) - \underset{(1.34)}{0.0043} \tfrac{1}{2}(K_{R-1} - K_{R-2})$$

$$+ \underset{(3.80)}{0.0429} \sum_{i=0}^{7} \mu_i S_{F-i-3} - \underset{(7.81)}{2.1042} \sum_{i=0}^{7} \mu_i RM_{MBCIND-i-3}$$

$$\bar{R}^2 = 0.810 \qquad S_e = 0.55 \qquad DW = 0.65 \qquad\qquad (5.31)$$

$$I_{BUS_O} = -35.72 + \underset{(6.27)}{0.1742 C_{-1}} - \underset{(3.31)}{0.0563 K_{O-1}}$$

$$+ \underset{(0.76)}{0.0363} \sum_{i=0}^{7} \mu_i C_{-i-2} + \underset{(5.20)}{2.396} \sum_{i=0}^{7} \mu_i (RM_{MBCIND} - RM_{CPAPER})_{-i-2},$$

$$\bar{R}^2 = 0.930 \qquad S_e = 1.05 \qquad DW = 0.73 \qquad\qquad (5.32)$$

[54] An updated version of the Wharton model with autoregressive transformations of the investment equations is being tested as this is written. The results of using these functions are described briefly on p. 237.

where

I_{BUS_M} = investment in plant and equipment, manufacturing, billions of 1958 dollars

I_{BUS_R} = investment in plant and equipment, regulated industry, billions of 1958 dollars

I_{BUS_O} = investment in plant and equipment, other nonfarm, billions of 1958 dollars

$JCAP_M$ = Wharton index of capacity utilization in manufacturing

X_M = output originating in manufacturing, billions of 1958 dollars

RE_M = retained earnings in manufacturing, billions of 1958 dollars

CCA_M = capital consumption allowances in manufacturing, billions of 1958 dollars

RM_{MBCIND} = Moody's average yield on corporate industrial bonds, percent

K_M = stock of capital in manufacturing, end of period, billions of 1958 dollars

μ_i = Almon distributed lag weights (0.074, 0.132, 0.170, 0.183, 0.171, 0.138, 0.091, 0.041)

S_F = final private sales, billions of 1958 dollars

K_R = stock of capital in regulated industry, end of period, billions of 1958 dollars

C = consumer expenditures, billions of 1958 dollars

K_O = stock of capital in residual nonfarm sector, end of period, billions of 1958 dollars

RM_{CPAPER} = rate on four- to six-month commercial paper, percent.

For the investment tax credit, the results (set out in Table 5-1) revealed that the rate of return on manufacturing investment would be lowered by one percentage point as a result of the suspension of the tax. This change is introduced into the complete solution by *raising* RM_{MBCIND} (the interest cost of borrowed capital) by one point in the equation for I_{BUS_M}, that is, by subtracting $1.158 \sum \mu_i (1.0)$ for each time period, using the distributed lag weights just given. The amount of summation is determined cumulatively as the projection progresses from period to period in the future.[55]

For regulated industry, the rate of return was reduced (raising RM_{MBCIND} by 0.39 point—see Table 5-1); $2.1042 \sum \mu_i (0.39)$ is subtracted for each period of the projection.

[55] As noted at the end of the previous section, the lag structures were shortened by one period because of the elimination of the recognition gap.

In the case of residual nonfarm investment, the equation estimated in the Wharton model uses the difference between long- and short-run interest rates, $RM_{MBCIND} - RM_{CPAPER}$, instead of the long-term rate alone, to show the tightness of the money market confronting borrowers. In order to assign a marginal value to the rate of return as a result of the credit suspension, we estimated a new regression equation in which $RM_{MBCIND} - RM_{CPAPER}$ was replaced by the short-term rate RM_{CPAPER}. This variable has a coefficient estimated at 0.9878, which was used to determine the effect of the change in the rate of return for the original equation in the model. Therefore, the interest cost was raised $0.9878 \sum \mu_i$ (0.24) and subtracted for each period of the projection. In this calculation, we placed the interest differential at 0.24, the difference in rates of return shown in Table 5-1. For the three industries combined, the rate of return effect in 1967—before considering feedbacks from the whole system, but including the temporary effect—is roughly $0.6 billion.

This discussion covers the first three points at which the October 1966 changes are introduced in the model. In the corporate tax equation, additive constants were introduced for each period so that taxes would be increased by $1.7 billion over the course of six quarters.[56] The appropriate function fitted to the period 1965–66 is:

$$TC = -4.26 + 0.46(Z_{B+IVA} - IVA), \qquad (5.33)$$

where

TC = corporate profits taxes in billions of current dollars

Z_{B+IVA} = corporate profits before taxes, adjusted for inventory valuation adjustment, in billions of current dollars

IVA = inventory valuation adjustment in billions of current dollars. (This variable includes some noncorporate IVA and is misspecified to that extent.)

The following amounts were added to the constant term of this equation:

1966:	4	0.8
1967:	1	1.3
	2	1.3
	3	1.3
	4	1.3
1968:	1	0.8

[56] We spread $1.7 billion over four (interior) quarters of 1967 and two half (external) quarters at the end of 1966 and the beginning of 1968. Changes were introduced in six different quarterly time periods, but the effective length of the changes is only five quarters.

The beginning and ending adjustments are gradual, and intermediate period values are stable, because, under the 1966 act, the availability of the credit depends on the date of order and not on the date of shipment. The effect of the adjustments in the model solutions is to reduce cash flow, which depends on profits after tax. The equation for manufacturing investment depends directly on cash flow. In the other two investment equations, the effect of taxes is more indirect, and occurs through the ultimate influence on output and expenditures.

Finally, the three depreciation equations associated with the three types of investment were modified to account for accelerated depreciation by the inclusion of dummy variables for the 1962 changes and shifts in constant terms for the 1966 changes. The depreciation equations are:

$$D_M = 0.29 + 0.0467 \sum_{i=0}^{N} (P_{\text{IBUS}} I_{\text{BUS}_M} - D_M)_{-i} + 2.952 \, DM Y_{\text{LIVES}}$$
$$\quad\quad (51.88) \quad\quad\quad\quad\quad\quad\quad\quad\quad\quad\quad (18.62)$$

$$\bar{R}^2 = 0.988 \quad\quad S_e = 0.43 \quad\quad DW = 0.28 \quad\quad\quad (5.34)$$

$$D_R = 1.27 + 0.0205 \sum_{i=0}^{N} (P_{\text{IBUS}} I_{\text{BUS}_R} - D_R)_{-i} + 0.249 \, DM Y_{\text{LIVES}}$$
$$\quad\quad (18.33) \quad\quad\quad\quad\quad\quad\quad\quad\quad\quad\quad (35.07)$$

$$\bar{R}^2 = 0.994 \quad\quad S_e = 0.17 \quad\quad DW = 0.15 \quad\quad\quad (5.35)$$

$$D_O = 3.54 + 0.0281 \sum_{i=0}^{N} (P_{\text{IBUS}} I_{\text{BUS}_O} - D_O)_{-i},$$
$$\quad\quad (46.83)$$

$$\bar{R}^2 = 0.962 \quad\quad S_e = 0.56 \quad\quad DW = 0.21 \quad\quad\quad (5.36)$$

$$\left.\begin{array}{c} D_M \\ D_R \\ D_O \end{array}\right\} = \text{depreciation (manufacturing, regulated, residual nonfarm), in billions of current dollars}$$

P_{IBUS} = implicit deflator for nonresidential fixed business investment, 1958 = 1.00

$DM Y_{\text{LIVES}}$ = dummy variable to account for 1962 changes in depreciation rules (equals zero before first quarter of 1962 and unity thereafter).

We have estimated that, as a result of the October 1966 suspensions, $0.8 billion is to be allocated among reductions to depreciation expense in proportion to shares of these three sectors in total eligible depreciation expense.

We reduced the constants for D_M by 0.196, for D_R by 0.294, and for D_O by 0.3097.

The cash flow effect on investment of the combination of suspension of accelerated depreciation and the investment tax credit is roughly $0.3 billion before any system feedback occurs. Nearly all of this comes from the tax credit. The rate of return and cash flow effect together amount to $0.9 billion. This figure should be compared with the complete system impact given below.

Tax Credit Suspension Simulations

The system was then solved over eight quarters, starting from the fourth quarter of 1966, in the following three ways; the differences among solutions indicate the impact of the credit.

NO SUSPENSION. Observed lag values were used for the whole system of equations in the third quarter of 1966 and earlier periods; assumed values were introduced for exogenous variables for the fourth quarter of 1966 and seven following quarters. The assumptions were predicated on the following conditions: continued fighting in Vietnam, with smaller defense increments after mid-1967; rising state and local government expenditures; three-fourths of the requested increments in social security payments approved for July 1967; continued expansion of world trade; no tax increases. In this calculation, there were no adjustments in the investment functions, the corporate tax function, or the depreciation functions for the suspension legislation of October 1966.

PERMANENT SUSPENSION. All lags and exogenous values were the same as in the previous calculation, but the investment functions were adjusted for the suspension of the credit, and the depreciation functions for the suspension of accelerated depreciation.

TEMPORARY SUSPENSION. The effect of a temporary suspension of the investment tax credit is stronger than that of a permanent suspension. In this case ad hoc allowances were made for the temporary nature of the suspension by increasing interest rates in the three investment equations as described above. It should be pointed out that the projections are made only for the nonfarm sector. Farm investment is set exogenously at forecast levels and is not changed in the three projections.

The results are shown in Table 5-2. In the calculations that assume no suspension of the credit or depreciation provisions, GNP (seasonally adjusted at annual rates in current dollars) rises about $5 billion to $6

TABLE 5-2. Estimated Values of Gross National Product and Investment for Varying Assumptions about Suspension of the Investment Tax Credit and Accelerated Depreciation, Fourth Quarter 1966 through Third Quarter 1968

(Seasonally adjusted annual rates in billions of dollars)

Year and quarter	No suspension		Permanent suspension		Temporary suspension	
	Gross national product	Gross fixed nonresidential investment	Gross national product	Gross fixed nonresidential investment	Gross national product	Gross fixed nonresidential investment
1966: 4	761.5	82.5	761.0	82.3	761.0	82.3
1967: 1	766.1	84.5	764.7	83.7	764.7	83.7
2	772.5	84.0	770.2	82.8	769.7	82.5
3	787.5	84.6	784.1	82.7	782.6	81.9
4	805.9	84.8	801.6	82.2	798.6	80.6
1968: 1	820.3	87.0	815.4	83.8	813.0	82.2
2	830.6	87.9	830.6	86.8	831.0	86.5
3	839.3	88.9	840.4	88.4	841.2	88.3

billion in each of the first two quarters of 1967; it continues to increase strongly through early 1968 and then eventually its rise slows. The added transfer payments in late 1967 make for rapid growth. Capital formation grows fairly substantially in early 1967 and continues to grow in 1968. The slower growth of GNP in early 1967 induces some unemployment, which fades as the economy picks up later in the year.

With a permanent suspension, there is a slower rate of growth in the value of output during early 1967, but a similar rapid recovery in the latter part of the year and continued growth during 1968, so that the final position of the economy is approximately what it would have been without any suspension at all. Compared with the previous solution, there is a drop in gross capital formation of $1.6 billion during calendar year 1967. The lower level of investment, resulting from the suspension provisions, is not fully offset by higher values in other components of the GNP accounts, and the consequence is a slower rate of economic growth during 1967 but a vigorous recovery in 1968, so that no permanent loss is imposed on the economy.

These calculations suggest, however, that even without the suspension the economy would have grown more slowly in 1967 than in 1966. The effect of the suspension appears to have been further to retard the growth rate.

TABLE 5-3. Estimated Value of Gross National Product and of Gross Fixed Nonresidential Investment, Assuming Restoration of the Investment Tax Credit and Accelerated Depreciation, July 1, 1967, and April 1, 1967

(Seasonally adjusted annual rates in billions of dollars)

Year and quarter	July 1, 1967		April 1, 1967	
	Gross national product	Gross fixed nonresidential investment	Gross national product	Gross fixed nonresidential investment
1967: 1	768.7	82.9	768.7	82.9
2	778.3	83.2	778.3	83.2
3	785.9	82.3	790.4	84.5
4	801.1	83.3	801.8	83.9
1968: 1	819.7	84.5	818.9	84.6
2	831.7	86.6	831.5	86.6
3	838.8	87.4	838.4	87.5
4	848.3	87.8	848.3	87.9

Temporary suspension, the calculations reveal, makes for even less capital formation, lower GNP values, and higher unemployment rates than permanent suspension. The recovery is, however, vigorous, and by late 1968 the same high level of activity as resulted from the two previous calculations is attained. The cutback in capital formation is now placed at $2.2 billion, as compared with $1.6 billion for the permanent suspension.

If solution of the model is started in the first quarter of 1967, instead of the fourth quarter of 1966, using actual instead of computed values of variables for the fourth quarter of 1966, our growth projections are slightly higher in early 1967—an increment of $10 billion per quarter in GNP, instead of $6 billion. These calculations were run with two basic assumptions: (1) that the investment incentives are restored at the beginning of the second quarter of 1967, and (2) that they are restored at the beginning of the third quarter. Table 5-3 shows that early restoration adds to capital formation which, with its multiplier effect, causes GNP to rise by more than $4.0 billion. Later in 1968 the two solutions—early and later restoration—converge to the same values.

Stimulative Tax Credit and Depreciation Simulations

The above calculations deal with the restrictive aspects of investment credit and accelerated depreciation policies. Analogous calculations can be made to assess the effects of these policies in stimulating investment and overall activity by considering complete system solutions in 1962, when the tax credit was introduced and allowable taxable asset lives were shortened. The Wharton model was solved for nine quarters, beginning with the fourth quarter of 1962. Again, there are three basic solutions:

NO CHANGE SOLUTION. It was assumed that the corporate tax and depreciation functions in the period 1962–64 were unchanged by the 1962 depreciation and credit provisions and that the parameter values were the same as in 1961. Lagged values of variables were fixed at their actual levels in periods before the fourth quarter of 1962. Exogenous variables were assigned their observed values over the period from the fourth quarter of 1962 through the fourth quarter of 1964. The provisions of the tax cut of 1964 were introduced in the solution for the appropriate quarters of 1964.

CREDIT/ACCELERATION I. In this calculation 1.15 was subtracted from the constant of the tax function to indicate the effect of the credit. This value was chosen so as to make the tax function fit the actual values of corporate tax liabilities and profits. The depreciation equations were raised by the jump values: $2,952 million in manufacturing and $249 million in regulated industry. In other respects the solution was the same as the no change solution. No provision was made for changes in the rate of return on investment as a result of the credit. Only changes in cash flow were introduced.

CREDIT/ACCELERATION II. This solution is like that in credit/acceleration I, but the adjustments to the investment functions for increases in rates of return were added. These were introduced as positive stimulants and were assumed to have nonzero effects from the fourth quarter of 1962. To allow for the Long amendment, the increases in rates of return were reduced by 20 percent. This figure was deduced from Terborgh's work.[57]

A major empirical reason for not introducing these additional changes in credit/acceleration I is that we knew from prior calculations that activity levels generally, and investment levels specifically, would be close to observed levels without this additional stimulus. In this third case of complete system

[57] George Terborgh, *New Investment Incentives*: *The Investment Credit and the New Depreciation System* (Washington: Machinery and Allied Products Institute, 1962).

solutions, the added effects push investment above actual levels. There is, of course, no analogue of the temporary nature of the credit suspension in 1967.

The no change solution begins with a GNP value that is about $0.3 billion below that of credit/acceleration I at the start of the simulation and builds up to a value that is $1.3 billion below it after nine quarters. Thus we estimate that the stimulus due to higher cash flow (reduced taxes and higher depreciation) eventually reaches $1.3 billion. This increase in GNP is accompanied by an increase in capital formation that reaches $0.7 billion after nine quarters.

If in credit/acceleration II terms are added to the three investment equations to reflect rate of return differentials (as in the 1966–67 simulations), there is an even greater expansion of GNP and capital formation. By the end of 1964, GNP is $4.6 billion greater and gross capital formation $3.5 billion greater than in the no change solution. As the other two solutions are closer to the actual values for gross capital formation at the end of 1964 than is the solution that allows for added rate of return stimulus, we feel that investment may not have been responding as vigorously to the stimulus in 1963–64 as to the deterrent suggested by our simulations in 1966–67. It is possible that we should reduce the estimate for 1967 of the impact of the suspension so that only cash flow is used. However, on the basis of predicted and actual investment, a rate of return restraint seems to be required. For the 1962–64 period, the investment figure of $69.1 billion for the simulation of credit/acceleration II seems unusually high. Therefore, we are inclined to place the impact of the 1962 legislation more at the order of magnitude of the differentials between the no change and credit/acceleration I simulations.

Simulations with Alternative Investment Functions

One final calculation is in order. As was pointed out earlier, the basic specification of the investment function in the Wharton model is estimated with serially dependent residuals, and second-order autoregressive transformations would be needed to give estimates that eliminate the computed serial dependence. In an updated variant of the Wharton model, not fully tested, we have estimated the investment function for manufacturing and regulated industry on the basis of second order autoregressive transformations that yield independent residual variations. The investment process in this model has a lag structure that more closely approximates Jorgenson's quarterly estimates of investment in which I_t is regressed on I_{t-1}, I_{t-2},

TABLE 5-4. Gross National Product and Gross Fixed Nonresidential Investment for 1963–64 Simulations

(Seasonally adjusted annual rates in billions of dollars)

Year and quarter	Actual values		No change		Credit/acceleration I		Credit/acceleration II	
	Gross national product	Gross fixed non-residential investment	Gross national product	Gross fixed non-residential investment	Gross national product	Gross fixed non-residential investment	Gross national product	Gross fixed non-residential investment
1962: 4	572.0	53.3	575.8	54.0	576.1	54.0	576.3	54.1
1963: 1	577.4	52.6	584.5	56.4	585.0	56.5	585.6	56.8
2	584.2	54.1	587.4	57.4	588.0	57.5	589.3	58.2
3	594.7	55.6	595.8	58.1	596.5	58.3	598.5	59.5
4	605.8	57.4	605.9	59.4	606.8	59.7	609.4	61.4
1964: 1	616.8	58.7	616.7	60.9	617.8	61.4	620.8	63.4
2	627.7	60.3	628.0	62.4	629.2	62.9	632.5	65.3
3	637.9	62.3	637.8	64.5	639.2	65.1	642.5	67.8
4	644.2	63.9	645.4	65.6	646.7	66.3	650.0	69.1

x_{t-3}, x_{t-4}, x_{t-5}.[58] The last three variables are measured as the change in the value of output deflated by an index of user cost. These latest estimates of investment functions have not only random residuals, but also different coefficients. Particularly to be noted is the fact that the interest rate coefficients are much larger (in absolute values). If we simulate our new, but untested, model over the 1963–64 period using the same controls as in the no change and credit/acceleration II solutions, we obtain differential levels of gross fixed investment of $5.4 billion and GNP of $7.5 billion by the fourth quarter of 1964. These contrast with $3.5 billion and $4.6 billion, shown in Table 5-4. The shift to a lag structure of the same length as Jorgenson's, included in the new model, brings us closer to the Hall and Jorgenson estimates of the effect of the investment incentives, but we still do not reach their high figures. More testing and experimentation is required with the new model version before we are prepared to stand behind these estimates, but they do provide interesting evidence for the problem at hand.

[58] Jorgenson, "Capital Theory and Investment Behavior."

Company Attitudes and Response to Investment Tax Credit and Accelerated Depreciation

IN ADDITION TO MAKING the usual kind of macroeconomic studies of time series statistics, we queried officers of individual corporations on how the legislative imposition or suspension of investment incentives has affected their own investment planning. The companies surveyed do not make up a representative sample, in any sense, of total U.S. investment activity or even of their own industries; but they are important companies accounting for significant portions of investment activity, and many are not atypical of their own industries. Twelve corporations responded to our questionnaire.

The questionnaire (pages 241–42) was answered before the reinstatement of the credit and accelerated depreciation. It was designed to gain knowledge about investment decision procedures in individual companies, the relevance of the tax credit and accelerated depreciation for such decisions, and the magnitude of the effect of the incentive provisions on their investment programs.

Timing in Investment Planning

Results varied on the time span from (a) investment decision to (b) order to (c) final installation, but none of the companies could complete the process for investment beyond standard, routine equipment in less than four months. Many decisions to invest in production equipment required up to two years to implement. In the case of plant facilities, the lags were much longer, usually extending from twelve to thirty-six months.

The fact that investment planning and implementation take time, often as much as three years, has meant that temporary legislation, such as that in the fall of 1966, which suspended the investment tax credit and restricted accelerated depreciation, has practically no effect on a significant part of investment. Firms that were in the midst of long-range investment projects with a time span exceeding the proposed suspension period found themselves continuing the long-range project beyond the time in which the suspension period was completed. Generally speaking, the companies in the sample did not feel sensitive to the temporary suspension of the investment tax credit and accelerated depreciation during 1966–67. They felt that the suspensions had little effect on their investment plans during the final quarter of 1966. In most cases, the companies were involved in projects of sufficient length that they did not want to disrupt them because of temporary legislation.

Use of Investment Incentives

The companies surveyed have all been investing on a substantial scale. Some spend more than $1 billion per year on capital formation and some spend little more than $1 million, but most spend several million dollars annually. In total they accounted for nearly 10 percent of nonresidential fixed investment in 1966. Since it became available in 1962, they have all made use of the investment tax credit. A comparison of their claims for credit with capital outlays discloses that none of the manufacturing companies claimed as much as 7 percent and none of the utility companies as much as 3 percent. In every case there is attrition as a result of the inclusion of ineligible investments in the total of gross capital outlays or as a result of maximum limitations on credit that can be claimed. We find justification here for our use of credits of 3.7 percent for manufacturing and 2.6 percent for regulated industry.

Little evidence developed of unused credit available to carry forward at the end of 1965 or 1966.

In the simulation calculations, we have assumed that the investment incentives added about 1 full percentage point to a typical firm's rate of return in manufacturing. This calculation is confirmed by responses to the questionnaire. There is no confirmation of the lower value placed on the rate of return by application of the incentives to utilities, but we feel that the rate is realistic.

Among the companies interviewed, the investment tax credit was more widely used than accelerated depreciation. Some of our respondents did not make use of accelerated depreciation and preferred to use straight-line methods. Many found it hard to determine how much their depreciation expense was currently increased by the use of acceleration. In those cases where estimates of the increment were made, the order of magnitude of the differential was between $5 million and $15 million. For the same companies, the claims for investment tax credit were also in this range. Since the depreciation differential does not accrue wholly to the benefit of the firm, it would seem that the investment tax credit has greater impact on investment behavior than provisions for accelerated depreciation.

Opinions on Investment Incentives

All the respondents were in favor of both types of investment incentives, but were guarded in their judgment of the effects. All wanted restoration of the incentives early in 1967 and thought that they should not have been suspended. They did not think that the incentives were of critical importance in the past, but they did approve of them and used them in most cases. The consensus was that there were minimal effects from suspension, in the short run, and that restoration would be only a moderate stimulus.

One view often expressed was that the incentives were not suitable as short-run instruments of economic policy. Respondents did not like the uncertainty caused by temporary changes in the incentive legislation and they felt that those making long-run investment decisions should not be confronted with short-run manipulation of investment incentives. The incentives, they believed, need not be fixed, but they should be varied on a long-term basis. To influence short-run policy decisions, the companies would have preferred the use of the general corporate income tax.

Questionnaire on Investment Tax Credit and Accelerated Depreciation

1. How much time elapses between original investment decision making, ordering, and final installation of capital goods in your case?
   a. Production equipment.
   b. General equipment.
   c. Plant facilities.

2. Have you made use of the investment tax credit since it became available in 1962?

 a. How much was your capital formation (investment expenditure) during 1965? During 1966?

 b. How much was your investment tax credit during 1965? During 1966?

 c. How much unused credit available for carry forward did you have at the end of 1965? At the end of 1966?

 d. Did the suspension of the credit affect your orders during the fourth quarter of 1966? In what way?

3. Have you made use of the provisions for accelerated depreciation since they became available in 1962?

 a. How much was your depreciation expense during 1965? During 1966?

 b. How much would your depreciation expense have been if you had used straight-line depreciation or 150 percent declining balance?

4. What is your opinion of the economic desirability of the investment tax credit? The provisions for accelerated depreciation?

 a. What has been the effect of these two measures on your capital planning since 1962?

 b. What has been the effect of the suspension of October 10, 1966, on your plans for 1967?

 c. In your opinion should the credit and depreciation provisions be restored or the suspension continued?

5. Consider your calculations of the rate of return on your capital facilities. How much is the rate of return increased for you by the existence of the investment tax credit and accelerated depreciation?

 a. How will your rate of return calculations be affected during 1967 if the suspensions are terminated December 31, 1967?

6. What are the main criteria that you use in reaching investment decisions under your programs of capital planning? For production equipment? For general equipment? For plant facilities?

CHAPTER VI

Discussion

FRANKLIN M. FISHER *Massachusetts Institute of Technology*

LEGEND HAS IT THAT WINSTON CHURCHILL once said, "Whenever I ask five economists a question, I get six answers—two from Mr. Keynes."

The four analyses presented in this book are all marked by high quality. Each applies sophisticated econometric tools to the empirical and theoretical analysis of an important problem; each does so in a professional and convincing manner; each sheds light where before there was darkness. If it were not for the inconvenient fact that the four analyses happen to concern the same problem and happen to contradict each other's findings, there would be little to discuss. Except for that, indeed, the contribution of each to economic science and to public policy seems assured.

I cannot pretend to resolve these contradictions here. But I can hope to promote their resolution by a systematic look at the four treatments and how they deal with certain economic and statistical issues.

Direct versus Indirect Tests of Tax Policy

The conflicting results reported in the four chapters reflect more than disagreement about the effectiveness of tax policy; they reflect an underlying, long-standing, and well-documented lack of agreement among economists about the determinants of investment. This lack of agreement arises in the present context because each of the authors has approached the problem by analyzing the determinants of investment rather than the effects of tax policy. Each reasons that tax policy affects investment behavior not independently but through such variables as cost of capital, rate of return, liquidity, and the like. Accordingly, changes in tax policy enter their models as changes in such variables assumed to be equivalent in every way, in their effects on investment, to equal changes in the same variables brought about by other forces.

The theoretical basis for such treatment of tax effects is strong. Nevertheless, it seems a dangerous way to proceed if the focus is on these very effects.

Suppose tax policies had not changed in the period considered by the authors. This would not mean that the variables through which tax policy is assumed to influence investment were likewise constant; rather, those variables might have altered considerably for a variety of reasons. Each of the authors could then have estimated his investment function and each could have made a prediction about the effects of tax policy on investment by considering the way in which changes in tax policy influence the variables entering the model. Such predictions would be reasonably based, but they would rest entirely on the assumption that the effects of tax policy could be represented as occurring completely and exclusively through the effects on the other variables and as indistinguishable from the effects of anything else causing the same changes in these variables. The trouble with such an assumption, however, is not that it is implausible, but that, in the circumstances described, it would be completely untested. The procedures just described would begin and end and that assumption would still be only an article of faith even though the crucial prediction rested on it.

Although the actual circumstances are not exactly like those just considered, they are uncomfortably similar. There were a few changes in tax policy in the period considered, but their contribution to variations in the rate of return, the extent of liquidity, and the cost of capital was minor compared with that of other causes. In such circumstances, to make no direct test of the influence of tax policy and to constrain its influence to its effects through other variables is again to ignore a matter of primary importance.[1]

---

[1] Robert Eisner, in "Tax Policy and Investment Behavior: Comment," *American Economic Review*, Vol. 59 (June 1969), pp. 379–88, makes this point in his criticism of an earlier paper of Hall and Jorgenson. See Robert E. Hall and Dale W. Jorgenson, "Tax Policy and Investment Behavior," *American Economic Review*, Vol. 57 (June 1967), pp. 391–414. Hall and Jorgenson may seem the most obviously vulnerable of the four

To point this up, suppose that the money price of a commodity in a demand study never changed in the period of the sample. A demand function for that commodity might nevertheless be estimated, because theory plainly says that what matters is the real price, and the real price would have changed through movements in the general price level. Despite the theoretical support for such a procedure, and even if the results fit the data, one would properly hesitate to use these results for a prediction of the effects of a change in the money price. People presumably look only at the real price, but real people have a funny habit of not doing what economists presume they do. Changes in the money price may signal reexamination of consumption patterns by calling sudden attention to the commodity.

The analogy is quite useful. Rational businessmen ought to treat changes in tax policy as identical with other changes resulting in the same values of the rate of return, the cost of capital, the liquidity position of the firm, and so forth. Were I in charge of the investment policy of a firm, I should certainly apply this principle, but I suspect that, at least in the short run, real businessmen behave differently. A change in the depreciation permitted for tax purposes may signal businessmen to reexamine the way in which they determine reactions to liquidity, rates of return, and cost of capital. Taking advantage of the change may, furthermore, involve a revision in accounting methods which is not costless. Finally, firms may simply take time to recognize that the results of such changes are equivalent to changes in other variables.

A case in point is the sluggish adoption of accelerated depreciation after 1954 despite its obvious profit advantages.[2] This behavior suggests that businessmen were slower to react to the changes wrought by tax policy in the variables entering the authors' investment models than they would have been to changes stemming from other sources. By now, many businessmen have come to treat accelerated depreciation rationally as another way of

---

sets of authors to the present criticisms, because in their model tax policy enters only through the cost of capital, which in turn enters only through a variable the movements of which are largely those of output. Nevertheless, the criticism applies directly to every paper presented at the conference.

[2] See Norman B. Ture, *Accelerated Depreciation in the United States, 1954–60* (Columbia University Press for the National Bureau of Economic Research, 1967); and Terence J. Wales, "The Effect of Accelerated Depreciation on Investment—An Empirical Study" (Ph.D. thesis, Massachusetts Institute of Technology, 1967).

improving rates of return, cost of capital, and liquidity, but some of them were an uncomfortably long time about it.[3]

What would have been the case had the conference that this book reports been held before the 1954 changes in the tax code? Each author could still have estimated his model, for tax policy enters such models only through variables that are moved by other, more important causes as well. Each author could have predicted the effects of the new accelerated depreciation methods. And each would have been dead wrong, because the effects of tax policy were not the same as the effects of differently inspired movements in the same variables of the same magnitude as theoretically would have been induced by the tax change.

Some of the authors have learned this lesson in part. Bischoff and Klein and Taubman make allowance for the fact that accelerated depreciation was not immediately adopted; they move the relevant variables by using measures of that fraction of assets actually depreciated according to the new methods. In omitting this appropriate refinement, Coen and Hall and Jorgenson have been remiss. Nevertheless, none of the authors goes further in taking account of possible discrepancies between theory and practice; none tests directly the effects of tax policy on investment.

All the conclusions about the effects of tax policy reported here would have been on firmer ground had these effects not been constrained by the assumption that they were the same as those produced by other, more volatile variables. Direct tests of that hypothesis and direct estimation of those effects would have been very desirable.

Such estimation and tests have been made by Robert Eisner for the model given by Hall and Jorgenson in their earlier paper.[4] The results are striking. Instead of the strong influence of tax policy on investment found by Hall and Jorgenson, Eisner, testing tax policy explicitly and separately from other changes in the cost of capital, found almost none. Closely related is the finding by Eisner and Nadiri of the powerful effect on the results stemming from the constraint in the Jorgenson investment model that the cost of capital enters the investment function only when combined with output in a single variable.[5] It may well be, therefore, that similar

[3] Among other things, the survey made by Klein and Taubman revealed that many companies ". . . found it hard to determine how much their depreciation expense was currently increased by the use of acceleration." See p. 241.

[4] Eisner, "Tax Policy and Investment Behavior: Comment," and Hall and Jorgenson, "Tax Policy and Investment Behavior."

[5] Robert Eisner and M. I. Nadiri, "Investment Behavior and Neo-Classical Theory," *Review of Economics and Statistics*, Vol. 50 (August 1968), pp. 369–82.

direct tests of the effects of tax policy made with the other models discussed in this volume would not lead to such drastic changes in the conclusions. Nevertheless, this cannot be guaranteed, and such direct tests ought to be made.[6]

Determinants of Desired Capital Stock: Theoretical Basis

How does each of the analyses treat the important problems in predicting the effects of tax policy on investment?

It is almost impossible to write down a sensible expression for desired capital stock for a firm without saying something about the nature of the production function that underlies or corresponds to that expression. Since there is a substantial literature on estimation of production functions, a natural way to proceed is to do so explicitly. To a large extent, Jorgenson pioneered in this regard and Hall and Jorgenson and Bischoff base their analyses on theories of maximizing behavior with particular types of production functions assumed.[7] Coen and Klein and Taubman, on the other hand, do not pay close attention to this issue. While this means that their work is not restricted by the implications of special assumptions concerning the production functions, it also means that the forms of their investment functions are derived from considerations theoretically less rigorous and possibly less satisfactory than those that underlie the functions used by Bischoff and Hall and Jorgenson.

It is not easy to decide where the weight of this criticism falls. On the one hand, there is a well-developed neoclassical theory of the demand for capital, largely attributable to Jorgenson, which uses the sort of assumptions and reaches the kind of elegant results that characterize much of microeconomic theory.[8] If its assumptions are met in practice, investment studies

---

[6] In attempting to estimate as parameters of his model the extent of adoption of accelerated depreciation and the effective rate of the tax credit, Bischoff has, to a certain extent, made such a test. His finding that wide variation in the values of these parameters makes little difference to the fit of his model can be considered a negative result on a somewhat more direct test of the effects of tax policy than those made by the other authors.

[7] Dale W. Jorgenson, "Capital Theory and Investment Behavior," in American Economic Association, *Papers and Proceedings of the Seventy-fifth Annual Meeting, 1962 (American Economic Review,* Vol. 53, May 1963), pp. 247–59; Dale W. Jorgenson, "Anticipations and Investment Behavior," in James S. Duesenberry, Gary Fromm, Lawrence R. Klein, and Edwin Kuh (eds.), *The Brookings Quarterly Econometric Model of the United States* (Chicago: Rand McNally, 1965; Amsterdam: North-Holland, 1965); and Hall and Jorgenson, "Tax Policy and Investment Behavior."

[8] *Ibid.*

based on that theory are obviously preferable to studies in which the form of the investment function and the nature of the variables entering it are dictated largely by the sort of ad hoc theorizing that too often mars econometric work. On the other hand, highly developed as that theory is, its assumptions may not be realistic and the very nature of its strong implications may allow little room for the operation of factors important in the real world and in the minds of businessmen. It is obviously sensible, for example, at least to test whether other factors, such as liquidity, really do affect investment.

In short, the analyst of investment behavior must compromise, drawing on the theoretical results so far as possible without unduly restricting the play of forces operating in the real world. Theory must be in a form in which special assumptions do not play much of a role or in which they are either plausible or subject to test. Variables must not, however, be included simply because they work.

Coming to the models of the four chapters, I find that Hall and Jorgenson rely most heavily on special theoretical assumptions, Klein and Taubman use the least underpinning provided by neoclassical theory, and Bischoff and Coen, in that order, fall in between.

Specifically, Hall and Jorgenson and Bischoff make heavy use of the production function-profit maximizing model. Hall and Jorgenson make the convenient but dubious assumption that the production function is of the Cobb-Douglas form. This leads to very strong restrictions on the way in which the cost of capital enters the investment function; as has been noted, these restrictions have been recently tested by Eisner and Nadiri and the results seem to depend on them rather heavily.[9]

Bischoff, on the other hand, assumes a much more realistic production relationship. In his model, the production function is of the type developed by Leif Johansen, in which there is substitutability ex ante but fixed coefficients ex post.[10] His ex ante production function is more general than the Cobb-Douglas form, being of the constant elasticity of substitution form. Allowance for technical change is also made.

While the Johansen model has yet to undergo extensive empirical testing, it has great inherent plausibility and the treatment given it by Bischoff is both elegant and powerful. From the point of view of the pure theory of

---

[9] Eisner and Nadiri, "Investment Behavior and Neo-Classical Theory."

[10] Leif Johansen, "Substitution versus Fixed Production Coefficients in the Theory of Economic Growth: A Synthesis," *Econometrica*, Vol. 27 (April 1959), pp. 157–76.

the determinants of desired capital stock by the firm, I find his analysis superior to the others.

Yet the pure theory of the firm's demand for capital derived from such considerations may be very satisfying and the resulting implications for the behavior of aggregate investment in the real world simply wrong. This may be for several reasons.

One reason has to do with aggregation. It is possible to construct a production function for manufacturing with, say, an aggregate capital stock as one of its arguments; but such a construction requires the extremely restrictive and unrealistic assumption of relatively little difference in technology among individual firms.[11] Even if all the other assumptions of the Jorgenson model are satisfied, such an aggregate cannot be treated as though it had a single production function.

This has significant implications for investment studies. Interest centers not directly on an aggregate production function but rather on aggregate investment behavior. By considering investment behavior at the firm level, the Jorgenson model can identify the variables likely to be important in explaining investment and thus aid considerably in doing so. Restrictions on the way in which such variables enter the aggregate investment function, however, are not valid if they depend on the assumption that the production functions of firms can be aggregated into a macrofunction. What must be aggregated is investment behavior, not the production functions from which it is derived. In this respect the theoretically rigorous treatments of Hall and Jorgenson and of Bischoff may not be appropriate.

Furthermore, some of the assumptions on which these treatments rest may not be valid. In particular, if substantial imperfections exist in the markets for capital and other factors, there is room for forces other than those accommodated by these theories in their pure form. In making allowance for these forces, Coen and Klein and Taubman have been wise. It is not enough to say that investment can be accurately predicted by a model making competitive assumptions. The crucial difficulty is that investment can be accurately predicted in more than one way.

Coen begins his analysis of desired capital stock with the Jorgenson model; he argues that Jorgenson's insertion of output into the investment

---

[11] It is even doubtful that good approximations can be obtained in this way. See, for example, Franklin M. Fisher, "Embodied Technical Change and the Existence of an Aggregate Capital Stock," *Review of Economic Studies*, Vol. 32 (October 1965), pp. 263–88; and Franklin M. Fisher, "Approximate Aggregation and the Leontief Conditions," *Econometrica*, Vol. 37 (July 1969), pp. 457–69.

function was illegitimate, but gets output in himself through a different door. He contends that the presence of inventories makes it possible for expected or planned sales to fall short of actual sales, and that a revision in plans is triggered when, for an extended period, sales remain high relative to expectations. To the extent that this is convincing, it is an argument for the inclusion of the difference between actual and expected sales in the investment function. Since this value cannot be observed, Coen puts in only the level of sales itself.[12]

I find this unconvincing. If Coen is correct about plan revisions, the variable to use is the backlog of unfilled orders, not orders, or the level of inventories (perhaps relative to sales), not the change in inventories. The new orders variable used by Coen works well; but any variable highly correlated with output would work well, and the theoretical (as opposed to empirical) underpinning of this part of Coen's model seems weak.

More generally, Coen's use of a production function is nonspecific. It leads him to a consideration of what variables belong in the investment function, but it puts practically no other restrictions on the form of his model. Again, such lack of theoretically derived restrictions can be either good or bad, depending on the verisimilitude of the model. I think it fair to say that the model used by Hall and Jorgenson is probably too restrictive in this regard.

The model used by Klein and Taubman, on the other hand, is hardly restrictive at all. Their investment function is not explicitly derived from Jorgenson's considerations of production functions and maximizing behavior. Rather, it represents a distillation of much of the econometric literature on investment. This is not to say that the variables they use are without theoretical foundation, only that the justification of them is relatively general and puts no strong restrictions on their model.

Lag Structures and Speeds of Adjustment

All the authors recognize that lags play an important role in the explanation of investment behavior. Lags come from three sources: the influence of past variables on expectations; the role replacement demand plays in investment demand; and the delay in translating investment appropriations into expenditures.

The lag structures used by the authors differ. Coen uses a Koyck geo-

[12] The variable actually used is new orders which, because of delay between orders and sales, reflect present rather than past demand in the output market.

metrically declining structure for the effect of desired capital stock on investment with three alternative sets of assumptions about the degree to which past variables influence desired capital stock through expectations. Hall and Jorgenson assume that all effects take place within five years and require the five nonzero lag coefficients to lie on a parabola. Bischoff uses a different but likewise flexible lag structure. Finally, Klein and Taubman use Shirley Almon's distributed lag weights for the lag between appropriations and expenditures, superimposed on a Koyck distributed lag.[13]

The issue is whether the imposition of strong assumptions about lags in these analyses pays off in efficiency or loses through misspecification. I think the evidence supporting use of the Almon lag structure ought not to be ignored. Whether the Koyck lag is as clearly indicated is questionable. While Eisner and Nadiri find that one Jorgenson model fitted with a relatively free lag structure gives best results with a Koyck lag, the evidence is weak.[14] I believe that Hall and Jorgenson and Bischoff were wise to allow some flexibility in their lag structure, and, of course, the Hall and Jorgenson parabolic lag structure is closely related to the Almon structure.

Since they make use of available specific information, the application of the Almon weights seems to me to be desirable. If the other lags in the process are flexibly specified, the resulting net lag structure can be estimated by an appropriately flexible procedure. Nevertheless, the use of the Almon lags places an appropriate restriction on the model and should improve the results. Whether a Koyck-type lag is an appropriate specification of even the remaining lag forces, however, is quite another matter.

Coen urges the assumption of a Koyck distributed lag (given expectations) by arguing that other, more rigid patterns can produce foolish results, leading firms to go on investing when desired and actual capital stock are already equal. This point is well taken when desired capital stock decreases and firms wish to cancel investment plans. Nevertheless, in a period in which desired capital stock has mainly been rising, that argument (which does not rule out all lag structures other than Koyck's) is weak, and the assumption of only a Koyck lag structure ignores the evidence of Almon's work. Coen's argument may imply different lag structures on the upswing and downswing, but he does not use such structures.

In allowing the speed in the adjustment of actual to desired capital stock to be influenced by the liquidity of the firms, Coen's model seems

[13] Shirley Almon, "The Distributed Lag between Capital Appropriations and Expenditures," *Econometrica*, Vol. 33 (January 1965), pp. 178–96.

[14] Eisner and Nadiri, "Investment Behavior and Neo-Classical Theory."

to me to be superior to the others discussed here. This is by no means the only way in which the liquidity variable can enter the investment function, but it appears to be the most plausible way.[15] If there is capital rationing or if, as Coen argues, firms prefer internal financing because, among other reasons, it affords more favorable tax treatment for capital gains and dividends to stockholders, the most sensible way for that preference to evidence itself is in the timing of investment expenditures. It is reasonable that, except for technologically determined delays in investment scheduling, the timing of investment expenditures should be influenced by the internal position of the firm rather than by an inflexible dependence on past decisions.[16] The way in which liquidity enters Coen's model is of crucial importance in his results. I believe it to be appropriate.[17]

Autocorrelation

The proper estimation of distributed lag relationships, whatever their specification, makes it especially important to consider the possibility that disturbances are autocorrelated. This is so not only because the presence of such autocorrelation affects the efficiency of estimates and may blur the estimates of the lag distribution, but also because the models may involve lagged endogenous variables as regressors. In particular, if lagged capital stock appears as a regressor, then lagged investment is involved on the right-hand side and autocorrelated disturbances will lead to inconsistency when ordinary least squares is used as the estimator, as they certainly will when lagged investment appears itself as a regressor. Further, if output should be considered endogenous (as is argued later), then the presence of autocorrelation means that the effects of simultaneity are not entirely escapable by establishing lagged instead of current output as a determinant of investment. Since disturbances are likely to be auto-

[15] In this matter, Coen follows Edward Greenberg, "A Stock-Adjustment Investment Model," *Econometrica*, Vol. 32 (July 1964), pp. 339–57; and Harold M. Hochman, "Some Aggregative Implications of Depreciation Acceleration," *Yale Economic Essays*, Vol. 6 (Spring 1966), pp. 217–74.

[16] I have argued elsewhere that decisions respond to the economic rather than Gregorian calendar. See Franklin M. Fisher, *A Priori Information and Time Series Analysis: Essays in Economic Theory and Measurement* (Amsterdam: North-Holland, 1962), Chap. 2.

[17] Liquidity variables also appear in the analysis by Klein and Taubman, but not exactly in this manner, see equation (5.17), p. 212. Bischoff and Hall and Jorgenson do not use them at all.

correlated, it is clearly desirable to use an estimation method that takes explicit account of the possibility of their serial correlation. This is particularly important when the timing of responses to tax policy is an issue, but the bias and inconsistency under discussion cannot safely be assumed to affect only the estimates of the dynamic structure of investment demand. While I do not believe that this problem is qualitatively serious in all the present cases (lagged capital stock is not the same as lagged investment, for one thing), it may well be serious enough to account for some of the differences among the chapters in estimates of the effects of tax policy.[18]

Hall and Jorgenson and Klein and Taubman make explicit allowance for the possibility of autocorrelation; Coen and Bischoff do not. The problem is much more serious for Coen than for Bischoff because lagged investment appears as a regressor in Coen's analysis, whereas inconsistency enters Bischoff's estimates from this source (if at all) only through the presence of lagged output.[19]

Coen notes the possibility of autocorrelation in the disturbances but assumes that his equation has nonautocorrelated disturbances in the form in which it is written for estimation after the Koyck transformation.[20] He recognizes that this implies autocorrelation of the disturbances of his original equations, but apparently commits the not uncommon error of believing that what matters is the manner in which the model is written rather than the true state of affairs. In view of the presence of lagged investment as such in his equations, this is a very serious slip.

Even though Hall and Jorgenson and Klein and Taubman are alert to the possibility of autocorrelation in the disturbances and use estimators that allow for it, it may still be detrimental to their results. This potential exists because the estimation methods that they use would be fully appropriate only if there were no lagged endogenous variables in their models. With such variables present, the estimates of the autocorrelation properties of the disturbances that they obtain will not be consistent.[21] This is obviously more serious for Klein and Taubman, who have lagged capital stock variables in their equation, than for Hall and Jorgenson, who

[18] Note, however, that it does not matter that capital stock is high relative to investment just because capital stock was high at the beginning of the sample period.

[19] Lagged capital stock does appear as a regressor in the alternative models with which Bischoff compares his own. This makes the comparison inconclusive.

[20] See Table 4-5, p. 168.

[21] The problem is the same as that posed when the Durbin-Watson statistic is used in an equation with a lagged endogenous variable estimated by least squares. If output is endogenous, Bischoff's Durbin-Watson statistics are affected.

have not. As with Bischoff, the problem enters the Hall and Jorgenson estimates only through the presence of the lagged output variables.

Simultaneity

This discussion raises the question of whether output is an endogenous variable. If it is, then simultaneous equation bias must be guarded against, particularly where output or output-related variables appear without a lag, as they do in the Hall and Jorgenson and Coen analyses.[22] The same problem, however, will arise when output appears with a lag because of the possibility of autocorrelation in the disturbances. The simultaneous equation problem cannot be overcome by the use of short lags. Lagged endogenous variables will still be endogenous (correlated with the disturbance from the equation to be estimated); treating them as predetermined begets inconsistency.

When output or similar variables on the right-hand side of investment demand functions are treated as exogenous, simultaneous equation trouble arises. There are two reasons for this, one at the level of the firm, the other at the level of the economy.

At the level of the firm, the difficulty is that output and desired capital stock are part of the same decision, granting the Jorgenson model, and it is not theoretically appropriate to take output as given and determining desired capital stock. This may not be a minor defect in a model claiming a sound theoretical foundation. Further, if the output-capital-employment decision of the firm is subject to random shock, then it may well be that the same shocks that, for example, cause output to deviate from plans also affect investment. In such a case, output is not uncorrelated with the disturbance in the investment relationship. This seems to me to be the true econometric objection to the insertion of output into the investment function through substitution in the profit-maximizing conditions (as is done by Hall and Jorgenson), although I have some doubts as to whether this is of much quantitative importance.[23]

There is, however, another, much more important reason for regarding output as endogenous to the investment relationship. This is the fact that

[22] Of course, these variables also appear with lags.

[23] Coen objects to that substitution for similar reasons (Chap. 4, p. 144), but since his remarks do not bear directly on estimation problems, the force of his objection is weakened. What matters is not whether the relationship to be estimated reflects causation but what the properties of the disturbances are.

investment expenditures by one firm themselves directly and indirectly generate orders and sales for other firms. Particularly when dealing with industry- or manufacturing-wide aggregates, the fact that output is generated by another equation in which investment expenditures appear ought not to be overlooked. Even if output appears with a lag in the investment function or even if some of the effects of investment on output take time, autocorrelation in the disturbances means that output and output-related variables ought not to be treated as exogenous in estimating the investment equation.

Every one of the four analyses is subject to this criticism to a greater or less degree. The problem is likely to be most serious for the analyses of Coen and Hall and Jorgenson, in which orders in the one case and output in the other appear unlagged as well as lagged; but it is a problem for Bischoff and Klein and Taubman as well.[24]

Conclusion

Each of the four contributions clearly contains something of unique value. It may nevertheless be incumbent upon me to single out the analysis I regard as least vulnerable to the criticisms I have made. With some hesitation, I suggest that the analyses by Bischoff and by Klein and Taubman withstand them better than those by Coen and by Hall and Jorgenson. The Hall and Jorgenson model imposes too many restrictive assumptions, and the estimation procedures and distributed lag specification of Coen leave too much to be desired. Furthermore, these authors neglect the phenomenon of the slow adoption of accelerated depreciation methods. Of four important contributions, consequently, I am slightly more disposed to accept the results of Bischoff and of Klein and Taubman than those of Coen and of Hall and Jorgenson.

[24] The analysis by Klein and Taubman is the only one in which the investment function is placed in the context of a complete model. It would be easier for them than for the other authors to reestimate, treating lagged output as endogenous. There can be no disagreement over their related point that the full effects of tax policy on investment can be assessed only in the context of a complete model where the multiplier effects of investment expenditures are taken into account.

CHAPTER VII

Discussion

ARNOLD C. HARBERGER *University of Chicago*

I CANNOT CONCEIVE THAT, even as little as five years ago, a book of this type would have come anywhere near this one in linking the discussion of concrete policy issues to the subtleties of modern economic theory, to the nuances of interpreting particular data series, and to the details of advanced econometric method. Economics is becoming more and more a science, and economists are more and more professional in its practice. These authors are among the leaders in this exceedingly healthy development.

Having said that, I cannot help reflecting on the disparity of the results emerging from the four treatments of the relation of tax incentives to investment behavior. It is naïve to expect there to be only one way in which economic science can be brought intelligently to bear upon a given set of data to answer a given question. Several models, each soundly based, may still have differing implications, because theory has yet to achieve—if, indeed, it ever will—a unique set of propositions on which all professional economists agree. And where divergent theories are tested on a given body of data, the data might not be sufficiently extensive or robust to show that one approach is superior to another. Alternative basic series may likewise exist, each with its own defects; economists may choose differently among them, and may elect alternative ways of adjusting and using the series to correct for the error components they conceive to be most important. Finally, the matter is still further complicated when distributed lags enter the postulated relationships in a significant way; here the choice of the precise type of lag distribution to be imposed can itself have strong bearing on the results.

The basic trouble is that, in much of their work, economists are destined to deal with a limited body of data. In statistical terms, they have limited degrees of freedom. For the data to tell them anything, they must make arbitrary judgments about specification of the model itself, forms of functional relationships, nature of lag distributions, and the like. Once the investigator makes these judgments, he is in a sense their prisoner; they become the "maintained hypotheses" under which his econometric exercises are carried out. Working within such a framework, the economist can find the results that yield him the best fit for a particular body of data; they may have high levels of significance and good explanatory power, and in this sense be better than any alternative results that can be drawn from the same data within the same framework. But they may, unfortunately, be closely tied up with the framework of maintained hypotheses, in the sense that a modest change in the latter may produce a quite different set of best results.

A long-standing commonplace of scientific method holds that there are in principle an infinite number of hypotheses capable of explaining a given finite body of data. Two points determine a straight line, but an infinite number of parabolas, circles, ellipses, and hyperbolas will also fit those points. In econometric work, complicated functional forms have traditionally been ruled out on essentially a priori grounds, but even so the specification of functions—their form, the determination of which explanatory variables will be introduced in them, and so forth—has been an extremely important issue. As analysts have moved forward to incorporate lag structures in their work, the number of possible hypotheses that might be entertained to explain a given body of data has multiplied as well, thus raising the probability that two—or even four or six—authors, approaching the same question with somewhat different basic models, will each come up with results indicating that his approach is consistent with the data.

Comparison of Approaches

These remarks are relevant to comparing the work under discussion. Of the four, the Klein and Taubman paper has the least restrictive investment function, in the sense that fewer restrictions derived from economic theory are imposed in the derivation of that function. Where distributed lags are used by Klein and Taubman, they are in the main arbitrarily drawn from Shirley Almon's study,[1] and applied to three distinct classes of industries (manufacturing, regulated, and other). But a few unexplained variations

---

[1] Shirley Almon, "The Distributed Lag between Capital Appropriations and Expenditures," *Econometrica*, Vol. 33 (January 1965), pp. 178–96.

occur in the treatment of different sectors. For manufacturing, an Almon-lagged capital stock variable is used, along with others, to explain investment; for the regulated industries an unweighted two-quarter moving average of lagged capital stock is used; for the remaining sector, the variable is simply last quarter's capital stock. A lagged capital utilization variable appears in the equation explaining manufacturing investment, but not in those for the other two sectors. A cash flow variable likewise appears in the manufacturing equation but not in the others. While these discrepancies of approach may have sound justifications, the failure of the authors to make them explicit leaves the reader wondering to what degree the equations presented were the result of an extensive process of experimentation, within a rather loose theoretical framework, in search of the best fit.

On the other hand, Klein and Taubman appear to have taken greater pains to justify the particular data series they have used, and to accommodate their analysis to the nuances of the investment-stimulating legislation, than have the other authors.

By way of contrast, the paper by Hall and Jorgenson adopts the explicit framework of neoclassical capital theory, and imposes on the model derived from that framework the restrictive assumptions of (1) competition, (2) Cobb-Douglas production functions, (3) exponential depreciation of capital goods, and (4) a constant before-tax discount rate. The solid theoretical foundation for Hall and Jorgenson's work strikes me as a distinct advantage. Except for the assumption of a constant before-tax discount rate, the other restrictions appear also to have some independent justification. The assumption of competition is clearly violated in the real world, but the results would be much the same if it were replaced by an assumed constant degree of monopoly; only if the degree of monopoly were itself a function of the tax changes would a serious problem be involved here. The Cobb-Douglas production functions are defended on the ground that a significant body of empirical evidence appears to be consistent with the Cobb-Douglas hypothesis, although the authors recognize that some studies suggest an elasticity of substitution between capital and labor of less than one. The assumption of the exponential depreciation of capital goods has great advantages of mathematical convenience in a model of the type Hall and Jorgenson employ, and appears, like the assumption of Cobb-Douglas production functions, at least not to have been controverted by the weight of existing evidence.

A constant before-tax discount rate is, however, another matter. In accepting it, Hall and Jorgenson implicitly make an extreme and implausible assumption about the shifting of the corporation tax, namely, that with the imposition of an increase in the tax, the after-tax rate of return will fall by the full amount of such increase, and will rise by the full amount with a decrease in the tax rate. This result would be plausible if the corporation income tax struck all income from capital equally, but it is not plausible for the U.S. case, in which the corporation income tax applies to the income from only about half the capital in the economy. All income from capital in unincorporated enterprise (predominantly housing and agricultural capital) is exempt from the corporation income tax, and that part of corporate capital that is financed by debt also is exempt. As a consequence, so long as equilibrium prevails in the capital market before and after a change in the corporation income tax, one would expect an increase in the corporation tax rates to depress the after-tax rate of return on all capital, and a decrease in the tax rate to enhance it. But it is indeed extreme to assume that the after-tax rate of return to corporate equity capital falls by the full amount of the tax, for then equilibrium in the capital market would require a corresponding fall in the rate of interest on debt capital and in the rate of return obtained in the noncorporate sector. Capital as a factor of production would under these circumstances bear substantially more than the full burden of the tax.[2] It is far more plausible to assume that capital bears approximately the full burden of the corporation income tax, which means that the after-tax rate of return to corporate equity capital would rise by approximately half of any decrease in the tax rate, or fall by approximately half of any increase in that rate, with the rates of return to noncorporate and corporate nonequity capital falling or rising equally with the after-tax yield on corporate capital in the case, respectively, of a rate increase or a rate decrease.

The effect of assuming a constant before-tax discount rate is therefore to exaggerate considerably the effect of tax stimuli upon investment, because it ignores their indirect influence on investment through rises in the rate of interest. I shall return to this issue.

Bischoff's paper is in much the same spirit as Hall and Jorgenson's, although somewhat less restrictive in its assumptions. The basic differences

[2] In the United States, the capital impact would be approximately twice the full tax burden. For an elaboration of this point see Arnold C. Harberger, "The Corporation Income Taxes," in *International Encyclopedia of the Social Sciences*, Vol. 15 (Macmillan, 1968); Arnold C. Harberger, "The Incidence of the Corporation Income Tax," *Journal of Political Economy*, Vol. 70 (June 1962), pp. 215–40; and John G. Cragg, Arnold C. Harberger, and Peter Mieszkowski, "Empirical Evidence on the Incidence of the Corporation Income Tax," *Journal of Political Economy*, Vol. 75 (December 1967), pp. 811–21.

are that (1) Bischoff does not impose a Cobb-Douglas production function but instead fits the more flexible constant-elasticity-of-substitution function; (2) Bischoff permits the lag pattern of investment response to changes in relative prices to be different from the lag pattern of response to output changes, whereas the Hall and Jorgenson procedure effectively imposes the same lag pattern in the two cases; and (3) Bischoff permits the discount rate governing investment decisions to respond to changes in market interest rates, whereas Hall and Jorgenson do not. Bischoff's estimates of the elasticity of substitution that yield the best fits are sufficiently close to unity that one cannot attribute significant differences between his results and those of Hall and Jorgenson to his relaxation of the Cobb-Douglas assumption.

Far more important is Bischoff's allowance for different lag patterns of response to changes in relative prices and in output. Bischoff's Table 3-11 reveals a rapid response of investment to output changes, initially more than double the steady-state response and remaining greater than the steady-state response for eleven quarters. On the other hand, Table 3-11 also indicates that the response of investment to price changes (which include changes in equipment cost, interest rate, and taxes) is slow, starting with a small negative effect relative to the steady-state response and taking nine quarters to build up to 90 percent and eleven quarters to reach 100 percent. These results suggest that Hall and Jorgenson have probably overestimated the effectiveness of the tax incentives in stimulating investment; their common pattern of lagged response of investment to changes in price and output probably approximates a weighted average of Bischoff's slow response to price changes and his rapid response to output changes, and hence overstates the speed of reaction to price changes and understates that to output movements.

Bischoff's approach also has an advantage over Hall and Jorgenson's in that it permits the cost-of-capital variable to be influenced by movements in the market interest rate and in the dividend yield on stocks, as well as by tax changes. It is quite clear that the estimates in both papers of investment responsiveness are dominated by output changes, Bischoff's probably substantially less so than Hall and Jorgenson's, as his price variable captures additional (and thoroughly valid) sources of movement in the cost of capital.

But let it be noted that, like Hall and Jorgenson's, Bischoff's estimates of the actual effect of tax concessions on investment fail to allow for the effects of the concessions on interest rates. Whereas Hall and Jorgenson assume the before-tax rate of return in corporate capital to be constant, and measure the influence of tax incentives on this basis, Bischoff assumes in effect that in the absence of tax concessions the interest rate and dividend yield would have followed the same time path as they actually did in the presence of the concessions. Bischoff's treatment of interest rates and stock yields as exogenous is thus subject to the same criticism as Hall and Jorgenson's treatment of the before-tax rate of return as given.

Coen's approach is more general than both Bischoff's and Hall and Jorgenson's in that (1) Coen does not postulate an explicit form for the production function; (2) Coen directly estimates separate coefficients for his new orders (corresponding to output) and price variables, whereas the user cost (price) variable and the output variable enter Bischoff's and Hall and Jorgenson's estimated equations multiplicatively, so that their separate influences are either equal (Hall and Jorgenson) or constrained by a single estimated coefficient (Bischoff); and (3) Coen introduces cash flow as a determinant of investment, while Bischoff and Hall and Jorgenson do not. Coen's model is less general than Bischoff's in that Coen imposes a single exponential lag structure according to which investment responds to price and output stimuli.

Unlike Klein and Taubman and like Hall and Jorgenson and Bischoff, Coen derives his estimated equation directly from a theoretical framework that incorporates profit maximization. He handles the cash flow variable (which is indeed difficult to incorporate in a maximizing model) most ingeniously, by postulating that variations in cash flow do not influence the target capital stock determined by price and output, but rather affect the speed with which that target level is approached. He differs from Bischoff and Hall and Jorgenson in imposing an exponential adjustment lag, whereas they obtain their lag structure from the data; but he adds some flexibility by incorporating a fitted expectations lag (the same for the price and new orders variables). I doubt, however, that these differences are of great importance in accounting for the differences in results.

I suspect that the important difference between Coen's approach on the one hand and Bischoff's and Hall and Jorgenson's on the other is the manner in which the user cost and output variables enter the equation; and it is difficult to say in this case that one approach is clearly better than the other. If the data were perfect, I think there would be little doubt that Coen's formulation would be preferable. For both Hall and Jorgenson and Bischoff, the lag-adjusted price and output series enter multiplicatively in the equation explaining investment; a single coefficient applies to their product. While admittedly something is lost in linearizing a product like, say, $(p/c)_t Q_t$ into $(\overline{p/c}) Q_t + (p/c)_t \overline{Q}$, I do not feel that the loss is likely to be great. And if it is not great, performing the linearization and introducing $(p/c)_t$ and Q_t separately can be regarded as a test of the validity of the fundamental assumption that $\overline{(p/c)}Q_t$ and $(p/c)_t\overline{Q}$ have the same coefficient. A formulation similar to Coen's can in this sense be regarded as providing a test of one of the basic assumptions of both Bischoff and Hall and Jorgenson, so long as the data are strong enough for this task.

Unfortunately, that is unlikely to be the case. Zvi Griliches, who first called this point to my attention, has expressed the judgment that the average measurement error in the user cost variables employed by these authors can easily be as high as 20 to 25 percent of the mean of such variables. In common, I believe, with most other observers, I share his qualms. If he is correct, when output and user cost are introduced as separate variables in a regression, the coefficient of user cost will be biased strongly toward zero because of its high error component. Coen's results, which indicate a much smaller effect of the tax stimuli than Bischoff's or Hall and Jorgenson's, can be explained in this way, provided one is willing to postulate a sufficiently high error component in his user cost variable.

The Hall and Jorgenson and Bischoff results are less influenced by this error, because by hypothesis they get information on the coefficient of user cost from variations in output as well as in user cost (price). Error variability is a significantly smaller fraction of the total variability of $(p/c)_t Q_t$ than it is of the total variability of $(p/c)_t$ alone; hence the coefficient of the $(p/c)_t Q_t$ variable is less biased than that of $(p/c)_t$. Similarly, one can say that the substantial variations in output that took place over the estimating period bring a lot more information to bear on the estimate of the user cost coefficient than Coen's approach will allow. Thus if one is willing to accept the theoretical framework of Bischoff or Hall and Jorgenson, with its implication that the output and price variables *should* be joined together, one can easily be led by econometric considerations to prefer their results to Coen's. But if one rejects the framework implying that $(p/c)_t Q_t$ is the right variable, or accepts that framework tentatively but judges the issue of measurement error to be of minor importance, then one would be inclined to regard Coen's results as superior.

My final point in connection with Coen's work is that he, like Hall and Jorgenson and Bischoff, measures partial rather than total effects of the tax incentives, in the sense that he does not allow for the effects of these incentives themselves on interest rates.

Consequences of the Tax Measures

This section explores the likely macroeconomic consequences of the series of tax measures under consideration, and inquires what the four papers have to say about them. It is not unfair to characterize most proponents of the legislation at the time of enactment as thinking that the measures would increase investment in the U.S. economy in relation to some measure of its overall scale, such as gross national product (GNP). The facts, however, quite clearly belie this key expectation. Whereas in the years 1955 through 1961, gross private domestic investment bore an average relationship to GNP of 15.3 percent, the corresponding average from 1962 onward (including the first half of 1967) is 15.0 percent.

How can this apparent failure of the tax stimuli actually to stimulate be explained? The answer lies largely in the truism that investment must equal savings for the economy as a whole. This means, in national accounting terms, that gross private domestic investment plus net foreign investment must equal gross private savings plus the government surplus. The tax measures under consideration, including the general tax reduction of 1964, produced no clear incentive to savings. Each entailed a reduction in the revenues the government might expect from a given level of GNP, and each entailed a corresponding rise in private disposable income out of a given GNP. But since increments to disposable income are not all saved, the net effect of the tax stimuli has very likely been a reduction in total saving (private plus government) as a fraction of GNP. This, indeed, is what the crude data show, with national saving averaging 16.0 percent of GNP in the 1955–61 period and 15.9 percent in the 1962–67 period. (The difference between national saving and gross private domestic investment is net foreign investment, which increased from an average 0.7 percent of GNP in 1955–61 to an average 0.9 percent in 1962–67.)

Once the issue of the savings rate is brought into the picture, it becomes quite obvious that those who expected the tax stimuli substantially to increase overall investment (and saving) in relation to GNP were doomed from the beginning to disappointment. This does not mean, however, that the measures must be written off as failures. Once the overall savings constraint is accepted, it is clear that the probable effect of the tax stimuli was a shift in the composition of total investment rather than a significant change in its relation to GNP. Such a compositional shift did in fact occur. From an average of 4.8 percent of GNP in the 1955–61 period, residential construction fell to an average 3.9 percent in the 1962–67 period. Counterbalancing this, other private domestic nonresidential investment (principally plant and equipment spending) rose from 9.8 percent of GNP in the earlier period to 10.2 percent in the later period, and was the principal beneficiary of all of the tax measures under consideration.

To the extent that the observed compositional shift of investment was the consequence of the tax stimuli, they should be given good marks, for it is obvious that the marginal productivity of capital in the nonresidential sector of the economy is substantially higher than it is in the housing sector. Tax provisions alone guarantee this; the relevant marginal productivity in the corporate sector is gross of corporate taxes, property taxes, and personal taxes, while in the bulk of the housing sector it does not even include personal taxes. To put it another way, the yield to an individual of a corporate investment is the marginal productivity of that investment less all the taxes that have to be paid out of that marginal product. In owner-occupied housing, the relevant yield is something like the mortgage rate, say 6 percent, reduced by the individual's marginal tax rate. Thus one can applaud the effects of the tax incentives to investment while recognizing that they may not have accomplished the global objective many believe they were intended to produce.[3]

What follows is an attempt, with the aid of some simple models, to isolate the effects of the tax stimuli on what may be called "covered investment," that is, those items of investment that benefited directly from the measures under consideration. In the first example, it is assumed that, in the absence of the tax stimuli, the monetary authorities would have been able to manage their policies so as to achieve the same level of income in each year as that actually attained. There is in this case no "income effect" of the tax measures, only a redistribution of investment from the noncovered to the covered category.

Figure 7-1 depicts investment I as a function of the interest rate r for both the covered c and noncovered n categories. It is assumed that, in the absence of the tax stimuli, the interest rate required to achieve the actual level of income would have been r^0. In the presence of the tax measures, the interest rate required to produce this same level of income is r^1. As a

---

[3] One should not make the mistake here of assuming that a stimulus to residential investment helps the poor at the expense of the rich. The available evidence on housing demand indicates an income elasticity in excess of unity. See Margaret G. Reid, *Housing and Income* (University of Chicago Press, 1962), and David Laidler, "Income Tax Incentives for Owner-Occupied Housing," in Arnold C. Harberger and Martin J. Bailey (eds.), *The Taxation of Income from Capital* (Brookings Institution, 1969).

FIGURE 7-1. Effects of Tax Incentives on Covered and Noncovered Investment, Assuming Actual Time Path of Income

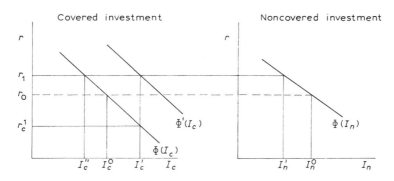

consequence of the tax measures, therefore, noncovered investment falls from I_n^0 to I_n'. Covered investment, however, is subject to two influences. As a consequence of the rise in the interest rate, it would normally tend to fall from I_c^0 to I_c'', but the tax measures shift the investment demand curve to the right, causing a net increase from I_c^0 to I_c'. Another way of interpreting the adjustment is to conceive of the tax stimuli as giving an implicit subsidy to covered investment. This subsidy can be converted into an equivalent reduction in the interest rate, equal to $(r^1 - r_c^1)$. Under this interpretation the effect of the rise in the interest rate itself would again be to reduce covered investment to I_c'', and the partial or direct effect of the tax stimuli would have been movement along $\Phi(I_c)$ increasing investment from I_c'' to I_c'.

All four analyses follow this second interpretation, in that they convert the tax measures into equivalent reductions in the interest rate or—what amounts to much the same thing—the user cost of capital. But three of the four take as the effect of the tax stimuli what I have called the partial or direct effect, and make no allowance for the rise in interest rates caused by these same tax measures. Thus, the Hall and Jorgenson, Bischoff, and Coen measures of the increase in investment caused by the stimuli correspond to $I_c' - I_c''$ in Figure 7-1, not to $I_c' - I_c^0$, which represents the total effect. Klein and Taubman, on the other hand, indicate that their results stem from inserting the tax stimulus $(r^1 - r_c^1)$ into the Wharton Econometric Forecasting Unit model, and solving for the resulting increase in gross fiscal nonresidential investment. Their answer thus corresponds, in a sense, to the general equilibrium answer of $I_c' - I_c^0$, but their underlying model was different from the one discussed here, as they obtain different time paths of GNP with and without the tax stimuli, while this model assumes the course of GNP to be unaffected by them.

In a second simple model, in which the tax measures can have an effect upon GNP, it is assumed that the time path of the quantity of money would have been the same in the presence or absence of the tax measures. This is analogous to saying that the *LM* curve of the traditional Keynesian or neo-Keynesian analysis would be unaffected by the policies in question. Here the tax stimuli result in a rightward shift of the *IS* curve, causing both income and the interest rate to rise. The effect on covered investment is depicted in Figure 7-2.

FIGURE 7-2. Effects of Tax Incentives on Covered Investment, Assuming Actual Time Path of Money Supply

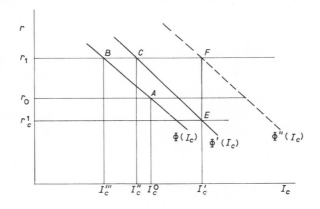

The indirect effect of the measures through the induced change in the interest rate is given by a movement along $\Phi(I_c)$ from A to B; the indirect effect through the induced change in income is given by a shift of the investment demand curve from $\phi(I_c)$ to $\phi'(I_c)$ and is reflected in a movement from B to C; and the direct price effect, which Hall and Jorgenson, Bischoff, and Coen attempt to measure, is given by a movement along $\phi'(I_c)$ from C to E. (This last step can equivalently be considered a shift of the investment demand from C to F.) The total effect of the tax stimuli on covered investment is thus given by $I'_c - I^0_c$. The effect on noncovered investment is indeterminate, consisting of a reduction caused by the rise in the interest rate and an increase caused by the rise in GNP.

A third possible policy alternative is that in the absence of the tax measures the time path of interest rates would have been the same as that which actually developed, a not implausible assumption in the light of the key role of the interest rate in the defense of the U.S. balance of payments. Under this alternative, no part of the upward drift of interest rates that has taken place since 1962 is attributed to the tax measures since, by assumption, it would have happened even in their absence. The role of the tax measures is then to prevent this tightening of credit markets from having the negative effect on economic activity that it would normally entail. Analytically, in this case, starting from the position (probably of less than full employment) that the economy would have reached with the same interest rate but in the absence of the tax measures, the effect of the measures is to produce a rightward shift of the *IS* curve, and a concomitant rightward shift of the *LM* curve, so as to permit equilibrium at a higher level of income with the same interest rate. The effect on covered investment is shown in Figure 7-3.

FIGURE 7-3. Effects of Tax Incentives on Covered Investment, Assuming Actual Time Path of Interest Rates

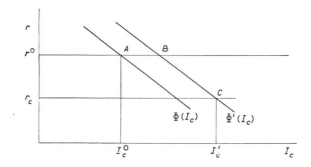

Here the change in this category of investment occasioned by the tax stimuli consists of two steps: a move from *A* to *B* occasioned by the induced increase in income, and a move from *B* to *C* representing the direct price effect of the tax incentives.

This discussion serves only to open up a series of issues that lamentably were not treated by any of the authors. Hall and Jorgenson, Bischoff, and Coen simply bypass all general equilibrium considerations and concentrate on attempting to measure the direct price effect of the incentives. They therefore cannot purport to say anything about the total effect. The total effect must be less than the direct effect where alternative monetary policy would have kept the time path of income the same; it must be greater than the direct effect where alternative monetary policy would have kept the time path of interest rates the same; and it can be either greater or less than the direct effect in the case where the alternative policy would have maintained the same time path of the money supply—all this in the context of the simple models outlined above, and referring only to covered investment.

Klein and Taubman, on the other hand, though unique in working within a general equilibrium framework, fail to spell out the key assumptions about policy and behavior underlying their solution, and do nothing at all to explore the implications of the tax incentives under different assumptions about monetary policy. On the first point, they are clearly in a better position than any reader to distinguish the key behavioral and policy forces that, in the Wharton model, contribute important elements to their solution. Had they done this, they could have given at least a rough idea of the nature, in their model, of the principal indirect effects of the tax stimuli on both covered and noncovered investment. They could also, of course, have stated explicitly the main policy assumptions on which their solution is based, so that readers could readily judge their plausibility.

On the second point, I would like to have seen alternative solutions based on different policy assumptions, analogous but not necessarily equivalent to the three cases discussed above. I have no doubt that with a sufficiently easy monetary policy the actual time path of GNP could have been approximately replicated even in the absence of the tax incentives. It is therefore of some interest to explore this case. On the other hand, the preoccupation of the monetary authorities with the balance of payments makes it unlikely that they would have pursued such a policy; on this ground the equal-interest-rate case is worth exploring. Even more interesting would be a model in which the actual time path of the balance of payments was replicated, and its consequences for GNP, interest rates, and covered and noncovered investment derived, on the assumption the tax incentives did not exist. But this is probably asking too much, as I know of no way reliably to capture, in an econometric equation, the volatile function explaining the capital account of the balance of payments. All the difficulties encountered in explaining private domestic investment—and many more— are present when the capital account is the dependent variable.

In sum, therefore, the quality of the work presented here is very high, but the analyses leave unfinished and unclear the picture of the quantitative effects of the tax incentives that have been examined. I remain prone to the same rough judgment about these incentives that I have held for several years: that they played an important role in permitting us to come reasonably close to full employment in the presence of a strong balance-of-payments constraint; that they accomplished this by creating a situation in which the interest rate level consistent with full employment was significantly higher than it otherwise would be; that, viewed against alternative ways of achieving full employment, these tax stimuli produced a massive shift of investment from the noncovered sector (principally residential housing) to the covered sector, without much change in total investment; and that, viewed against the alternative of maintaining the same interest-rate or balance-of-payments posture that obtained, the incentives probably accounted for a significant increase in total investment and in income.

Symbols

a_i	= parameters in investment relationships
A	= proportionality or technological change factor
A'_j	= parameters of polynomial distributed lag
$\left.\begin{array}{l} A_1, A_2, A_3, \\ A'_1, A'_2, A'_3, \\ B_1, B_2, B_3, \\ B'_1, B'_2, B'_3, \\ C_1, C_2, C_3, C_4 \end{array}\right\}$	= Almon polynomial distributed lag coefficients
b	= reaction coefficient, proportion
b'	= dividend reaction coefficient, proportion
b''	= coefficient of additional reaction, proportion
b_{i_t}	= reaction coefficient of firm i in period t
B'_j	= parameters of polynomial distributed lag
c	= rental price of capital (termed user cost by Coen)
c_i	= rental price or cost of the ith factor
c_1	= rental price of capital equipment
c_{j_t}	= rental price in period t using the jth depreciation method (termed user cost by Coen)
c^B	= rental price that would have prevailed had there been no change in tax policy
C	= personal consumption expenditures

CCA	= capital consumption allowances (subscript M denotes manufacturing)
CDT	= investment tax credit, millions of dollars
$COST$	= total cost of production
d	= total differentiation operator
d_i	= parameters in desired capital relationships
D	= depreciation (subscripts M, R, and O denote depreciation in manufacturing, regulated, and other nonfarm sectors, respectively)
D^A	= depreciation after adoption of accelerated methods, millions of dollars
D^B	= depreciation before adoption of accelerated methods (straight-line before 1954), millions of dollars
$D(s-t)$	= depreciation per dollar of initial investment (q_t) allowable for tax purposes as a deduction from income at time t on an asset of age $s-t$ (sometimes written as $D(s)$ with t assumed equal to zero)
DIV	= dividends, millions of dollars
$DIV/PRICE$	= Moody's industrial dividend-price ratio
DMY_{LIVES}	= dummy variable to account for 1962 changes in depreciation guidelines (equals zero before the first quarter of 1962 and unity thereafter)
DW	= Durbin-Watson coefficient
e	= Napierian constant
E	= price elasticity of demand for output
E_j	= price elasticity of supply of factor j
f	= function operator
F	= internally generated cash flow or profits after taxes plus depreciation
F^B	= internally generated cash flow or profits after taxes plus depreciation before adoption of accelerated methods or other tax policy changes
F_A	= cash flow generated by project A
F_B	= cash flow generated by project B
$\mathscr{F}$	= likelihood ratio test statistic
G	= criterion function for parameter estimation
GNP	= gross national product
GNP^{58}	= gross national product in 1958 dollars
h'	= parameter reflecting exponential rate of technical change

h = parameter reflecting technical change, that over time, augments the amount of output from a given input

h_1 = technical change parameter for capital equipment (see h_i)

I = gross investment

I_c = gross investment in sectors covered by tax incentives

I_n = gross investment in sectors not covered by tax incentives

$\breve{I}_t$ = autoregressively transformed values of gross investment

$\hat{I}$ = predicted value of gross investment

$\hat{I}^\mathrm{B}$ = predicted value of gross investment without policy changes (sometimes shown without $\hat{\ }$)

$\hat{I}^r$ = predicted value of gross investment when the bond yield and dividend-price ratio are held constant at 3.75 percent and 4.39 percent, respectively

$\hat{I}^{V'}$ = predicted value of gross investment when V' is held constant at 5.79

I^{58} = gross investment in 1958 dollars

I^* = planned gross investment in dollars

I_BUS = gross fixed nonresidential investment (subscripts M, R, and O denote plant and equipment expenditures in manufacturing, regulated, and other nonfarm industries, respectively)

I_N = net investment (subscript MD denotes net investment in durable manufacturing)

I_QK = gross investment measured in capacity-output units

I_QK^* = planned gross investment measured in capacity-output units

IO = investment orders

IVA = inventory valuation adjustment

$JCAP_M$ = Wharton capacity utilization index for manufacturing

k = rate of investment tax credit, proportion

k^* = a priori specified value of k

k' = rate of investment tax credit deductible from depreciation, proportion

K = capital stock (if no time index is shown, generally assumed to be at end of period $t-1$)

K_t^* = desired or optimum level of capital stock at the end of period t

$\tilde{K}_t^*$	= autogressively transformed values of desired capital stock
K_{t-1}	= actual level of capital stock at the end of period $t-1$
K	= capital stock in manufacturing (subscripts M, R, and O denote depreciation in manufacturing, regulated, and other nonfarm sectors, respectively)
L	= quantity of labor input
L^*	= desired or optimum quantity of labor input
m	= number of factors
m_1	= number of parameters to be estimated without constraints
m_0	= number of parameters to be estimated with constraints taken into account
m_2	= number of observations
m_3	= number of parameters to be estimated
M	= rate of markup on marginal or minimum average costs
MP_j	= marginal productivity of factor j
n	= maximum length of lag distribution
O	= manufacturers' new orders received
p	= price of output
p_j	= price of factor j
P_{IBUS}	= implicit deflator for nonresidential fixed business investment
q	= price of new capital goods
Q	= quantity of output
Q^*	= expected, planned, or desired output
Q_K	= level of capacity measured in output units
Q_K^*	= level of desired capacity measured in output units
r	= interest or discount rate
r'	= rate of return after taxes
r^a	= rate of interest or return after tax credit
r^b	= market rate of interest on bonds
r^e	= implicit rate of interest that must be paid for equity capital
r_c	= implicit interest rate for sector covered by investment tax incentives
r_0	= parameter, constant term in Bischoff cost of capital equation

r_1	= parameter on Moody's industrial bond yield in Bischoff cost of capital equation
r_2	= parameter on Moody's industrial dividend yield in Bischoff cost of capital equation
r_3	= parameter on time in Bischoff cost of capital equation
r_4	= parameter on tax rate in Bischoff cost of capital equation
R	= profits or gross business income before taxes plus depreciation
R_{ZA}	= rate of profits after taxes earned on sales, proportion
RE_M	= retained earnings in manufacturing
RES_{NB}	= unborrowed reserves
RM_{CPAPER}	= rate on four- to six-month commercial paper
RM_{GBL}	= long-term government bond yield
RM_{MBCIND}	= Moody's corporate industrial bond yield
R_I^2	= ratio of explained sum of squares to total sum of squares for gross investment
R_N^2	= ratio of explained sum of squares to total sum of squares for net investment
R^2	= coefficient of determination not corrected for degrees of freedom
$\bar{R}^2$	= coefficient of determination corrected for degrees of freedom
s	= a time index
S	= lag operator, for example, $SK_t = K_{t-1}$, $S^2K_t = K_{t-2}$
S_e	= standard error of estimate
S_F	= final sales (GNP minus inventory change)
S_R	= realized level of sales
t	= the present time period
T	= depreciable lifetime of an asset
$T*$	= optimal switchover point (in years) from declining-balance to straight-line depreciation
TC	= corporate profits taxes
$TIME$	= time trend
u	= statutory tax rate on income
$u-\tilde{u}$	= tax rate cuts equivalent to reductions in user cost that actually occurred
u^B	= statutory tax rate on income before tax cut, proportion
v	= proportion of depreciation for tax purposes to replacement

v_1, v_2 = constant exponential parameters

V = factor proportions or relative price of factor inputs

V' = modified concept of V (see text, p. 82).

V^* = desired factor proportions

w = wage rate or price of labor input

$\dot{w}$ = rate of change of wage rates

w_0 = wage rate in initial period

W = net worth

x = any time series variable

X_i = input of the ith factor

X_1 = input of capital equipment

X_M = output orginating in manufacturing (subscript MD, instead of M, denotes durable manufacturing)

z = discounted value of deductions from fully depreciating an asset with an initial cost of one dollar, over its lifetime

z^* = discounted value of economic depreciation (z calculated with an exponential rate of depreciation equal to δ)

z^B = discounted value of depreciation deductions before reduction in useful lives

z_{j_t} = discounted value of depreciation deductions in period t using method j

z_{SL} = discounted value of straight-line depreciation deductions (z calculated with rate of depreciation equal to $1/T$)

z_{SYD} = discounted value of sum-of-the-years-digits depreciation deductions (z calculated with rate of depreciation equal to $2(T-s)/T^2$)

Z = profits

Z_A = profits after taxes

Z_B = profits before taxes

Z'_B = modified concept of profits before taxes (defined as the difference between current revenue and current outlay less the rental value of capital services)

Z_{B+IVA} = corporate profits before taxes adjusted for inventory valuation changes

α = elasticity of output with respect to capital input

α' = parameter relating investment to changes in output

α_i = parameter relating output to input of the ith factor

α_1 = parameter relating output to input of capital equipment

$\boldsymbol{\beta}$ = set of β_{ij} parameters

$\hat{\boldsymbol{\beta}}$ = estimated set of β_{ij} parameters

β_1 = desired capital-output ratio, proportion

β_2 = optimum utilization rate of capital, proportion

β_3 = desired dividend-profit payout ratio, proportion

β_4 = proportion of gross investment to be financed externally

β_i = a constant parameter

β_{ij} = parameter in Bischoff distributed lag

β_τ = parameters in polynomial distributed lag

$\beta(S)$ = polynomial distributed lag operator

$\gamma(S)$ = polynomial distributed lag operator

δ = rate of real depreciation or rate of economic obsolescence, proportion

∂ = partial differentiation operator

$\boldsymbol{\partial}$ = matrix of partial derivatives

$\varDelta$ = backwards first-difference operator which subtracts the value of a variable at time $t-1$ from its value at time t

ε = error term distributed serially independently and uniformly over time

$\varepsilon_0, \varepsilon_1$ = residuals in constrained estimate equation

$\hat{\varepsilon}_{k*}$ = estimated residuals when k is specified at an a priori value $k*$

$\hat{\varepsilon}_k$ = estimated residuals when k is estimated with other parameters

ζ^* = desired capacity-output ratio

η = a time index

θ = ratio of rate of declining-balance depreciation to rate of straight-line depreciation

κ = order of polynomial

λ_ι = parameter in Bischoff distributed lag of effect of changes in relative factor prices on investment

$\varLambda$ = Lagrangian parameter

μ^i = Almon lag distribution weights

μ_j = parameter in Bischoff distributed lag of effect of changes in output on investment

$\mu(S)$	=	time sequence of investment project completions or expenditures (in some cases restricted to a polynomial distributed lag)
$\mu(12)$	=	twelve-quarter inverted-V distributed lag in Coen investment function
ν	=	autoregressive error term
ξ	=	distributed lag on output
π_i	=	parameters in polynomial distributed lag
ρ	=	before-tax rate of return
ρ_1	=	first-order autoregression coefficient
ρ_2	=	second-order autoregression coefficient
$\rho\{x\}$	=	autoregressive transformation of variable x
σ	=	elasticity of substitution
ς	=	proportion of depreciation taken by accelerated methods
τ	=	a time index
υ	=	efficiency parameter
φ	=	distributed lag on output
Φ	=	a function operator (sometimes with subscript)
ψ_j	=	distributed lag on installation of investment orders, or the proportion of capacity ordered in period t that is installed in period j
χ	=	distributed lag on factor proportions
ω_1	=	autocorrelation parameter, second term in $\omega(S)$ polynomial
$\hat{\omega}_1$	=	first-round estimator of the autocorrelation parameter ω_1
$\omega(S)$	=	polynomial distributed lag operator

Conference Participants

Albert Ando
  University of Pennsylvania

Charles W. Bischoff
  Yale University

William C. Brainard
  Yale University

Gerard M. Brannon
  U.S. Treasury Department

John A. Brittain
  The Brookings Institution

E. Cary Brown
  Massachusetts Institute of
  Technology

Murray Brown
  University of Buffalo

Samuel B. Chase, Jr.
  University of Montana

Robert M. Coen
  Stanford University

Sheldon S. Cohen
  Cohen & Uretz

Phoebus J. Dhrymes
  University of Pennsylvania

Otto Eckstein
  Harvard University

Robert Eisner
  Northwestern University

Franklin M. Fisher
  Massachusetts Institute of
  Technology

Gary Fromm
  American University

Zvi Griliches
  Harvard University

Robert E. Hall
    Massachusetts Institute
    of Technology

Arnold C. Harberger
    University of Chicago

Bert G. Hickman
    Stanford University

Hendrik S. Houthakker
    Council of Economic Advisers

Dale W. Jorgenson
    Harvard University

Lawrence R. Klein
    University of Pennsylvania

Edwin Kuh
    Massachusetts Institute of
    Technology

Ta-Chung Liu
    Cornell University

Guy Orcutt
    Yale University

Joseph A. Pechman
    The Brookings Institution

George L. Perry
    The Brookings Institution

Richard E. Slitor
    U.S. Treasury Department

Stanley S. Surrey
    Harvard University

Paul Taubman
    University of Pennsylvania

Melvin I. White
    City University of New York

Selected Bibliography

Almon, Shirley. "The Distributed Lag between Capital Appropriations and Expenditures," *Econometrica*, Vol. 33 (January 1965), pp. 178–96.

———. "Lags between Investment Decisions and Their Causes," *Review of Economics and Statistics*, Vol. 50 (May 1968), pp. 193–206.

Anderson, W. H. Locke. *Corporate Finance and Fixed Investment*. Boston: Harvard University, Graduate School of Business Administration, Division of Research, 1964.

Ando, Albert, E. Cary Brown, Robert M. Solow, and John Karaken. "Lags in Fiscal and Monetary Policy," in Commission on Money and Credit, *Stabilization Policies*. Englewood Cliffs, N.J.: Prentice-Hall, 1963.

Angell, James W., "Uncertainty, Likelihoods and Investment Decisions," *Quarterly Journal of Economics*, Vol. 75 (February 1960), pp. 1–28.

Arrow, Kenneth J. "Optimal Capital Policy with Irreversible Investment," in James N. Wolfe (ed.), *Values, Capital and Growth: Papers in Honour of Sir John Hicks*. Edinburgh: Edinburgh University Press, 1968.

———, Hollis B. Chenery, B. S. Minhas, and Robert M. Solow. "Capital-Labor Substitution and Economic Efficiency," *Review of Economics and Statistics*, Vol. 43 (August 1961), pp. 225–50.

Bailey, Martin J. "Formal Criteria for Investment Decisions," *Journal of Political Economy*, Vol. 67 (October 1959), pp. 476–88.

Bardhan, Pranab K., and Ronald Britto. "Properties of Equilibrium in a Growth Model with Economic Obsolescence; Some Micro-Economic Properties of Vintage-Type Capital Models." Processed. Paper presented to the North

American Regional Conference of the Econometric Society, Washington, December 1967.

Black, J. "Investment Allowances, Initial Allowances and Cheap Loans as Means of Encouraging Investment," *Review of Economic Studies*, Vol. 27 (October 1959), pp. 44–49.

Boot, J. C. G., and G. M. De Wit. "Investment Demand: An Empirical Contribution to the Aggregation Problem," *International Economic Review*, Vol. 1 (January 1960), pp. 3–30.

Borch, Karl. "Equilibrium in a Reinsurance Market," *Econometrica*, Vol. 30 (July 1962), pp. 424–44.

Bowman, Mary J. (ed.) *Expectations, Uncertainty and Business Behavior.* New York: Social Science Research Council, Committee on Business Enterprise Research, 1958.

Bowman, Raymond T., and Almarin Phillips. "The Capacity Concept and Induced Investment," *Canadian Journal of Economics and Political Science*, Vol. 21 (May 1955), pp. 190–203.

Bridge, Lawrence. "The Financing of Investment by New Firms," in Universities-National Bureau Committee for Economic Research, *Conference on Research in Business Finance.* New York: National Bureau of Economic Research, 1952.

Brockie, Melvin D., and Arthur L. Grey, Jr. "The Marginal Efficiency of Capital and Investment Programming," *Economic Journal*, Vol. 66 (December 1956), pp. 662–75.

Broster, E. J. "An Economic Analysis of Fixed Investment," *Economic Journal*, Vol. 68 (December 1958), pp. 768–79.

Brown, E. Cary. "Business-Income Taxation and Investment Incentives," in Lloyd A. Metzler and others, *Income, Employment and Public Policy: Essays in Honor of Alvin H. Hansen.* New York: W. W. Norton and Co., 1948.

———. "Purposes and Functions of Depreciation under the Income Tax," in E. Cary Brown and others, *Depreciation and Taxes.* Symposium conducted by the Tax Institute. Princeton: Tax Institute, 1959.

———. "Tax Incentives for Investment," in American Economic Association, *Papers and Proceedings of the Seventy-fourth Annual Meeting, 1961 (American Economic Review*, Vol. 52, May 1962), pp. 335–45.

Brown, Murray. "Profit, Output and Liquidity in the Theory of Fixed Investment," *International Economic Review*, Vol. 2 (January 1961), pp. 110–21.

———, and Herman Roseman. "Cross-Section Analysis of Manufacturing Investment During 1951–55," in American Statistical Association, *Proceedings of the Business and Economic Statistics Section, 1957*, pp. 344–51.

Campagna, Anthony S. "Capital Appropriations and the Investment Decision," *Review of Economics and Statistics*, Vol. 50 (May 1968), pp. 207–14.

Carter, C. F., G. P. Meredith, and G. L. S. Shackle (eds.). *Uncertainty and Business Decisions; A Symposium.* Liverpool: University Press of Liverpool, 1954.

Chase, Sam B., Jr. "Tax Credits for Investment Spending," *National Tax Journal,* Vol. 15 (March 1962), pp. 32–52.

Chawner, Lowell J. "Capital Expenditures for Manufacturing Plant and Equipment—1915–1940," *Survey of Current Business,* Vol. 21 (March 1941), pp. 9–15.

Chenery, Hollis B. "Overcapacity and the Acceleration Principle," *Econometrica,* Vol. 20 (January 1952), pp. 1–28.

Clower, R. W. "An Investigation into the Dynamics of Investment," *American Economic Review,* Vol. 44 (March 1954), pp. 64–81.

Coen, Robert M. "Tax Policy and Investment Behavior: Comment," *American Economic Review,* Vol. 59 (June 1969), pp. 370–79.

———, and Bert G. Hickman. "Aggregative Demand Functions for Capital and Labor in the U.S. Economy." Processed. Research Memorandum No. 74. Stanford University Research Center in Economic Growth, July 1969.

Cohen, Morris. "Anticipations Data in the Capital Goods Field," in American Statistical Association, *Proceedings of the Business and Economic Statistics Section, 1957,* pp. 193–97.

Colm, Gerhard. "Tax Policy and Capital Formation," in National Industrial Conference Board, *Capital Formation and Its Elements.* New York: NICB, 1939.

Cragg, John G., Arnold C. Harberger, and Peter Mieszkowski. "Empirical Evidence on the Incidence of the Corporation Income Tax," *Journal of Political Economy,* Vol. 75 (December 1967), pp. 811–21.

Creamer, Daniel B. *Capital Expansion and Capacity in Postwar Manufacturing.* Studies in Business Economics, No. 72. New York: National Industrial Conference Board, 1961.

———. *Capital and Output Trends in Manufacturing Industries, 1880–1948.* Occasional Paper 41. New York: National Bureau of Economic Research, 1954.

———. "Postwar Trends in the Relation of Capital to Output in Manufactures," in American Economic Association, *Papers and Proceedings of the Seventieth Annual Meeting, 1957 (American Economic Review,* Vol. 48, May 1958), pp. 249–59.

———, Sergei Dobrovolsky, and Israel Borenstein. *Capital in Manufacturing and Mining: Its Formation and Financing.* Princeton: Princeton University Press for the National Bureau of Economic Research, 1960.

Crockett, Jean Bronfenbrenner. "Effect of Current Operating Experience on the Realization of Investment Plans," paper presented to the December 1953 meeting of the Econometric Society, Washington. Abstracted in *Econometrica,* Vol. 22 (October 1954), pp. 525–26.

Cunningham, N. J. "Business Investment and the Marginal Cost of Funds," Pts. 1 and 2, *Metroeconomica,* Vol. 10 (August 1958), pp. 60–73, and Vol. 10 (December 1958), pp. 155–81.

Darling, Paul G. "Surrogative Measurements of Expectations: An Example in Estimating the Liquidity Influence on Investment," *Review of Economics and Statistics,* Vol. 38 (November 1956), pp. 413–26.

de Leeuw, Frank. "The Demand for Capital Goods by Manufacturers: A Study of Quarterly Time Series," *Econometrica*, Vol. 30 (July 1962), pp. 407–23.

Dhrymes, Phoebus J., and Mordecai Kurz. "Investment, Dividend, and External Finance Behavior of Firms," in Robert Ferber (ed.), *Determinants of Investment Behavior*. A Conference of the Universities-National Bureau Committee for Economic Research. New York: Columbia University Press for the National Bureau of Economic Research, 1967.

Dobrovolsky, Sergei P. "Capital Formation and Financing Trends in Manufacturing and Mining, 1900–1953," *Journal of Finance*, Vol. 10 (May 1955), pp. 250–65.

———. "Depreciation Policies and Investment Decisions," *American Economic Review*, Vol. 41 (December 1951), pp. 906–14.

———. "Economics of Corporate Internal and External Financing," *Journal of Finance*, Vol. 13 (March 1958), pp. 35–47.

Domar, Evsey D. "The Case for Accelerated Depreciation," *Quarterly Journal of Economics*, Vol. 67 (November 1953), pp. 493–519.

Durand, David. "The Cost of Capital, Corporation Finance, and the Theory of Investment: Comment," *American Economic Review*, Vol. 49 (September 1959), pp. 639–55.

Eckaus, R. S. "The Acceleration Principle Reconsidered," *Quarterly Journal of Economics*, Vol. 67 (May 1953), pp. 209–30.

———, and Louis Lefeber. "Capital Formation: A Theoretical and Empirical Analysis," *Review of Economics and Statistics*, Vol. 44 (May 1962), pp. 113–22.

Eckstein, Otto. "Manufacturing Investment and Business Expectations: Extensions of de Leeuw's Results," *Econometrica*, Vol. 33 (April 1965), pp. 420–24.

Egerton, R. A. D. *Investment Decisions under Uncertainty*. Liverpool: University Press of Liverpool, 1960.

———. "Investment, Uncertainty and Expectations," *Review of Economic Studies*, Vol. 22, No. 2 (1955), pp. 143–50.

Eisner, Robert. "Accelerated Amortization, Growth, and Net Profits," *Quarterly Journal of Economics*, Vol. 66 (November 1952), pp. 533–44.

———. "Accelerated Depreciation: Some Further Thoughts," *Quarterly Journal of Economics*, Vol. 69 (May 1955), pp. 285–96.

———. "An Appraisal of Proposals for Tax Differentials Affecting Investment," in Dan Throop Smith and others, *Income Tax Differentials*. Princeton: Tax Institute, 1958.

———. "Capital and Labor in Production: Some Direct Estimates," in Murray Brown (ed.), *The Theory and Empirical Analysis of Production*. Studies in Income and Wealth, Vol. 31. New York: Columbia University Press for the National Bureau of Economic Research, 1967.

———. "Capital Expenditures, Profits, and the Acceleration Principle," in National Bureau of Economic Research, *Models of Income Determination*. Studies in Income and Wealth, Vol. 28. Princeton: Princeton University Press for the National Bureau of Economic Research, 1964.

Eisner, Robert. "Determinants of Capital Expenditures: An Interview Study." Studies in Business Expectations and Planning, No. 2. University of Illinois, 1956.

———. "A Distributed Lag Investment Function," *Econometrica*, Vol. 28 (January 1960), pp. 1–29.

———. "Expectations, Plans, and Capital Expenditures: A Synthesis of Ex Post and Ex Ante Data," in Mary J. Bowman (ed.), *Expectations, Uncertainty and Business Behavior*. New York: Social Science Research Council, Committee on Business Enterprise Research, 1958.

———. "Interview and Other Survey Techniques and the Study of Investment," in National Bureau of Economic Research, *Problems of Capital Formation*. Studies in Income and Wealth, Vol. 19. Princeton: Princeton University Press for the National Bureau of Economic Research, 1957.

———. "Investment and the Frustrations of Econometricians." Paper presented to the joint session of the American Economic Association and the Econometric Society, Chicago, December 1968.

———. "Investment: Fact and Fancy," in American Economic Association, *Papers and Proceedings of the Seventy-fifth Annual Meeting, 1962 (American Economic Review*, Vol. 53, May 1963), pp. 237–46.

———. "Investment Plans and Realizations," in American Economic Association, *Papers and Proceedings of the Seventy-fourth Annual Meeting, 1961 (American Economic Review*, Vol. 52, May 1962), pp. 190–203.

———. "A Permanent Income Theory for Investment: Some Empirical Explorations," *American Economic Review*, Vol. 57 (June 1967), pp. 363–90.

———. "Realization of Investment Anticipations," in James S. Duesenberry, Gary Fromm, Lawrence R. Klein, and Edwin Kuh (eds.), *The Brookings Quarterly Econometric Model of the United States*. Chicago: Rand McNally and Co., 1965; Amsterdam: North-Holland, 1965.

———. "Tax Policy and Investment Behavior: Comment," *American Economic Review*, Vol. 59 (June 1969), pp. 379–88.

———, and M. I. Nadiri. "Investment Behavior and Neo-Classical Theory," *Review of Economics and Statistics*, Vol. 50 (August 1968), pp. 369–82.

Eisner, Robert, and Robert H. Strotz. "Determinants of Business Investment," in Commission on Money and Credit, *Impacts of Monetary Policy*. Englewood Cliffs, N.J.: Prentice-Hall, 1963.

Evans, Michael K. "A Study of Industry Investment Decisions," *Review of Economics and Statistics*, Vol. 49 (May 1967), pp. 151–64.

———, and Edward W. Green. "The Relative Efficacy of Investment Anticipations," *Journal of the American Statistical Association*, Vol. 61 (March 1966), pp. 104–16.

Fisher, Franklin M. "Embodied Technical Change and the Existence of an Aggregate Capital Stock," *Review of Economic Studies*, Vol. 32 (October 1965), pp. 263–88.

Fisher, Gene H. "Endogenous and Exogenous Investment in Macro-Economic Models," *Review of Economics and Statistics*, Vol. 35 (August 1953), pp. 211–20.

Foss, Murray F. "The Utilization of Capital Equipment: Postwar Compared with Prewar," *Survey of Current Business*, Vol. 43 (June 1963), pp. 8–16.

————, and Vito Natrella. "The Structure and Realization of Business Investment Anticipations," in Universities-National Bureau Committee for Economic Research, *The Quality and Economic Significance of Anticipations Data*. Princeton: Princeton University Press for the National Bureau of Economic Research, 1960.

————, and ————. "Ten Years' Experience with Business Investment Anticipations," *Survey of Current Business*, Vol. 37 (January 1957), pp. 16–24.

Friend, Irwin, and Jean Bronfenbrenner. "Business Investment Programs and their Realization," *Survey of Current Business*, Vol. 30 (December 1950), pp. 11–22.

————, and ————. "Plant and Equipment Programs and their Realization," in *Short-Term Economic Forecasting*. Studies in Income and Wealth, Vol. 17. Princeton: Princeton University Press for the National Bureau of Economic Research, 1955.

Friend, Irwin, and Irving B. Kravis. "Entrepreneurial Income, Saving and Investment," *American Economic Review*, Vol. 47 (June 1957), pp. 269–301.

Gehrels, Franz, and Suzanne Wiggins. "Interest Rates and Manufacturers' Fixed Investment," *American Economic Review*, Vol. 47 (March 1957), pp. 79–92.

Goode, Richard. "Accelerated Depreciation Allowances as a Stimulus to Investment," *Quarterly Journal of Economics*, Vol. 69 (May 1955), pp. 191–220.

————. "Special Tax Measures To Restrain Investment," *International Monetary Fund Staff Papers*, Vol. 5 (February 1957), pp. 434–48.

Goodwin, Richard M. "Secular and Cyclical Aspects of the Multiplier and the Accelerator," in Lloyd A. Metzler and others, *Income, Employment and Public Policy: Essays in Honor of Alvin H. Hansen*. New York: W. W. Norton, 1948.

Gordon, Myron J. "The Savings Investment and Valuation of a Corporation," *Review of Economics and Statistics*, Vol. 44 (February 1962), pp. 37–51.

————. "Security and a Financial Theory of Investment," *Quarterly Journal of Economics*, Vol. 74 (August 1960), pp. 472–92.

Gordon, Robert J. "$45 Billion of U.S. Private Investment Has Been Mislaid," *American Economic Review*, Vol. 59 (June 1969), pp. 221–38.

————. "The Incidence of the Corporation Income Tax in U.S. Manufacturing, 1925–62," *American Economic Review*, Vol. 57 (September 1967), pp. 731–58.

Goris, Hendrieke, and Leen M. Koyck. "The Prices of Investment Goods and the Volume of Production in the United States," *Review of Economics and Statistics*, Vol. 35 (February 1953), pp. 59–66.

Gould, John P. "Market Value and the Theory of Investment of the Firm," *American Economic Review*, Vol. 57 (September 1967), pp. 910–13.

————. "The Use of Endogenous Variables in Dynamic Models of Investment," *Quarterly Journal of Economics*, Vol. 83 (November 1969), pp. 580–99.

Greenberg, Edward. "A Stock-Adjustment Investment Model," *Econometrica*, Vol. 32 (July 1964), pp. 339–57.

Griliches, Zvi. "Capital Stock in Investment Functions: Some Problems of Concept and Measurement," in Carl F. Christ and others, *Measurement in Economics: Studies in Mathematical Economics and Econometrics in Memory of Yehuda Grunfeld*. Stanford: Stanford University Press, 1963.

————. "The Demand for a Durable Input: Farm Tractors in the United States, 1921–57," in Arnold C. Harberger (ed.), *The Demand for Durable Goods*. Chicago: University of Chicago Press, 1960.

————. "Production Functions in Manufacturing: Some Preliminary Results," in Murray Brown (ed.), *The Theory and Empirical Analysis of Production*. New York: Columbia University Press for the National Bureau of Economic Research, 1967.

————, and Neil Wallace. "The Determinants of Investment Revisited," *International Economic Review*, Vol. 6 (September 1965), pp. 311–29.

Grosse, Robert N. *Capital Requirements for the Expansion of Industrial Capacity*. Vol. 1, Pts. 1 and 2. Washington: U.S. Bureau of the Budget, November 30, 1953.

————. "The Structure of Capital," in Wassily Leontief and others, *Studies in the Structure of the American Economy: Theoretical and Empirical Explorations in Input-Output Analysis*. New York: Oxford University Press, 1953.

————, and Edward B. Berman. "Estimating Future Purchases of Capital Equipment for Replacement," in National Bureau of Economic Research, *Problems of Capital Formation: Concepts, Measurement, and Controlling Factors*. Studies in Income and Wealth, Vol. 19. Princeton: Princeton University Press for the National Bureau of Economic Research, 1957.

Grunfeld, Yehuda. "The Determinants of Corporate Investment," in Arnold C. Harberger (ed.), *The Demand for Durable Goods*. Chicago: University of Chicago Press, 1960.

————, and Zvi Griliches. "Is Aggregation Necessarily Bad?" *Review of Economics and Statistics*, Vol. 42 (February 1960), pp. 1–13.

Haavelmo, Trygve. "The Effect of the Rate of Interest on Investment: A Note," *Review of Economic Statistics*, Vol. 23 (February 1941), pp. 49–52.

————. "A Note on the Theory of Investment," *Review of Economic Studies*, Vol. 16 (1949–50), pp. 78–81.

————. *A Study in the Theory of Investment*. Chicago: University of Chicago Press, 1960.

Hall, Robert E. "Technical Change and Capital from the Point of View of the Dual," *Review of Economic Studies*, Vol. 35 (January 1968), pp. 35–46.

Hall, Robert E., and Dale W. Jorgenson. "The Role of Taxation in Stabilizing Private Investment," in Vincent P. Rock (ed.). *Policymakers and Model Builders: Cases and Concepts.* (New York: Gordon and Breach, 1969).

————, and ————. "Tax Policy and Investment Behavior," *American Economic Review*, Vol. 57 (June 1967), pp. 391–414.

————, and ————. "Tax Policy and Investment Behavior: Reply and Further Results," *American Economic Review*, Vol. 59 (June 1969), pp. 388–401.

Hart, Albert G. *Anticipations, Uncertainty, and Dynamic Planning.* Chicago: University of Chicago Press, 1940.

————. "Uncertainty and Inducements To Invest," *Review of Economic Studies*, Vol. 8 (October 1940), pp. 49–53.

Hayek, Friedrich von. *Profits, Interest and Investment, and Other Essays on the Theory of Industrial Fluctuations.* London: George Routledge and Sons, 1939.

Heins, A. James, and Case M. Sprenkle. "A Comment on the Modigliani-Miller Cost of Capital Thesis," and Franco Modigliani and Merton H. Miller, "Reply to Heins and Sprenkle," *American Economic Review*, Vol. 59, (September 1969), pp. 590–92 and 592–95, respectively.

Helliwell, John F. *Public Policies and Private Investment.* Oxford: Clarendon Press, 1968.

Hickman, Bert G. "Diffusion, Acceleration, and Business Cycles," *American Economic Review*, Vol. 49 (September 1959), pp. 535–65.

————. *Investment Demand and U.S. Economic Growth.* Washington: Brookings Institution, 1965.

Hochman, Harold M. "Some Aggregative Implications of Depreciation Acceleration," *Yale Economic Essays*, Vol. 6 (Spring 1966), pp. 217–74.

Howrey, E. Philip. "A Note on the Damping of Pure Replacement Cycles," *Review of Economics and Statistics*, Vol. 47 (August 1965), pp. 334–37.

Hurwicz, Leonid. "Theory of the Firm and of Investment," *Econometrica*, Vol. 14 (April 1946), pp. 109–36.

Jaszi, George, Robert C. Wasson, and Lawrence Grose. "Expansion of Fixed Business Capital in the United States," *Survey of Current Business*, Vol. 42 (November 1962), pp. 9–18, 28.

Jensen, Arne. "Application of Stochastic Processes to an Investment Plan," *Metroeconomica*, Vol. 5 (December 1953), pp. 129–37.

Johansen, Leif. "Substitution Versus Fixed Production Coefficients in the Theory of Economic Growth: A Synthesis," *Econometrica*, Vol. 27 (April 1959), pp. 157–76.

Jorgenson, Dale W. "Anticipations and Investment Behavior," in James S. Duesenberry, Gary Fromm, Lawrence R. Klein, and Edwin Kuh (eds.), *The Brookings Quarterly Econometric Model of the United States.* Chicago: Rand McNally and Co., 1965; Amsterdam: North-Holland, 1965.

————. "Capital Theory and Investment Behavior," in American Economic Association, *Papers and Proceedings of the Seventy-fifth Annual Meeting, 1962,*

(*American Economic Review*, Vol. 53, May 1963), pp. 247–59. Reprinted in American Economic Association, *Readings in Business Cycles*. Homewood, Ill.: Richard D. Irwin, 1965.

Jorgenson, Dale W. "The Theory of Investment Behavior," in Robert Ferber (ed.), *Determinants of Investment Behavior*. A Conference of the Universities-National Bureau Committee for Economic Research. New York: Columbia University Press for the National Bureau of Economic Research, 1967.

————, Jerald Hunter, and M. Ishag Nadiri. "A Comparison of Alternative Econometric Models of Quarterly Investment Behavior," *Econometrica*, Vol. 38 (March 1970), pp. 187–212.

————, ————, and ————. "The Predictive Performance of Econometric Models of Quarterly Investment Behavior," *Econometrica*, Vol. 38 (March 1970), pp. 213–24.

Jorgenson, Dale W., and Calvin D. Siebert. "A Comparison of Alternative Theories of Corporate Investment Behavior," *American Economic Review*, Vol. 58 (September 1968), pp. 681–712.

————, and ————. "Optimal Capital Accumulation and Corporate Investment Behavior," *Journal of Political Economy*, Vol. 76 (November–December 1968), pp. 1123–51.

Jorgenson, Dale W., and James A. Stephenson. "Anticipations and Investment Behavior in U.S. Manufacturing, 1947–1960," *Journal of the American Statistical Association*, Vol. 64 (March 1969), pp. 67–89.

————, and ————. "Investment Behavior in U.S. Manufacturing, 1947–1960," *Econometrica*, Vol. 35 (April 1967), pp. 169–220.

————, and ————. "Issues in the Development of the Neo-Classical Theory of Investment Behavior." Processed. Working Papers in Economic Theory and Econometrics, No. 145. University of California, Berkeley, Institute of Business and Economic Research, Center for Research in Management Science, February 1969.

————, and ————. "The Time Structure of Investment Behavior in United States Manufacturing, 1947–1960," *Review of Economics and Statistics*, Vol. 49 (February 1967), pp. 16–27.

Kalecki, Michal. "A Macrodynamic Theory of Business Cycles," *Econometrica*, Vol. 3 (July 1935), pp. 327–44.

————. *Theory of Economic Dynamics: An Essay on Cyclical and Long-run Changes in Capitalist Economy*. New York: Rinehart and Co., 1954.

Kemp, Murray C., and Phạm Chí Thành. "On a Class of Growth Models," *Econometrica*, Vol. 34 (April 1966), pp. 257–82.

Kendrick, John W. *Productivity Trends in the United States*. Princeton: Princeton University Press for the National Bureau of Economic Research, 1961.

Keynes, John Maynard. *The General Theory of Employment, Interest and Money*. New York: Harcourt, Brace and Co., 1936.

Klein, Lawrence R. "Notes on the Theory of Investment," *Kyklos*, Vol. 2, Fasc. 2 (1948), pp. 97–117.

———. "Pitfalls in the Statistical Determination of the Investment Schedule," *Econometrica*, Vol. 11 (July–October 1943), pp. 246–58.

———. "Studies in Investment Behavior," in Universities-National Bureau Committee for Economic Research, *Conference on Business Cycles*. New York: National Bureau of Economic Research, 1951.

Knox, A. D. "The Acceleration Principle and the Theory of Investment: A Survey," *Economica*, Vol. 19 (August 1952), pp. 269–97.

Koyck, L. M. *Distributed Lags and Investment Analysis*. Amsterdam: North-Holland, 1954.

Krzyzaniak, Marian, and Richard A. Musgrave. *The Shifting of the Corporation Income Tax: An Empirical Study of Its Short-run Effect upon the Rate of Return*. Baltimore: Johns Hopkins Press, 1963.

Kuh, Edwin. *Capital Stock Growth: A Micro-Econometric Approach*. Amsterdam: North-Holland, 1963.

———. "Capital Theory and Capital Budgeting," *Metroeconomica*, Vol. 12 (August–December 1960), pp. 64–80.

———. "Theory and Institutions in the Study of Investment Behavior," in American Economic Association, *Papers and Proceedings of the Seventy-fifth Annual Meeting, 1962* (*American Economic Review*, Vol. 53, May 1963), pp. 260–68.

———. "A Time Series Approach to Cross-Section Investment Behavior," paper presented at the meeting of the Econometric Society, Cleveland, December 1956. Abstracted in "Report of the Cleveland Meeting," *Econometrica*, Vol. 25 (October 1957), p. 609.

———, and John R. Meyer. "Investment, Liquidity, and Monetary Policy," in Commission on Money and Credit, *Impacts of Monetary Policy*. Englewood Cliffs, N.J.: Prentice-Hall, 1963.

Kuznets, Simon. *Capital in the American Economy: Its Formation and Financing*. Princeton: Princeton University Press for the National Bureau of Economic Research, 1961.

———. "Relation between Capital Goods and Finished Products in the Business Cycle," in *Economic Essays in Honor of Wesley Clair Mitchell*. New York: Columbia University Press, 1935.

Levine, Robert A. "Capital Expenditures Forecasts by Individual Firms," in Universities-National Bureau Committee for Economic Research, *The Quality and Economic Significance of Anticipations Data*. Princeton: Princeton University Press, 1960.

———. "Plant and Equipment Expenditures Surveys: Intentions and Fulfillment." Cowles Foundation Discussion Paper 17. Processed. New Haven, Conn.: Cowles Foundation, 1956.

Liebling, Herman I. "Financing Business in Recession and Expansion," *Survey of Current Business*, Vol. 38 (October 1958), pp. 15–20.

———. "Financing the Expansion of Business," *Survey of Current Business*, Vol. 37 (September 1957), pp. 6–14.

Lindsay, Robert. "The Stability of Business Capital Outlays," *Review of Economics and Statistics*, Vol. 40 (May 1958), pp. 159–63.

Lintner, John. "Dividends, Earnings, Leverage, Stock Prices, and the Supply of Capital to Corporations," *Review of Economics and Statistics*, Vol. 44 (August 1962), pp. 243–69.

———. "Effect of Corporate Taxation on Real Investment," in American Economic Association, *Papers and Proceedings of the Sixty-sixth Annual Meeting, 1953* (*American Economic Review*, Vol. 44, May 1954), pp. 520–34.

Liu, Ta-Chung, and Ching-Gwan Chang. "U.S. Consumption and Investment Propensities: Prewar and Postwar, U.S.," *American Economic Review*, Vol. 40 (September 1950), pp. 565–82.

Livingston, S. Morris. "The Demand for Producers' Durable Equipment," *Survey of Current Business*, Vol. 29 (June 1949), pp. 8–18.

Lutz, Friedrich A. "The Criterion of Maximum Profits in the Theory of Investment," *Quarterly Journal of Economics*, Vol. 60 (November 1945), pp. 56–77.

———. "The Interest Rate and Investment in a Dynamic Economy," *American Economic Review*, Vol. 35 (December 1945), pp. 811–30.

———. *The Theory of Capital*. Proceedings of a Conference held by the International Economic Association. New York: St. Martin's Press, 1961.

———, and Vera Lutz. *The Theory of Investment of the Firm*. Princeton: Princeton University Press, 1951.

Lydall, H. F. "The Impact of the Credit Squeeze on Small and Medium-Sized Manufacturing Firms," *Economic Journal*, Vol. 67 (September 1957), pp. 415–31.

Manne, Alan S. "Capacity Expansion and Probabilistic Growth," *Econometrica*, Vol. 29 (October 1961), pp. 632–49.

———. "Some Notes on the Acceleration Principle," *Review of Economic Statistics*, Vol. 27 (May 1945), pp. 93–99.

Marston, A., R. Winfrey, and J. D. Hempstead. *Engineering Evaluation and Depreciation*. 2nd ed. New York: McGraw-Hill, 1953.

Massé, Pierre. *Optimal Investment Decisions: Rules for Action and Criteria for Choice*. Englewood Cliffs, N.J.: Prentice-Hall, 1962.

Massell, Benton F. "Investment, Innovation, and Growth," *Econometrica*, Vol. 30 (April 1962), pp. 239–52.

Mayer, Thomas. "Input Lead Times for Capital Coefficients." Inter-Industry Research Item No. 52. Processed. Washington: U.S. Bureau of Mines, 1953.

———. "Plant and Equipment Lead Times," *Journal of Business*, Vol. 33 (April 1960), pp. 127–32.

Mayer, Thomas, and Sidney Sonenblum. "Lead Times for Fixed Investment," *Review of Economics and Statistics*, Vol. 37 (August 1955), pp. 300–04.

Meade, James E., and P. W. S. Andrews. "Summary of Replies to Questions on Effects of Interest Rates," *Oxford Economic Papers*, No. 1 (October 1938), pp. 14–31.

Meyer, John R., and Robert R. Glauber. *Investment Decisions, Economic Forecasting, and Public Policy*. Boston: Harvard University, Graduate School of Business Administration, Division of Research, 1964.

Meyer, John R., and Edwin Kuh. "Acceleration and Related Theories of Investment: An Empirical Inquiry," *Review of Economics and Statistics*, Vol. 37 (August 1955), pp. 217–30.

———, and ———. "Further Comments on the Empirical Study of Investment Functions," *Review of Economics and Statistics*, Vol. 39 (May 1957), pp. 218–22.

———, and ———. *The Investment Decision: An Empirical Study*. Cambridge: Harvard University Press, 1957.

Miller, John Perry. "The Pricing Effects of Accelerated Amortization," *Review of Economics and Statistics*, Vol. 34 (February 1952), pp. 10–17.

Miller, Merton H. "The Corporation Income Tax and Corporate Financial Policies," in Commission on Money and Credit, *Stabilization Policies*. Englewood Cliffs, N.J.: Prentice-Hall, 1963.

———, and Franco Modigliani. "Some Estimates of the Cost of Capital to the Electric Utility Industry, 1954–57," *American Economic Review*, Vol. 56 (June 1966), pp. 333–91.

Modigliani, Franco, and Kalman J. Cohen. *The Role of Anticipations and Plans in Economic Behavior and Their Use in Economic Analysis and Forecasting*. Urbana: University of Illinois, 1961.

Modigliani, Franco, and Merton H. Miller. "Corporate Income Taxes and the Cost of Capital: A Correction," *American Economic Review*, Vol. 53 (June 1963), pp. 433–43.

———, and ———. "The Cost of Capital, Corporation Finance and the Theory of Investment," *American Economic Review*, Vol. 48 (June 1958), pp. 261–97.

———, and ———. "The Cost of Capital, Corporation Finance, and the Theory of Investment: Reply," *American Economic Review*, Vol. 55 (June 1965), pp. 524–27.

———, and ———. "Reply to Heins and Sprenkle," *American Economic Review*, Vol. 59 (September 1969), pp. 592–95.

Modigliani, Franco, and H. M. Weingartner. "Forecasting Uses of Anticipatory Data on Investment and Sales," *Quarterly Journal of Economics*, Vol. 72 (February 1958), pp. 23–54.

———, and ———. "Forecasting Uses of Anticipatory Data: Reply," *Quarterly Journal of Economics*, Vol. 73 (February 1959), pp. 171–72.

Modigliani, Franco, and Morton Zeman. "The Effect of the Availability of Funds and the Terms Thereof on Business Investment," in Universities-National Bureau Committee for Economic Research, *Conference on Research in Business Finance.* New York: National Bureau of Economic Research, 1952.

Morrissett, Irving. "A Note on the Empirical Study of Acceleration and Related Theories of Investment," *Review of Economics and Statistics,* Vol. 39 (February 1957), pp. 91–93.

Musgrave, Richard A. "Effects of Tax Policy on Private Capital Formation," in Commission on Money and Credit, *Fiscal and Debt Management Policies.* Englewood Cliffs, N.J.: Prentice-Hall, 1963.

National Bureau of Economic Research. *Problems of Capital Formation: Concepts, Measurement, and Controlling Factors.* Studies in Income and Wealth, Vol. 19. Princeton: Princeton University Press for the National Bureau of Economic Research, 1957.

National Bureau of Economic Research. Universities-National Bureau Committee for Economic Research. *Capital Formation and Economic Growth.* Princeton: Princeton University Press for the National Bureau of Economic Research, 1955.

———. *Conference on Business Cycles.* New York: National Bureau of Economic Research, 1951.

———. *Conference on Research in Business Finance.* New York: National Bureau of Economic Research, 1952.

———. *The Quality and Economic Significance of Anticipations Data.* Princeton: Princeton University Press for the National Bureau of Economic Research, 1960.

———. *Regularization of Business Investment.* Princeton: Princeton University Press for the National Bureau of Economic Research, 1954.

National Industrial Conference Board. *Capital Formation and Its Elements.* A Series of Papers Presented at a Symposium Conducted by the Conference Board. New York: NICB, 1939.

———. *Controlling Capital Expenditures.* Studies in Business Policy, No. 62. New York: NICB, 1953.

Natrella, Vito. "Forecasting Plant and Equipment Expenditures from Businessmen's Expectations," in American Statistical Association, *Proceedings of the Business and Economic Statistics Section, 1956,* pp. 121–32.

Nerlove, Marc. "Recent Empirical Studies of the CES and Related Production Functions," in Murray Brown (ed.), *The Theory and Empirical Analysis of Production.* New York: Columbia University Press for the National Bureau of Economic Research, 1967.

Norton, Frank E. "The Accelerator and the Overinvestment and Underconsumption Models," *Economic Journal,* Vol. 66 (March 1956), pp. 49–65.

———. "Some Cross-Section Explorations in Investment Behavior," *Southern Economic Journal,* Vol. 22 (January 1956), pp. 330–38.

Novozhilov, V. V. "On Choosing between Investment Projects," *International*

Economics Papers, Vol. 6 (1956), pp. 66–87. First published in Russian, 1939 and 1946.

Okun, Arthur M. "The Predictive Value of Surveys of Business Intentions," in American Economic Association, *Papers and Proceedings of the Seventy-Fourth Annual Meeting, 1961* (*American Economic Review*, Vol. 52, May 1962), pp. 218–25.

Phelps, Edmund S. "Substitution, Fixed Proportions, Growth, and Distribution," *International Economic Review*, Vol. 4 (September 1963), pp. 254–88.

Phillips, Almarin. "An Appraisal of Measures of Capacity," in American Economic Association, *Papers and Proceedings of the Seventy-fifth Annual Meeting, 1962* (*American Economic Review*, Vol. 53, May 1963), pp. 275–92.

Popkin, Joel. "Comment on 'The Distributed Lag between Capital Appropriations and Expenditures,' " *Econometrica*, Vol. 34 (July 1966), pp. 719–23.

———. "The Relationship between New Orders and Shipments: An Analysis of the Machinery and Equipment Industries," *Survey of Current Business*, Vol. 45 (March 1965), pp. 24–32.

Puthucheary, J. "Investment Incentive and Income Tax," *Public Finance*, Vol. 14, No. 3–4 (1959), pp. 218–33.

Roos, Charles F. "The Demand for Investment Goods," in American Economic Association, *Papers and Proceedings of the Sixtieth Annual Meeting, 1947* (*American Economic Review*, Vol. 38, May 1948), pp. 311–20.

———, and Victor S. Von Szeliski. "The Demand for Durable Goods," *Econometrica*, Vol. 11 (April 1943), pp. 97–122.

Sachs, Reynold, and Albert G. Hart. "Anticipations and Investment Behavior: An Econometric Study of Quarterly Time Series for Large Firms in Durable Goods Manufacturing," in Robert Ferber (ed.), *Determinants of Investment Behavior*. A Conference of the Universities-National Bureau Committee for Economic Research. New York: Columbia University Press for the National Bureau of Economic Research, 1967.

Samuelson, Paul A. "Tax Deductibility of Economic Depreciation To Insure Invariant Valuations," *Journal of Political Economy*, Vol. 72 (December 1964), pp. 604–06.

Scott, A. D. "Notes on User Cost," *Economic Journal*, Vol. 63 (June 1953), pp. 368–84.

Shackle, G. L. S. "Business Men on Business Decisions," *Scottish Journal of Political Economy*, Vol. 2 (February 1955), pp. 32–46.

———. *Expectation in Economics*. London: Cambridge University Press, 1949.

———. *Expectations, Investment and Income*. London: Oxford University Press, 1938.

———. "Interest Rates and the Pace of Investment," *Economic Journal*, Vol. 56 (March 1946), pp. 1–17.

———. "The Nature of the Inducement To Invest," *Review of Economic Studies*, Vol. 8 (October 1940), pp. 44–48.

Shackle, G. L. S. "The Nature and Role of Profit," *Metroeconomica*, Vol. 3 (December 1951), pp. 101–07.

———. "On the Meaning and Measure of Uncertainty," Pts. 1 and 2, *Metroeconomica*, Vol. 4 (December 1952), pp. 87–104, and Vol. 5 (December 1953), pp. 97–115.

———. "Recent Theories Concerning the Nature and Role of Interest," *Economic Journal*, Vol. 71 (June 1961), pp. 209–54.

———. "A Theory of Investment-Decisions," *Oxford Economic Papers*, Vol. 6 (April 1942), pp. 77–94.

Smith, Kenneth R. "The Determinants of Excess Capacity." Paper presented to the North American Regional Conference of the Econometric Society, Washington, December 1967.

Smith, Vernon L. *Investment and Production: A Study in the Theory of the Capital-Using Enterprise.* Cambridge: Harvard University Press, 1961.

———. "Tax Depreciation Policy and Investment Theory," *International Economic Review*, Vol. 4 (January 1963), pp. 80–91.

Solow, Robert M. "Investment and Technical Progress," in Kenneth J. Arrow, Samuel Karlin, and Patrick Suppes (eds.), *Mathematical Methods in the Social Sciences, 1959.* Proceedings of the First Stanford Symposium. Stanford: Stanford University Press, 1960.

———. "Substitution and Fixed Proportions in the Theory of Capital," *Review of Economic Studies*, Vol. 29 (June 1962), pp. 207–18.

———. "Technical Progress, Capital Formation, and Economic Growth," in American Economic Association, *Papers and Proceedings of the Seventy-fourth Annual Meeting, 1961 (American Economic Review*, Vol. 52, May 1962), pp. 76–86.

Stekler, H. O. "Forecasting with Econometric Models: An Evaluation," *Econometrica*, Vol. 36 (July–October 1968), pp. 437–63.

Stockfisch, J. A. "The Capitalization, Allocation, and Investment Effects of Asset Taxation," *Southern Economic Journal*, Vol. 22 (January 1956), pp. 317–29.

———. "Investment Incentive, Taxation, and Accelerated Depreciation," *Southern Economic Journal*, Vol. 24 (July 1957), pp. 28–40.

———. "The Relationships between Money Cost, Investment, and the Rate of Return," *Quarterly Journal of Economics*, Vol. 70 (May 1956), pp. 295–302.

———. "Uncertainty, the Capitalization Theory and Investment Behavior," *Metroeconomica*, Vol. 7 (August 1955), pp. 73–84.

Stone, Richard, and D. A. Rowe. "The Market Demand for Durable Goods," *Econometrica*, Vol. 25 (July 1957), pp. 423–43.

Streever, Donald. *Capacity Utilization and Business Investment Bulletin.* Bulletin Series No. 86. Urbana: University of Illinois, Bureau of Economic and Business Research, 1960.

Strumilin, S. G. "The Time Factor in Capital Investment Projects," *International*

Economic Papers, Vol. 1 (1951), pp. 160–85. First published in Russian, 1946.

Taubman, Paul. "Personal Saving: A Time Series Analysis of Three Measures of the Same Conceptual Series," *Review of Economics and Statistics*, Vol. 50 (February 1968), pp. 125–29.

————, and Maurice Wilkinson. "User Cost, Capital Utilization and Investment Theory," *International Economic Review*, Vol. 11 (June 1970), pp. 209–15.

Terborgh, George. *Business Investment Policy: A MAPI Study and Manual.* Washington: Machinery and Allied Products Institute, 1960.

————. "Business Investment for Stability and Growth," in American Economic Association, *Papers and Proceedings of the Sixty-ninth Annual Meeting, 1956* (*American Economic Review*, Vol. 47, May 1957), pp. 132–34.

————. *Dynamic Equipment Policy.* New York: McGraw-Hill, 1949.

————. *New Investment Incentives: The Investment Credit and the New Depreciation System.* Washington: Machinery and Allied Products Institute, 1962.

————. *Realistic Depreciation Policy.* Chicago: Machinery and Allied Products Institute, 1954.

————. *Studies in the Analysis of Business Investment Projects.* Washington: Machinery and Allied Products Institute, 1960.

Tew, Brian. "The Finance of Investment," *Oxford Economic Papers*, N.S., Vol. 4 (July 1952), pp. 108–20.

Thurow, Lester C. "A Disequilibrium Neoclassical Investment Function," *Review of Economics and Statistics*, Vol. 51 (November 1969), pp. 431–35.

Tinbergen, Jan. "Statistical Evidence on the Acceleration Principle," *Economica*, N.S., Vol. 5 (May 1938), pp. 164–76.

————. *Statistical Testing of Business-Cycle Theories.* Vol. 1: *A Method and Its Application to Investment Activity.* Geneva: League of Nations, 1939.

————, and J. J. Polak. *The Dynamics of Business Cycles; A Study in Economic Fluctuations.* Chicago: University of Chicago Press, 1950.

Tinsley, P. A. "An Application of Variable Weight Distributed Lags," *Journal of the American Statistical Association*, Vol. 62 (December 1967), pp. 1277–89.

Tsiang, S. C. "Accelerator Theory of the Firm and the Business Cycle," *Quarterly Journal of Economics*, Vol. 65 (August 1951), pp. 325–41.

————. "Rehabilitation of Time Dimension of Investment in Macrodynamic Analysis," *Economica*, Vol. 16 (August 1949), pp. 204–17.

Tucker, Donald P. "Dynamic Income Adjustment to Money-Supply Changes," *American Economic Review*, Vol. 56 (June 1966), pp. 433–49.

Ture, Norman B. *Accelerated Depreciation in the United States, 1954–60.* New York: Columbia University Press for the National Bureau of Economic Research, 1967.

————. "Tax Reform: Depreciation Problems," in American Economic Association, *Papers and Proceedings of the Seventy-fifth Annual Meeting, 1962* (*American Economic Review*, Vol. 53, May 1963), pp. 334–53.

Ulmer, Melville J. *Capital in Transportation, Communications, and Public Utilities:*

Its Formation and Financing. Princeton: Princeton University Press for the National Bureau of Economic Research, 1960.

U.S. Bureau of the Budget. Office of Statistical Standards. "An Appraisal of OBE-SEC Estimates of Plant and Equipment Expenditures, 1947–1958." Statistical Evaluation Report No. 1, prepared by Raymond Nassimbene and Benjamin T. Teeter. Washington: Bureau of the Budget, 1959 (revised 1961).

U.S. Congress. Joint Economic Committee. *The Federal Tax System: Facts and Problems, 1964*. 88 Cong. 2 sess. Washington: Government Printing Office, 1964.

Wales, Terence. "Estimation of an Accelerated Depreciation Learning Function," *Journal of the American Statistical Association*, Vol. 61 (December 1966), pp. 995–1009.

Wallich, Henry C. "Effect of Taxation on Investment," *Harvard Business Review*, Vol. 23 (Summer 1945), pp. 442–50.

Walters, A. A. "Production and Cost Functions: An Econometric Survey," *Econometrica*, Vol. 31 (January–April 1963), pp. 1–66.

Wellisz, Stanislaw H. "Entrepreneur's Risk, Lender's Risk, and Investment," *Review of Economic Studies*, Vol. 20, No. 2 (1953), pp. 105–14.

White, William H. "The Changing Criteria in Investment Planning," in Joint Economic Committee, *Variability of Private Investment in Plant and Equipment*. Pt. 2. 87 Cong. 2 sess. Washington: Government Printing Office, 1962.

————. "Illusions in the Marginal Investment Subsidy," *National Tax Journal*, Vol. 15 (March 1962), pp. 26–31.

————. "Interest Inelasticity of Investment Demand—The Case from Business Attitude Surveys Re-examined," *American Economic Review*, Vol. 46 (September 1956), pp. 565–87.

————. "The Rate of Interest, the Marginal Efficiency of Capital and Investment Programming," *Economic Journal*, Vol. 68 (March 1958), pp. 51–59.

Wilson, D. Stevens. "Planned Capital Outlays and Financing," *Survey of Current Business*, Vol. 25 (July 1945), pp. 15–23.

Wilson, Thomas. "Cyclical and Autonomous Inducements To Invest," *Oxford Economic Papers*, N.S., Vol. 5 (March 1953), pp. 65–89.

————, and P. W. S. Andrews (eds.). *Oxford Studies in the Price Mechanism*. New York: Oxford University Press, 1951.

Wilson, Thomas A. *Capital Investment and the Cost of Capital: A Dynamic Analysis*. Studies of the Royal Commission on Taxation, No. 30. Ottawa: Queen's Printer, 1967.

Winding, Poul. *Some Aspects of the Acceleration Principle*. Amsterdam: North-Holland, 1957.

Wiseman, Jack. "Public Policy and the Investment Tax Credit," *National Tax Journal*, Vol. 16 (March 1963), pp. 36–40.

Wooden, Donald G., and Robert C. Wasson. "Manufacturing Investment Since 1929 in Relation to Employment, Output, and Income," *Survey of Current Business*, Vol. 36 (November 1956), pp. 8–20.

Index